Hermeneutics in the Genre of *Mukhtaṣar*

Hermeneutics in the Genre of *Mukhtaṣar*

Civil and Commercial Law in Islamic Law

Husain Kassim

LEXINGTON BOOKS
Lanham • Boulder • New York • London

Published by Lexington Books
An imprint of The Rowman & Littlefield Publishing Group, Inc.
4501 Forbes Boulevard, Suite 200, Lanham, Maryland 20706
www.rowman.com

6 Tinworth Street, London SE11 5AL, United Kingdom

British Library Cataloguing in Publication Information Available

Library of Congress Cataloging-in-Publication Data

Names: Kassim, Husain, 1939- author.
Title: Hermeneutics in the genre of *mukhtaṣar*: civil and commercial law in Islamic law / Husain Kassim.
Description: Lanham : Lexington Books, 2019. | Includes bibliographical references and index.
Identifiers: LCCN 2018042654 (print) | LCCN 2018043220 (ebook) | ISBN 9781498512169 (Electronic) | ISBN 9781498512152 (cloth : alk. paper)
Subjects: LCSH: Islamic law—Interpretation and construction. | Commercial law (Islamic law)
Classification: LCC KBP461 (ebook) | LCC KBP461 .K37 2019 (print) | DDC 340.5/925—dc23
LC record available at https://lccn.loc.gov/2018042654

∞™ The paper used in this publication meets the minimum requirements of American National Standard for Information Sciences—Permanence of Paper for Printed Library Materials, ANSI/NISO Z39.48-1992.

Printed in the United States of America

Contents

Acknowledgments

I wish to record my thanks to the Oxford Center for Islamic Studies for the Fellowship and releasing time from teaching at my home institution, University of Central Florida.

Introduction

Theoretical Framework of the Islamic Legal System in Accommodating Civil and Commercial law and the Relevance of Hermeneutical Compositions of *Mukhtaṣar*

This investigation is situated in the wider theoretical framework in accommodating the civil and commercial law regarding the tensions and conflicts between the Islamic legal system and the modern Western legal system. The modern Western legal system was superimposed in the colonial period on the previously existing Islamic legal system in the Muslim countries. During that period both these legal systems existed side by side. It is in this context and wider theoretical framework this work shows the relevance, significance, and import for continuing the hermeneutical approach of the genre of *Mukhtaṣar*.

The introduction of the Western legal system in the Muslim territories during the colonial period, to a large extent, ignored the traditions and legacy of the Islamic legal system, which was in operation in the Muslim countries until the sixteenth/seventeenth century. The Islamic legal system and the modern Western legal system had quite different origins and backgrounds. The Islamic legal system was deeply rooted in its own legal traditions and norms, whereas the modern Western legal system was grounded in its traditions and legacy. The development of these two legal systems had different backgrounds. In short, they both were entirely incompatible with each other.

During colonial rule in the Muslim world, from the seventeenth century onward, the previously existing Islamic legal system existed side by side with the modern Western legal system without any systematic interactions. Their domain of legal operations was entirely different, resulting in tensions and conflicts. During colonial rule, the Islamic legal system concerning civil and commercial law, which was hermeneutically developed as will be shown in our investigation of the selected compositions of *Mukhtaṣar*, existed side by side with the modern Western civil and commercial laws operating in most cases in the same place—we will briefly mention here the cases of Egypt and India.

In Egypt, the Islamic law of *sharīʿa* and the modern Western system coupled with the colonial political, economic, and hegemonic interests existed side by side with the Islamic legal system. As a result, the tensions and conflicts arose between the Mixed Courts and the National Courts of Egypt regarding the inheritance law that the property of an estate does not pass unless the debts of *praepositus* have been settled according to the Islamic legal system. Such cases were considered by the Mixed Courts as the domain of *sharīʿa* law. Similarly, the transformation of the traditional Islamic law into the Anglo-Mohammadan law occurred under the impact of colonial legal administration in India. This broke the ties with the Islamic legal system of the Indian judicial system inherited from the Mughal Indian judicial system of the past.[1] There were no systematic interrelations or interactions, or what Niklas Luhman in his article "Operational Closer and Structural Coupling" calls "communication."[2] Thus, the modern Western legal system had no positive and contributive effect for the continuity of hermeneutical approach for further developing the Islamic legal system that could have entailed all the essential expanded additional elements, which had occurred over the course of time during the entire colonial period and afterward.

It is in this context and wider theoretical framework, the significance and import of the compositions of *Mukhtaṣar* is to be situated for their relevance to the ongoing discussions about how hermeneutical approach of the composition of *Mukhtaṣar* can meet the demands of the modern times and look back into the Islamic legal resources and traditions. The continuity of the hermeneutical approach as it was done in the past until the thirteenth century by the authors of the compositions of *Mukhtaṣar* provides the Muslim jurists at present a concrete direction for incorporating hermeneutically the changes and conditions that have occurred in the modern times for the formation of Islamic legal system comprehensively.

The attempts to bring changes that have been introduced recently by the Muslim jurists under the impact of modern Western legal system have either turned out to be the "patchworks" or not "comprehensive" enough as discussed below:

Ottoman Turkey in the mid-nineteenth century wanted to join the Club of Europe and, under the pressure of European countries, introduced the *Tanẓīmāt* reforms. From 1839 to 1879, Turkey enacted the Swiss code of civil and commercial law, but without any amendments in the code. It was neither used nor did it prove effective in any way. This is to be attributed primarily to the fact that it was incompatible with the existing Islamic legal system in Turkey. Consequently, it was replaced by the civil and commercial law called *Majallāt-i-Aḥkāmī al-ʿAdalīya*, composed by Qādir Pasha. It was promulgated in 1875–76 and was applied throughout the Ottoman territories.[3]

The *Majallāt*, following the *Hidāya* composed by Buhrān al-Dīn al-Ḥasan ʿAlī Abū Bakr al-Marghīnānī (593/1197), who had chosen *Mukhtaṣar* of Abū al-Ḥusayn Muḥammad bin Aḥmad ibn Jaʿfar bin Hamdān al-Qudūrī (392/1037) for the composition of *Hidāya*, restated the rules and regulations for all civil and commercial transactions in a codified form. These transactions are hermeneutically based on and derived from the Islamic legal system. It is said that the codification was copied in the *Majallā* from the French legal system, but its entire content is based on al-Qudūrī's text, which goes back to the Islamic legal traditions giving it the character of Islamic legal system in the modern coded form. This is considered itself a great achievement. But, Qādir Pasha brings in the *Majallā* not much of the recent developments that have occurred during the colonial period, subjecting them hermeneutically according to the Islamic legal system, and incorporating them in it comprehensively.

Sanhurī's Code, which was promulgated in Egypt in 1949 and, thereafter, subsequently in Iraq and Syria, aims to incorporate the modern theory of civil and commercial law consistent with the Islamic legal system. According to Sanhūrī, the rules of civil and commercial law were not sufficiently developed within the traditional Islamic legal system to meet the demands of modern times.[4] This is true, since after the seventeenth/eighteenth century the Islamic legal hermeneutical approach had ceased to function under the colonial rule. Therefore, Sanhūrī's Code borrows the theory of civil and commercial law from the modern Western legal system and tries to integrate it into the Islamic legal system or rather "amalgamate" it in the Code with the past Islamic legal system. No wonder, according to some critics of Sanhūrī's Code such as Anderson,[5] who observes that several principles and provisions taken or borrowed from the modern Western legal system of different of Western countries make it impossible to maintain the harmony of legal system,[6] Or Sfeir, who thinks that it is certainly based on the French legal system.[7] Even some members of the Egyptian parliament considered it not Islamic.

Instead of borrowing civil and commercial law from the modern Western legal systems, Sanhūrī in his Code could have grounded it from within the Islamic traditions. In the Islamic legal traditions these concepts are hermeneutically developed comparable to those in the modern Western legal systems, though they reflect the agricultural society of Muslim countries. However, such concepts in the Islamic legal system have been developed beginning from Muḥammad bin Idrīs al-Shāfiʿī (204/820), and which was subsequently further developed hermeneutically by the Muslim jurists as we have explored and shown in our investigation of the selected compositions of *Mukhtaṣar*. To mention, these concepts are: the nature and concept of contract (*ʿaqd*), contracts of sale (*ʿaqd al-bayʿ*) *ṣarf* sale, *salam* sale, *ribā*, partnership (*shirka*), lease-hire (*ijāra*), right of option (*khiyār*), seller makes an offer and the purchaser can either accept it or reject it, after the contract is drawn the parties to the contract must abide by the stipulations in the contract, etc. This hermeneutical approach provides a direction and reopens the door for the hermeneutical formation of Islamic legal system that entails all the essential expanded elements and changes which had occurred over the course of time in the colonial period and thereafter, giving a character and identity of the Islamic legal system, considering *sharīa* the main source rather than considering it only a "residual source of law, the role of which is mediation, integration, unity, and conceptual homogeneity" as does Sanhūri.[8]

HERMENEUTICS IN THE GENRE OF *MUKHTAṢAR*

This book is about not well-known genre of *Mukhtaṣar* in Islamic law, and much less of the significance of its emergence in the hermeneutical formation of Islamic law. These compositions of *Mukhtaṣar* are authored texts by individual jurists claiming independently to personal hermeneutical interpretations in producing them.[9] They are not just abridgment, which the literal translation of the word "*mukhtaṣar*" suggests. These compositions of *Mukhtaṣar* do not simply reproduce the legal opinions of the eponyms of schools of law in an abridged form as it has traditionally been understood. Most importantly, the purpose for which they were composed was to provide the hermeneutical account of the formation of Islamic legal system incorporating all the essential expanded additional elements which had occurred developed over the course of time. The authors of the compositions of *Mukhtaṣar* in the production and reproduction continue hermeneutical formation of Islamic legal system Thus, in a very broad sense, these compositions of *Mukhtaṣar* can be characterized as hermeneutics like the nature of entire Islamic law.

Muḥammad bin Idrīs al-Shāfiʻī (204/820) was the first major figure who endeavored hermeneutically to systematize comprehensively the Islamic legal system in his pioneer work *Risāla*, a ninth-century preserved work, which offers a sustained treatment of al-Shāfiʻī's concept of hermeneutics. The originality of *Risāla* lies in its departure from the previous approach in the study of Islamic law. According to al-Shāfiʻī, the Islamic law as a comprehensive and coherent set of rules is dictated entirely by God, which is accessible to human beings through the textual recorded revelation provided in the *Qur'ān* and the prophetic *Ḥadīth* reports. According to al-Shāfiʻī, the *Qur'ān* and the prophetic *Ḥadīth* reports are effectively on a par per se. Al-Shāfiʻī's hermeneutics was designed to bring changes in the existing Islamic legal system. When one is talking about bringing changes, one must keep in mind the context in which al-Shāfi'ī intended to bring changes hermeneutically as a method to determine the legal rulings in accordance with the legal canons within the parameter set by the revealed sources. By this time the broad consensus was already formed about the general ideas of Islamic law. Thus, it was in the slowly evolving legal discourse in which changes could be brought methodologically to systematize comprehensively the Islamic legal system. Al-Shāfi'ī's hermeneutics was gradually accepted in all four Sunni schools of law.

Briefly described, in this hermeneutical task one employs the exegetic categories of orders (*awāmir*, pl. of *amr*) and prohibitions (*nawāhī*, pl. of *nahī*) and their implications, general and specific (*'āmm)* and specific (*khāṣṣ*), clarity (*mubayyan*) and ambiguity (*mujmal*), apparent (*ẓāhir*) and non-apparent (*mu'awwal*), expressed (*manṭūq*) and implicated (*mafhūm*), absolute (*muṭlaq*) and restricted (*muqayyad*), abrogation (*naskh*), and *qiyās*.[10]

The compositions of *Mukhtaṣar* represent continual effort by the Muslim jurists' hermeneutical task in the interpretative process between the authoritative texts and law. The compositions of *Mukhtaṣar* are the culmination of hermeneutical formation of Islamic legal system. The word "*mukhtaṣar*" is generally translated as "abridgment" or "summary" and was traditionally understood in that sense. This literal translation, though correct, fails to convey the real nature and the main purpose for which they were composed. This creates a false impression of Islamic law being static and unchanging. It undermines the significance of the role hermeneutics has played in the formation of Islamic law, not only in the compositions of *Mukhtaṣar*, but also in the entire *corpus* of Islamic jurisprudence.

In the compositions of *Mukhtaṣar*, the authors in the process of hermeneutical interpretations formulate the legal rulings and state them in a shorter and abridged form entailing all the expanded additional essential elements that could have occurred over the course of time. Thus, the compositions of *Mukhtaṣar* in the hermeneutical interpretative process manifest varied aspects in the formation of the Islamic legal system.

The compositions of *Mukhtaṣar* deal with all aspects of law, including religious laws (*aḥkām al-dīn*) and nonreligious laws (*aḥkām al-dunyā*), though the rulings related to the nonreligious matters are also determined according to or consistent with the dictates of the *Qur'ān* and the prophetic *Ḥadīth* reports. Our focus is strictly the analysis of the civil and commercial laws of human beings. Such matters fall under the analysis of the human beings that are expressed through the human language and its varied ways of stating the meanings and implications on the specific legal problems. They involve human utterances, effecting the contracts drawn in writing or expressed verbally such as offer and acceptance of the contract by both parties to the contract, stating the price, quality, quantity, measurement, weight of the commodity, etc. All such transactions are stated in human language, expression of the intention and purpose of the contract.[11] Besides such written words and verbal utterances, the gestures and signs of indications are used, such as nodding, pointing to the article of sale, and standing up during the meeting suggesting the deal is unacceptable.

In our investigation, we are going to explore and examine the nature of contract (*'aqd*), *ṣarf* sale, *salam* sale, right of option (*khiyār*), defects (*'uyūb*), *ribā,* partnership (*shirka*), and lease-hire (*ijāra*) in the compositions of *Mukhtaṣar* in the four Sunni schools of law.

PART I: HERMENEUTICS, AND THE GENRE OF *MUKHTAṢAR*

Part I contains al-Shāfi'ī's concept of hermeneutics and the role it has played in the formation of Islamic legal system, its subsequent developments over the course of time, and the nature and significance of the compositions of *Mukhtaṣar.*

Chapter 1 introduces readers with the concept of al-Shāfi'ī's hermeneutics and its significance in the formation of Islamic law. Al-Shāfi'ī expounds this concept of hermeneutics as method in the *Risāla.* It is the only second/eight century preserved work. For al-Shāfi'ī, God has dictated Islamic law in the revealed sources of the *Qur'ān* and the prophetic *Ḥadīth* reports. They are exclusively two sources of authority and does not include the *ijmā'* of the inhabitants of Medina that Mālik Anas (179/795) claimed to employ.

Al-Shāfi'ī's hermeneutics as a method is designed to hermeneutically systematize Islamic law at the epistemological level. According to Lowry, at the heart of al-Shāfi'ī's *Risāla* is the concept of *Bayān*, the primary legal theoretical concept expounded in detail. All legal rulings are derived from and expounded by one of the following combinations: (i) The *Qur'ān* alone, (ii) the *Qur'ān* and the prophetic *Ḥadīth* reports together, (iii) the *Qur'ān* and the prophetic *Ḥadīth* reports, (iv) the prophetic *Ḥadīth* reports independently alone, and (v) neither the *Qur'ān* nor the prophetic *Ḥadīth* reports, then *qiyās*.

After this, al-Shāfi'ī describes in the *Bayān* four modalities of the legislative statements of law: (i) the *Qur'ān* spells out an obligation and prohibition in the explicit text, (ii) the legislative statements affirmed in the *Qur'ān* and then explained by the prophetic *Ḥadīth* report, (iii) the legislative statement established by the Prophet's practice (*Sunna*) as God has imposed an obligation to obey the Prophet, (iv) when there is no specific legislative statement in either the *Qur'ān* or the prophetic *Ḥadīth,* then one must use *qiyās*.

As Lowry remarks the prophetic *Ḥadīth* reports, though they are co-source with the *Qur'ān*, they belong to different levels. The *Qur'ān* is ontologically primary and the function of the prophetic *Ḥadīth* reports is epistemologically to govern, clarify, and make explicit the intended meaning of the *Qur'ān*. When it comes to the civil and commercial laws in the compositions of *Mukhtaṣar*, the prophetic *Ḥadīth* reports play epistemologically a greater part than the *Qur'ān* as they are most widely used epistemologically for determining the legal rulings related to the legal canons.

After describing the four modalities of the legislative statements, al-Shāfi'ī illustrates following ways of hermeneutically interpreting the legal meaning of the Qur'ānic text by establishing the internal textual relationships: (i) the Qur'ānic verse can be made clear by another Qur'ānic verse, (ii) the Qur'ānic verse can be further elaborated or modified by another Qur'ānic verse, (iii) the prophetic *Ḥadīth* report can elaborate when it is not detailed enough, (iv) the legislative statement can be established by the practices of the Prophet (*Sunna)*, which the *Qur'ān* does not address and they can be considered as the elaboration of the *Qur'ān*, since the *Qur'ān* itself commands obedience to the Prophet, (v) when neither the *Qur'ān* nor the prophetic *Ḥadīth* reports describe any specific legislative statements, then one must as a believer exercise *qiyās*.

Al-Shāfi'ī describes for legislative statements five semantic features of Arabic language as a condition: (i) one must know Arabic language as the *Qur'ān* is revealed in Arabic. Al-Shāfi'ī makes it the basis for the assertion of the ambiguous nature of existing revealed text, especially, its semantic features, besides other four conditions, (ii) the legislative statements which seems to be unrestricted, but in which restricted sense is intended, (iii) unrestricted legislative statements whose apparent meaning is seemingly understood, but understood as restricted, (iv) the legislative statements that are understood from the context of the discourse, (v) the legislative statements not verbally expressed, but indicated by the gestures and signs.

Al-Shāfi'ī discusses specific forms of ambiguity under the term general (*'āmm)* and particular (*khāṣṣ*), the summary speech (*jumla*), and the abrogation (*naskh*) in determining hermeneutically the legal ruling in accordance to the *Qur'ān* and prophetic *Ḥadīth* reports.

Since our investigation deals with the civil and commercial laws in which epistemologically the prophetic *Ḥadīth* reports play a greater role, we would describe here their epistemological functions in determining the legal rulings hermeneutically: (i) the prophetic *Ḥadīth* reports can extend the authority of the *Qur'ān* not mentioned in the *Qur'ān* itself, (ii) the prophetic *Ḥadīth* reports can also help in determining which Qur'ānic verses to abrogate which other Qur'ānic verses, (iii) The prophetic *Ḥadīth* reports can elaborate the summary speech requirements, (iv) the prophetic *Ḥadīth* can function alone in determining the legal rulings.

Chapter 2 is about the nature and the purpose for which the compositions of *Mukhtaṣar* were written. Briefly stated, it juristically clarifies and defines as entailing all the essential additional expanded elements in a previously larger transmitted statement in a shorter statement in a comprehensive form, and the changes that could have occurred over the course of time in the society. The compositions of *Mukhtaṣar* are not "abridgment" as the literal translation of the word "mukhtaṣar" suggests.

For our investigation, we have selected for our investigation compositions of *Mukhtaṣar* from all four Sunni schools of law. The authors of these compositions of *Mukhtaṣar* try to hermeneutically systematize Islamic legal system representing the continuity of the hermeneutical interpretive process by producing and reproducing the compositions of *Mukhtaṣar*.

Our analysis of the contents of the compositions of *Mukhtaṣar* of the selected topics concerning the civil and commercial law shows how their nature, unfolding themselves in varied aspects in the hermeneutical interpretative process. The genre of *Mukhtaṣar* represents the continuity of hermeneutical approach in the formation of Islamic law. This hermeneutical formation of Islamic legal system continues incorporating *progressively* all the extended additional essential elements that have occurred over the course of time from one jurist to the next jurist of the composition of *Mukhtaṣar* as manifested here in al-Muzani's *Mukhtaṣar*, and al-Shīrāzī's *Tanbīh* in the Shāfiʿī school of law, in al-Ṭaḥāwī's *Mukhtaṣar*, al-Qudūrī's *Mukhtaṣar*, and al-Marghīnānī's *Hidāya* in the Ḥanafī school of law, al-Kiraqī's *Mukhtaṣar* in the Ḥanbalī school of law, finally culminating in Khalīl's *Mukhtaṣar* in the Mālikī school of law. Khalīl's *Mukhtaṣar* contains only the hermeneutically *mashhūr* (well-known) legal rulings regardless from which individual jurist or school of law.

PART II: HERMENEUTICS IN THE GENRE OF *MUKHTAṢAR*

Part II is about the genre of *Mukhtaṣar* in four Sunni schools of law and the "Differences of Opinion among the jurists (*Ikhtilāf al-Fuqhā'*)." The translation of each composition of *Mukhtaṣar* is rendered staying closer to the Arabic text.

The main purpose of our investigation is to show that the authors of compositions of *Mukhtaṣar* in the four Sunni schools of law comprehensively incorporate the expanded additional elements continuing the hermeneutical interpretative process in the formation of Islamic law. We are going to highlight the hermeneutical general features followed by the contents in each theme related to the transactions.

In the beginning, the characteristic text of the compositions of *Mukhtaṣar* represent relating hermeneutically the legal rulings to the legal cannons as revealed in the authoritative sources, but gradually this hermeneutical interpretative process develops incorporating increasingly more expanded additional elements. Thus, the authors of the compositions of *Mukhtaṣar* continue to develop *progressively* the hermeneutical process of interpretations in the formation of the Islamic legal system.

In chapter 3 we would deal with al-Shāfi'ī's concept of hermeneutics as reflected in the composition of *Mukhtaṣar* in the Shāfi'ī school of law. They are al-Muzanī's composition of *Mukhtaṣar* and al-Shīrāzī's composition of *Tanbīḥ*.

According to al-Shāfi'ī and al-Muzanī, a contract of sale is valid when both parties to the contract agree to the stipulations to the contract. It becomes binding for both parties upon its being concluded, except if defect is found in the article of sale. The article of sale must be according to the description (*ṣifa*). It should be in existence and is possible to be delivered. The contract of sale should be concluded without breaking the meeting (*majlis*). Al-Muzanī clarifies the right of seeing (*khiyār al-ru'ya*) is valid which al-Shāfi'ī in his earlier works considered not permitted, but in his later writings permitted it.

Al-Shīrāzī specifies the contract of sale by the wordings of offer by the seller and its acceptance by the purchaser. According to al-Shīrāzī, no extraneous conditions should be attached to the contract after it is concluded. He allows the extension of three days regarding the esculent articles.

Al-Shāfi'ī's and al-Muzanī's account of right of option is based on the prophetic *Ḥadīth* reports as they are considered co-source of authority and they serve epistemological function. Al-Shāfi'ī and al-Muzanī recognized the custom as it was practiced by the residents of Ḥijāz.

According to al-Muzanī, it is valid if after the contract has expired, one of the parties to the contract allows the other extension of the right of option. If one purchases a female slave and emancipates her before breaking meeting or if he hastens to perform cardinal intercourse, the seller has right to cancel the contract and the price becomes incumbent on the purchaser. If one of the partners to the contract dies prior to breaking meeting, his authorized representative can execute the right of option. If an animal gives birth to an offspring prior to the separation of the parties from each other, it belongs to the purchaser. In addition, al-Muzanī describes that if madness takes over one party prior to the separation of the parties to the contract, then the ruler (*Ḥākim*) takes over the case.

Al-Shīrāzī brings an expanded additional element regarding when the period of the right of option begins. There are two juristic opinions (*qawlān*).

According to one juristic opinion, the period of the right of option is determined on the day the contract was drawn. According to another juristic opinion, the right of option is determined upon the separation of the parties to the contract.

Al-Muzanī's and al-Shāfi'ī's account of *ribā* and *ṣarf* sale is based on the prophetic *Ḥadīth* reports, which is one of the authoritative sources along with the *Qur'ān* in determining legal rulings. This shows the epistemological significance of the prophetic *Ḥadīth* reports in the formation of the Islamic legal system. Al-Muzanī shows a greater awareness of al-Shāfi'ī's idea of classification of articles into genus (*jins*), species (*ṣanf*), and kind (*nau'*) such as milk and meat of one animal in exchange for milk and meat of another animal. Regarding it, we find differences of opinion among the four Sunni schools of law, which are the result of hermeneutical interpretations. Al-Muzanī in his account exercises *qiyās* as jurist on his own right. There is no *ribā* except in exchange of gold, silver, and esculent articles. In exchange of *dīnārs* and *dirhams*, it is valid to accept *falūs* (currency in use). However, the tax (*zakāt*) is not levied on it.

The *salaf* sale in the esculent articles is invalid. The suspension of payment to a future specified time in exchange of one article for two articles is not objectionable. However, it is not valid in the esculent articles belonging to the same species, except if they are of two different species as well as by estimate. Any two things that share the same proper name (*ism khāṣṣ*) are considered of the same species.

Al-Shīrāzī describes the unlawfulness of *ribā* in exchange of gold and silver as they belong to the same species based on the reason (*'lla*) that they determine the price of other things, likewise, in case of exchange of food and drinks at an unequal rate is based on the reason that they belong to the same species. However, if they belong to different species of food, it is valid.

According to al-Muzanī, the *salam* sale is considered one of the species of the contract of sale. It is based on the prophetic *Ḥadīth* report.

Al-Muzanī presents the material in an abridged form but, following al-Shāfi'ī, he narrates the rulings for different articles separately case by case and not in a general statement. Al-Shīrāzī packs them together in a general statement.

According to al-Shīrāzī, the *salam* sale in partnership and the friendly partnership is not valid. He brings some expanded additional elements in his account of *salam* sale such as the invalidity of ornaments and shells but considers the validity of other articles such as cheese with diffusing odor. In the *salam* sale, the suspension of payment to a future specified time is not valid. However, the suspension of payment in the *salam* sale in two installments is valid. If the *salam* sale is concluded at a certain place, then the description of the place of delivery of the article is not necessary. No extraneous conditions to the stipulations of the contract are allowed. The article of *salam* should be existing at the time of its delivery. If the article of *salam* sale delivered is of better quality or it is delivered before it is due, it is incumbent on the purchaser to accept it. If the purchaser claims against the seller that the article delivered was less in weight or quantity or it was not according to the description, his word is not accepted except with an oath.

Al-Shāfi'ī's account of partnership is very short and hermeneutically not quite developed. He does not cite any Qur'ānic verses or the prophetic *Ḥadīth* reports in support of its validity. Al-Shāfi'ī does not recognize partnership in reciprocity (*shirka mufāwada*), it is considered void (*bāṭil*), though he recognizes the partnership in traffic (*shirka al-'aynān*), and partnership in workmanship (*shirka abdān*). In the partnership, the profit is divided as stipulated in the contract. It is not valid that the partners spend the property in partnership on the personal needs, except for business purpose.

Al-Muzanī bases the validity of partnership on the prophetic narration. The Prophet considered booty acquired in the battle to be shared among the participants in the battle.

Al-Muzanī and al-Shīrāzī both bring expanded additional elements comprehensively incorporating them in their accounts. Some of the main features are described here.

According to al-Muzanī, if one of the partners dies, the partnership is dissolved, and the distribution of the profit acquired in partnership is commissioned to an authorized legal representative. If the inheritor is of legal age, he can become shareholder in partnership. If one of the partners purchases an article and it is found defective, he can return it or if the other partner can keep it, if he likes it. If one of the partners makes a purchase, the claim against him for the price lies on him and not on the other partner. If one of the partners commits treason, it is incumbent on the other partner to bring evidence against him.

Al-Shīrāzī, like al-Muzanī, declares that the validity of partnership is based on the *Sunna*. According to al-Shīrāzī, no partner should be in debt.

Al-Shīrāzī's account of lease-hire is comprehensive and very extensive covering all the essential expanded additional elements. The contract of lease-hire should be indicated clearly by describing it as the lease-hire, the usufruct of the thing being hired-leased and the wages for the work to be performed as recompense. According to Al-Shīrāzī, the contract of lease-hire is one of the species of the contract of sale. He justifies its validity based on the Qur'ānic verse (65: 6). What is valid or invalid in the contract of sale is valid or invalid in the contract of lease-hire. The subject of lease-hire is the usufruct of the thing being hired-leased. Al-Shāfi'ī describes leasing-hiring of a dog for hunting, a male camel for riding on a female camel, the singing girl or musician for entertainment is invalid. It is valid to lease-hire wet nurse for suckling a child, performance of pilgrimage to Mecca, a camel for riding, and hiring of a person for selling and purchasing things. The attainment of the purpose of work is the responsibility of the lessor. The leasing-hiring of an object is not valid, if the usufruct of it is not possible such as the land for cultivation, if water is cut off from reaching it. If a Muslim hires-leases land for cultivation to a *dhimmī*, the tax (*zakāt*) is levied on him, but not the tithe (*'ushar*).

Al-Shīrāzī describes two juristic opinions regarding the validity of the duration of lease-hire. According to one opinion, it is terminated at the end of each year. According to another legal opinion, it is terminated at the end of each three years. This is again the result of hermeneutical interpretative process. If the contract of lease-hire is not specified, the stipulations of right of option and meeting are not valid. The usufruct of certain objects such as house key, camel halter, girdle when they are let on hire-lease is the responsibility of lessor. There is no need to establish the wages for cleaning the pimples, cleaning the sewer, etc. If one leases-hires land for cultivation, he can cultivate any kind of crops. Similarly, if one leases-hires a camel for riding, then he can ride on it for bringing animals to drink water and carry fodder. If one hires-leases an animal to ride to a certain place, it is obligatory to specify the place of destination and wages. If he travels on it a longer distance than specified and the animal becomes destroyed, he is responsible for its price. If one hires-leases an article, it is not valid for him to sublease it. If the article of hire-lease is destroyed, the lessor can cancel the contract for the remaining duration of lease. If the article of lease-hire is usurped until the duration of lease-hire expires, it is considered as destroyed before it was taken into possession. If the lessor dies and the inheritor is not of legal age to whom it has passed, according to one juristic opinion the contract is canceled. According to another juristic opinion, it is not dissolved, and the third party as an agent takes it over. If a hireling goes to perform pilgrimage and dies or is restrained from performing pilgrimage, he is not entitled to wages. However, if he dies after performing pilgrimage, he is entitled to the wages, but the lessor is not responsible for his death. If he dies after performing certain rituals, then wages are determined in proportion to the rituals he has performed. If the leased-hired animal runs away and the lessee leaves it, he is responsible for its price plus the wages. If the property in the hands of a workman becomes destroyed, he is not responsible for it, because he is only a custodian. If the lessor sells the property under lease, the lease-hire is not terminated, but the lessor must fulfill the duration of the lease. If the duration of lease has expired and the tenant has left seedling behind in soil, then he is forced to cut it and level off the soil. If he does not do it, the wages for cutting seedling and clearing soil becomes incumbent on him.

Chapter 4 is about the genre *Mukhtaṣar* in the Ḥanafī school of law. It discusses Abū Ja'far Aḥmad Muḥammad al-Ṭaḥāwī's *Mukhtaṣar*, Abū al-Ḥasan Aḥmad al-Qudūrī's *Mukhtaṣar* supplemented with Buhrān al-Dīn Abū al-Ḥasan 'Alī bin 'Abd al-Jalīl al-Marghīnānī's *Hidāya.*

Al-Shaybānī does not use the term *'aqd* (contract) to signify its legal import. He neither describes the nature of the contract nor does he describe the stipulation of the contract. Al-Ṭaḥāwī's account of the concept of contract describes its nature and stipulations and is hermeneutically closer to that of al-Shāfi'ī.

Al-Ṭaḥāwī refers to the *Sunna* of the Prophet for the validity of the contract. He generally prefers the opinions of two disciples of Abū Ḥanīfa. Al-Ṭaḥāwī and al-Qudūrī both use al-Shāfi'ī's hermeneutical technique in expressing the declaration and acceptance of the contract by gesture or pointing the object of contract of sale. The sale of fruits with the condition of certain *riṭls* exempted is not valid.

Concerning the right of option, al-Shaybānī was accused of by al-Shāfi'ī for using *istiḥsān*, but al-Qudūrī and al-Marghīnānī make use of it explicitly. The stipulation of three days can be extended on the condition that a future time is specified. The three days right of option does not relinquish the ownership of the article of exchange by the parties to the contract.

According to al-Qudūrī, if the article with defect is returned, there is no right of option to exact compensation for the loss.

Al-Shaybānī and al-Qudūrī describe many kinds of defects in the article of sale as to when it is valid or invalid to return them. Al-Shaybānī also describes that it is valid to return the articles of defect which are countable such as walnuts, melons, cucumber, etc.

If one purchases cloth and gives it to dye in a certain color and finds defect in it, he can return it for the compensation. If one purchases a slave and he dies in the possession of the purchaser and later he comes to know of the defect, he is entitled to the compensation. If a person purchases an article and sells it to another person who returns it because of the defect, then the (first) purchaser is not entitled to return it to the seller from whom he had purchased it.

As to the *ribā*, al-Qudūrī establishes unlawfulness of *ribā* by using the word *taḥrīm* based on the Qur'ānic verse. He acknowledges custom as one of the sources of law, but it is considered inferior to the declaration based on the revealed sources of *Qur'ān* and prophetic *Ḥadīth* reports.

Al-Ṭaḥāwī hermeneutically incorporates al-Shāfi'ī's classification of things in genus *(jins)*, species (*ṣanf)*, and kind (*nau'*). The exchange of an excellent quality of article for an inferior quality of article is not permitted. Unlawfulness in everything in respect to the excess (*tafāḍul*) of one article of sale to other article of the same species has been established by the textual evidence (*naṣṣ*). It is considered forever of that nature, no matter how humankind forsakes this kind of mode of estimation, because the custom of the people is inferior to the revealed sources.

The *ṣarf* sale is valid based on the prophetic *Ḥadīth* report and was recognized by the Prophet. In the *ṣarf* sale, the articles of exchange, such as gold in exchange for gold, are permitted when they are of equal weight and measurement.

According to al-Qudūrī, the right of option in the *ṣarf* sale is invalid. In case of jewelry and ornaments to which gold or silver is attached, the price of gold or silver is considered valid. If the articles are of different species, then the *ṣarf* sale in exchange of one article for the other article at an unequal is valid.

Al-Qudūrī summarily puts all seven conditions of a valid *salam* together: (i) description of species, (ii) kind, (iii) quality, (iv) weight, (v) measurement, (vi) place of delivery, and (vii) the price of article of the *salam* sale received by the seller.

Al-Marghīnānī explicitly cites the validity of *salam* sale based on the prophetic *Ḥadīth* report. The weight, measurement, specified period of the delivery of the article of *salam* sale should be stipulated. The *salam* sale is valid of the articles of the same species which do not differ in their units. The *salam* sale of animal flesh and fresh fish is not valid. The usufruct of article of *salam* sale is invalid prior to the possession of article. The seller of the article of *salam* sale takes the price or takes the possession of the exchange of article prior to breaking meeting. The article of *salam* sale must be existing at the time when the contract is concluded and at the time of its delivery. If the article does not require expense of porterage, it is not necessary to describe the place of delivery. If the place of delivery was not specified, then the purchaser is obligated to accept the delivery of article.

The *salam* sale of dog or hawk is not valid. Likewise, the *salam* sale of honeybees is not valid, if not protected.

According to al-Shīrāzī and al-Marghīnānī, if anyone ask worker to make a thing, he has right of option to accept or reject it, because it was purchased without seeing it.

According to al-Marghīnānī, the *salam* sale of pearls and shells is invalid. The purchaser does not become proprietor of the article unless he himself has weighed or measured the article of *salam* sale. The price of the article of *salam* sale is incumbent on the purchaser or seller in whose possession it was, if it is destroyed.

Only in the Ḥanafī school of law, the partnership in reciprocity (*shirka mufāwada*) and partnership on personal credit (*shirka wujūh*) are acknowledged. It was only later that Mālikī jurist Khalīl acknowledges them in the *Mukhtaṣar* as we would see in chapter 6.

Al-Shaybānī discusses only the partnership in reciprocity (*shirka mufāwada*) and that too only briefly. Al-Ṭaḥāwī's, al-Qudūrī, and al-Marghīnānī deal with all four kinds of partnerships.

Al-Marghīnānī states the validity of partnership is based on the prophetic *Ḥadīth* report. In the time of Prophet people were accustomed to have transactions in partnership and the Prophet confirmed it.

According to al-Shaybānī, al-Ṭaḥāwī, and al-Qudūrī, partnership in reciprocity is valid between two Muslims or two *dhimmīs* since equality exists between them, but not between a free person and a slave, an adult and a minor of not legal age, and a Muslim and an unbeliever. Abū Ḥanīfa considers that the partnership between a Muslim and an unbeliever is not valid, but the two disciples allow it. The partnership can be contracted only in *dīnārs* and *dirhams* and no wares.

The partnership in traffic consists of having only goods and effects between two partners to purchase and sell in proportion to the same amount of goods and effects. It comprehends only agency (*wakāla*) and not bail (*kafāla*). If the property of one partner exceeds the property of other partner and the profit is shared at an unequal rate, it is valid based on the prophetic narration. If one of the partners makes a purchase with his property and afterward the property of other partner is destroyed, the thing purchased is considered in partnership between two of them. The partnership in traffic is valid between a Muslim and an unbeliever. The partnership in traffic between an owner and his slave with the limited permission is valid. If a person in partnership in traffic makes a purchase, he is responsible for its price in case there is a claim against him for it. No specified amount of profit is allowed for any partner in it. Each partner is at liberty in partnership in traffic and partnership in reciprocity to give the portion of profit (*bayḍa*) in the manner to lodge it as deposit or pledge in security.

The partnership in workmanship consists of when two persons join in partnership by agreement to work and share their earnings between them. The partnership in workmanship is valid in all what is valid in the contract of sale valid in respect to agency and what is invalid in respect to bail. The partnership in traffic between two females and two males, and between a male and a female is valid.

The partnership on personal credit is valid, if two persons having no property become partners on their personal credit to purchase and sell and each partner become both agent and bail for other partner for what each partner purchase or sell with the stipulation that it shall be of equal of profit and loss. If the profit is stipulated of an unequal amount between them, it is invalid. If one of the partners become apostate, or join the enemy territory, the partnership is annulled.

The contract of lease-hire in al-Shaybānī, al-Ṭaḥāwī, and al-Qudūrī are in substance not much different, except each one of them hermeneutically brings together entailing some expanded additional elements comprehensively.

Al-Qudūrī tries to hermeneutically incorporate expanded additional elements comprehensively not found in the writings of al-Shaybānī. He uses the prophetic *Ḥadīth* report in support for the validity of the contract of lease-hire and one of the techniques indicating the place by pointing it out. Al-Shaybānī makes use of the doctrine of *istiḥsān*.

Al-Qudūrī defines the contract of lease-hire as the profit (*munāfi'a*) in exchange for the usufruct of the article of lease-hire. For a valid contract of lease-hire, the usufruct and the wages must be specified based on the prophetic *Ḥadīth* report.

According to al-Shaybānī, al-Ṭaḥāwī, and Qudūrī, the contract of lease-hire is one of the species of contract of sale.

As to the time, al-Marghīnānī states that the recompense does not become due at the time of concluding the contract, contrary to al-Shāfi'ī's opinion. It can be claimed in advance, or as the consequence of the leaseholder obtaining the article of lease-hire, or by the previous agreement.

According to Abū Ḥanīfa and Abū Yūsuf, it is not valid for the lessor to demand rent (recompense) unless it is due. If the lease-hire is terminated before it has expired, the lessor returns rent for the remaining period of lease-hire.

According to al-Ṭaḥāwī, if one of the parties to the contract dies, the contract of lease-hire is void.

According to al-Shaybānī, if a person leases-hires land for cultivation of wheat and instead he cultivates fresh dates and if there is a loss, he is responsible for it and rent becomes incumbent on him.

According to Qudūrī, it is valid to lease-hire field to build a structure on it, or plant trees and when the lease-hire expires, he is responsible to tear down the structure on it, cut down the trees and level off the field.

According to al-Qudūrī, if one leases-hires an animal to ride on it, he can give it to another person to ride on it.

According to al-Ṭaḥāwī, if one leases-hires an animal to ride on it to a certain place and if he travels longer distance than specified, he is responsible for the rent of that additional distance. If the animal is destroyed by traveling, the lessee is responsible for the price of the animal. If one leases-hires cloth to wear and gives it to someone else to wear it, it is valid and, likewise, in such other things. In the same manner, it is valid if one leases-hires house and gives it to someone else to reside in it. If a person leases-hires house and after taking its possession it becomes damaged, he has right of option to keep it renting or he can invalidate the lease-hire.

According to al-Qudūrī and al-Ṭaḥāwī, there are two kinds of lease-hire: (i) common lease-hire (*ajīr mushrak*) and (ii) particular lease-hire (*ajīr khāṣṣ*).

The common lease- hire is when the contract of lease-hire is concluded for work and there is no requisite mentioned such as in case of dyeing or bleaching cloth. In such a case, the article given for the work is considered deposit and if the article becomes destroyed the worker is considered not responsible for it, but he is not entitled to the wages. This is the juristic opinion of Abū Ḥanīfa. According to the two disciples, the worker is entitled to the recompense.

The particular lease-hire is in which the worker is entitled to recompense by submitting himself or herself for a certain term such as for certain time such as for one month for the specified services, but not including any other things.

If a person leases-hires a shop and afterward becomes poor and gets involved in debt not enabling him to pay rent, then the Ḥākim takes over the case and sells the property of shopkeeper for the payment of debt.

Al-Ṭaḥāwī describes various kinds of defects due to which it is valid or not valid to return the defective articles. Returning of such as the female slave having bad smell in the mouth or she is habituated to adultery she is returned, but the same defect occurs in a male slave, it is not valid to return him.

Chapter 5 deals with al-Khiraqī's composition of *Mukhtaṣar* in the Ḥanbalī school of law. Although Aḥmad ibn Ḥanbal is considered the founder of the Ḥanbalī school of law, he is primarily a traditionist (*muḥaddīth*) and in the second place a jurisprudent to the extent his juristic *dicta* (*qāla*) are based on the prophetic *Ḥadīth* reports as required by Al-Shāfi'ī's concept of hermeneutics, but without further hermeneutical interpretations. The jurists in succeeding generations in the Ḥanbalī school of law, such as ʿOmar ibn Ḥusayn al-Khiraqī and others, incorporated expanded additional elements in the formation of the Islamic system.

Al-Khiraqī's composition of *Mukhtaṣar* is the first in the Ḥanbalī school of law after the acceptance of al-Shāfi'ī's concept of hermeneutics. Al-Khiraqī comprehensively incorporates the expanded additional elements in the formation of the Islamic legal system in the manner of the compositions of *Mukhtaṣar* of other Sunni schools of law. As a result, al-Khiraqī brings little of his own expanded additional elements comprehensively. Those expanded additional elements to mention are as follows:

It is not valid in the *salam* sale to take as security (*rahan*) or surety (*kafīl*) from a person to whom the article of *salam* sale is to be delivered.

The partnership, friendly partnership, and transfer of the property are considered the species of contract of sale, but not cancellation (*iqāla*), in contrast to it Aḥmad ibn Ḥanbal maintains that the cancellation is also one of the species of contract of sale.

If the silent partner (*muḍārib*) commissions a person to trade with the capital, then he is not permitted to commission another person to trade with it, because in that case the loss would incur for the first person whom he has commissioned. If he does it and the profit occur in the trade, it is returned to the first person whom he has commissioned.

If a person purchases food in lump, he is not entitled to sell it, unless it is transferred to him and knows its exact measurement.

In chapter 6, we have discussed al-Shāfiʿī's concept of the hermeneutics as reflected in Khalīl's *Mukhtaṣar*. Here we would explain briefly the most unique and striking feature of Khalīl's *Mukhtaṣar*. According to Khalīl, *Mukhtaṣar* denotes shortening or abridgment of a statement by which jurists mean replacing a longer statement with a shorter statement, which entails comprehensively all the expanded essential elements included in a larger statement. It is called *Mukhtaṣar* when the shorter statement indicates the meaning in entirety contained in thc longer statement. Khalīl expresses them in a shorter phrase or word denoting the legal rulings containing legal opinions from Mālik ibn Anas and bin Saʿīd Saḥnūn, and expanded additional elements developed from the jurists in earlier generations until Khalīl compiled the *Mukhtaṣar*. Another unique feature of Khalīl's *Mukhtaṣar* is that it contains only the *mashhūr* legal opinions regardless of which individual jurists or schools of law they are. When no definite ruling has been transmitted or not discussed by the jurists from earlier generations, Khalīl shows hesitation (*tarddud*) and does not give any legal opinion.

As Khalīl's *Mukhtaṣar* contains only the *mashhūr* legal opinions which had already been hermeneutically related to the legal canons, we would in this summary account mention only those elements which are expanded additional elements, or they specify clearly the rulings.

Khalīl defines the contract of sale precisely by using the wordings "offer of sale by the seller" and "acceptance of it" by the purchaser. In addition, he clarifies that the parties who draw the contract should be in the right frame of mind, not overcome by madness, and be of legal age. The contract of sale is not forced upon either of the parties to the contract.

The delay is granted in the execution of emancipation of slave by a Muslim and in case of an unbeliever, he is asked to expedite it.

If the seller is absent and far away, it is permitted to sell the slave by a person who has become Muslim. According to Khalīl, there has been transmitted no legal opinion from the jurists of earlier generations (*tarddud*).

The object of the contract of sale must be pure and lawful not such as manure, contaminated oil, or something of no use. It is not valid, if the price or value of the article of sale is not known.

It is valid to sell in the amount of four *riṭls* of meat of an animal as an exemption. If the animal dies after the purchaser has enjoyed meat, he owes its price.

If the seller knows the measurement and quantity of an article of sale and the purchaser did not know it, then he is given choice to accept it or return it. If he is informed of it later, then the sale is void such as in case of the singing girl for whose services the charges to be paid are informed later. If both parties to the contract know or think the land sold was leveled, it is valid. However, if they come to know of it later that it was not leveled or have doubt about it, then the seller has a choice to reduce the price of land or increase land in measurement.

It is not valid to sell living sparrows confined to the cage by estimate, because they do not fall in the category of estimate.

It is valid when the description of the articles is known by seeing similar of its kind (*mithlī*).

If a person buys an article relying upon the testimony that it is corresponding to the entry in the official register and claims that it was found different from what is recorded in it, then the word rests with the seller with an oath confirming that it was corresponding to the description as recorded in the register.

If one purchases an article which he has seen before and claims that a change was made in the description of an article, then the word rests with the seller with an oath.

It is valid to sell specified article with the known description in the absence of seller from the place where the contract was drawn. If the seller is not far away and it was not possible to see the article of sale without encountering any difficulty, the contract is void with only the description of article.

It is valid for the seller to expedite the payment of sale of an immovable property. It is the responsibility of the purchaser. Affecting an immovable property, it is valid to sell it in exchange for *dīnārs* in the absence of seller with the stipulation making it requisite that the purchaser expedite the payment within the near future (e.g., two days). In case, there is a dispute from the side of purchaser affecting the sale of moveable property whether it is destroyed or damaged, or existing, or regarding its description, the word rests with him with an oath.

It is absolutely (*muṭlaq*) unlawful in the *ṣarf* sale that one of the parties to the contract makes the payment immediately and the other makes payment at a future specified time.

It is invalid if *dirhams* are deposited and they become damaged or destroyed for which different kinds of *dirhams* are given as substitutes.

It is unlawful to combine sale and *ṣarf* sale in one contract. It is prohibited to expedite *ṣarf* sale, nor is it allowed to combine *dīnārs* from the purchaser and *dirhams* and wares from the seller. However, it is valid that *dīnārs* and *dirhams* to be payable at a future specified time to expedite sale of wares.

If a person gives silver to the goldsmith to make jewelry or *dīnārs* to make gold nuggets, the wages for it can be realized in two ways: either he can purchase silver or gold from the goldsmith and leave it with him to make jewelry or to make gold nuggets and pays wages. In this there is no *ribā* or *nisā'* or he can purchase jewelry molded in gold or silver and in addition to it pays wages. In this case, only *ribā* is involved. If there were no additional wages in the first case, it is valid and preferably in the second case it is not allowed.

If a person has exchanged *dīnārs* for *dirhams* in the sale with another person and says to him, "I permit it for more *dirhams* or differed payment," it is valid as the contract of sale and the contract of *ṣarf* sale becomes void. If the defect appears only in the original (*aṣl*) exchange of *dīnārs*, they are returned, but if it appears afterward, they are not returned, since they are with the increase or differed payment. It is invalid absolutely to return increase of *dirhams* if defect is found, except if it was made incumbent on the person who permitted *dīnārs* for increase in *dirhams.*

If there is a dispute regarding the corruption in *raṣāṣ*, the sale is resorted by substituting it. If there is a lapse of a long time between the appearance of defect and the time when the contract was concluded, and it was specified that if there is a lapse of long time between the appearance of the defect and when the contract was concluded, the contract is void.

The *ṣarf* sale for a smaller amount of *dīnārs* is invalidated when they are not combined with a larger amount of *dīnārs*, but it does not invalidate for a larger amount of *dīnārs*. However, if the *dīnārs* are different, the *ṣarf* sale of all *dīnārs* becomes invalidated. This is *mashhūr.*

If the substitute for defect is stipulated in the *ṣarf* sale when articles are not of the same species, it is invalid, except if they are combined in the contract of sale and in the contract of *ṣarf* sale.

It is valid to sell gold or silver attached to the *Qur'ān,* sword, or cloth after it is taken out from it. However, it is forbidden if it is attached to the inkwell, weapons used in the holy war excepting sword, saddle, riding animals, and man's clothing. If the ornament is nailed in with silver in the bag or bowl and it is not decomposed in its structure, then it has no effect on the permissibility to sell it. If an ornament is molded with gold or silver, it is not valid to sell it in exchange for gold or silver by weight, except if gold or silver is one-third combined in exchange for lesser. If an ornament is molded in gold or silver with any other metal, it is not valid to sell it. The substitute of lower quality of gold or silver in exchange for excellent quality of gold or silver lesser in weight is not allowed.

If the price of sold *dīnārs* or *dirhams* is arranged as the responsibility of purchaser to execute it, it is considered as the execution of debt or loan. If *falūs, dīnārs*, or *dirhams* fall in disuse in business transactions after it was arranged as the responsibility of purchaser or if their prices change continually in business transactions, then it is considered as *rahan* and there is nothing incumbent on the purchaser. If a person owes *falūs* from borrowing and they fall in disuse, then it is considered as if there was no borrowing.

Regarding the duration of time, Khalīl's *Mukhtaṣar* incorporates following expanded additional elements developed over the course of time:

According to Khalīl, the duration of right of option in general is one month in the sale of house, but some say two months. But, the ruling for the duration of two months applies in the sale of land and some say three or four months, because in the sale of land more time is required. In case of house, the purchaser has right of option to stay in the house overnight to get familiar with the neighborhood without occupying it and bringing his family and possessions in it. The rent for it is incumbent on the seller. It is valid in the sale of an animal to ride on it for a day during the time of right of option. Some jurists allow it for two or three days.

The right of option combining slave, his service, wages, and usufruct all together is valid.

It is not objectionable to stipulate riding on animal to bring messages from one place to other place and return.

The right of option takes place after the purchaser has settled in the house and the sale is considered to become sale with the right of option.

The stipulation of right of option concerning consultation in the absence of seller when he is far away from the place of contract and it is not known how to reach him, then it is interpreted according to the original (*aṣl*) right of option and agreement.

It is invalid to stipulate right of option in the sale of a piece of cloth without measuring it. If the purchaser after wearing it brings it defiled to return it to the seller after the expiration of duration of right of option, because of the responsibility of seller to measure it, then one of the parties in whose possession that piece of cloth is, is considered responsible for it.

It is invalid to defer price in the sale at the end of duration of right of option.

The lease-hire of land for cultivation not protected from calamity cancels the contract, if it is not replaced and brought to safety.

The lease-hire to begin after a month or more than one month is invalid.

If the purchaser buys one piece of the two pieces of cloth and takes them into his possession to choose one of them and return the other, he can by the stipulation of right of option purchase one of them and return other. However, the purchaser is responsible for the price of both pieces of cloth, if seller did not ask him to take both into his possession. If the purchaser claims that one piece of the cloths is destroyed, he is responsible for half of the price.

Regarding the absoluteness of responsibility such as loan or payment of debt, he has choice to keep one-third and pays two-thirds assuming as if two-thirds were destroyed.

The article of sale is returned, if it was not for the purpose for which it was bought. If the article s found not in accordance with the description, it is returned.

The sold article is returned, if it is found with defect because its price is reduced.

If the bisexuality in male or female slave is displayed, he or she is returned. The bisexuality is displayed by the mutual sexual act of male with another male and bisexuality in female is displayed by the mutual sexual act of female with another female, they are not returned because of doubtful resemblance from their speech or movement. Khalīl restricts it to the display of baseness in character as a defect. The hermaphrodite is considered defect. The male slave lacking hardness in the sexual organ and the female slave having depressed sexual organ are considered defects. Similarly, the defect in an animal such as wound inside its hoof preventing smooth walk and making it stumble, stubbornness in an animal, excessive aversion of eating less food, camel capable of not running fast or one cannot sit on it because of its slenderness, and an animal having disease called *sawas* are all considered defects.

The price of house is not returned because of the small defects such as the collapse of balcony and sinking of payment when the price of house is neither reduced or is it returned. Instead, in such a case the repair costs are deducted from the price of house.

If the female slave says to the purchaser, "I am the mother of seller's child" and a fortiori a free person and if it becomes established with the evidence before or after she has been sold, then the seller is liable for one-third of the price or compensation.

Khalīl also narrates seven conditions of the valid *salam* sale, as did Ḥanafī jurists al-Qudūrī in the *Mukhtaṣar* and al-Marghīnānī in the *Hidāya.*

The *salam* sale of a larger grown up animal in exchange for a smaller animal until it grows to become a larger and grown up animal is not valid, because there is a risk and gamble involved in it. However, the *salam* sale of two small animals in exchange for one larger animal in the same species is valid, if their usufructs are different.

The *salam* sale of one article known in exchange for another unknown article relying upon the knowledge gained by information is valid.

According to Mālik, difference of male and female in animals and humans is of no consequence. However, jurists from the earlier generations have disagreed with Mālik's opinion, because the usufructs of male and female in humans are different.

There is no difference in the knowledge of arithmetic and writing of slave, because both are of the same description. Writing includes reading, trading, dress making and such other things.

If the delivery of *salam* is specified to a different place at a distance away of two days in journey, then it is delivered on the third day. The postponement of the delivery of article for a month or two is counted by the first day of the appearance of new moon.

The article of *salam* sale is measured or weighed according to the custom of people.

It is not valid to sell two loads of wood packed in a bundle, because of the uncertainty (*gharar*) due to the difference of heaviness and lightness of wood packed in the bundle.

Taking price of the article sold in the *salam* sale into possession in advance ensures that there would be no loss due to the delay in the delivery of article.

Khalīl discusses at great length the descriptions of articles in the *salam* sale because of which their prices can differ in humans such as whether the slave is Roman or black man, whether he is of excellent or average quality. Some jurists claim that such descriptions are acknowledged in all articles of the *salam* sale. Other jurists claim that more descriptions are required in animals, cloths, honey etc. More descriptions are needed in case of palm dates and fish imported from different places, whether of superior or inferior quality, old or recently grown, and the description of their species. In brief, Khalīl comprehensively incorporates all these expanded elements in his account of *salam* sale.

According to Khalīl, there are seven kinds of partnership: partnership in reciprocity, partnership in traffic, partnership in restoration, partnership in workmanship, partnership in responsibility or on credit, silent partnership, and partnership in borrowing or loan. In the partnership in reciprocity, partnership in traffic, partnership in workmanship, and partnership on credit are already included other partnerships.

It is important to note from hermeneutical point of view that Khalīl acknowledges the partnership in reciprocity contrary to the opinion of Mālik and Malikī jurists. This is not to be considered simply the "difference of opinion" between the tenets of the school of law. In fact, Khalīl considers the partnership in reciprocity valid because of the hermeneutical interpretative process resulting into that of difference of opinion.

If a person in partnership deposits property in partnership without any good reason and it becomes destroyed or stolen, he is responsible for it.

It is valid if one of the partners takes out one-third from his property in partnership and keeps remaining two-thirds in the partnership.

It is valid if one of the partners sells the property on credit, but he is not permitted to purchase it on credit.

If one of the partners takes one hundred *dīnārs* from the partnership and claims that he has returned them in the partnership and dispute arises after a lapse of long time has elapsed when the contract was concluded, then the word of the one who claimed that he has returned them is accepted with an oath.

If a person in partnership relinquishes expenses for food and cloth from the partnership residing at a place, then expenses are determined according to the custom. The expenses for food and clothing for his personal and his family members are eliminated, if the ages and numbers of family members of two partner are residing at two different places where prices are different.

It is invalid in the partnership in traffic to require that a partner can have usufruct of the property in partnership in the presence of another partner.

It is invalid, if a person in the partnership in workmanship claims that the earnings made were only for him and not for the other.

The partnership in workmanship requires that the workmanship of both partners is compatible with each other.

Khalīl describes several reasons from different jurists of the invalidity of partnership on credit. According to Ibn Rushd, the profit follows responsibility, but in the partnership on credit each partner borrows from the other partner. It is like the workmanship of one partner brings capital and not the other.

The tools in the partnership in workmanship remain in the partnership after deducting the expenses and profit of each partner.

It is not valid in the partnership in traffic that one partner brings rooster and the other hens, and they are in debt, that is, the persons in the partnership in traffic should not be in debt.

If one partner in the partnership in workmanship falls sick or dies, then it is incumbent on the other partner to complete the work.

The revenues are not to be singled out exclusive for the owner. If it is stipulated in the contract by the owner of animals that his representative works with his animals and the revenues generated from it are for him and he pays wages to him for the work, it is invalid.

Two persons sharing structure in partnership, one residing upstairs and the other downstairs, and the roof of structure breaks down, then the owner of the structure of upstairs is responsible to repair it, and if the wall of lower part is destroyed, then the owner of the structure of downstairs is responsible to repair it.

In the account of lease-hire, Khalīl specifies as a general statement that there are three constitutive elements (*arkān* pl. of *rukn*): contract of lease-hire between two parties, the specified amount of wages, and the usufruct of the thing leased-hired.

The contract of lease-hire and the wages in one contract is invalid according to the *mashhūr* legal opinions, because, as Ibn Rushd says, the contract of lease-hire is not concluded except with the specified wages. Similarly, the contract of lease-hire in combination with the contract of sale is invalid.

It is not valid to lease-hire wet nurse for breast-feeding an infant, except after her own young child has become a one-year-old.

It is invalid, if one leases-hires any one to pick up the fallen olives or pressing them in exchange for one-third portion from it as wages or portion from the extracted olive oil as wages, because of not knowing the quantity of fallen olives or the description of oil from olives.

The lease-hire of land to cultivate in exchange for food is invalid, except for growing something other than food such as cotton, linen, flex, etc.

According to Mālik, it is not objectionable to lease-hire to grow wood. He meant with it Indian wood, sandal wood, fire wood, and tree stems, because they are easy to grow, and they last long time.

According to Mālik, if one leases-hires a person for sewing cloth today for a *dirham* and if he does it tomorrow for half of it, it is not valid and if he sews Roman garment for a *dirham* and if he sews Persian garment for half of it, it is not valid because these are two different contracts combined in one contract.

According to Mālik, it is valid if one sells to a person half of cloth or other things on the condition to sell other half later at an appointed time, except in case of food. According to Saḥnūn, it is not valid because the possession of wages is not known with specification.

Mālik said that it is valid if one rents an animal for a *dīnār* to ride on it to a certain place on the condition that the rent is calculated at the place of arrival as designated or known. According Ibn Rushd as he heard from Ibn al-Qāsim, it is valid if one rents a house for a year on the condition that if the lessee vacates it before it, then the rent is calculated according to the time of his residency in it.

It is valid that the lessor permits the lessee differed payment of rent or exempt it in exchange for any usufruct or exempt it before the next term of lease is transferred, assuming it would remain the same.

According to Ibn Yūnus, leasing land for thirty years for cash or differed payment is valid, because it is reliable in such things that there would be no change.

It is valid to rent a thing for two years for the known wages without specifying the rent for each month of the year.

It is valid to rent land for a mosque for a certain time and after the expiration of lease, if the structure is destroyed, it is valid for the owner of land to take stone, wood, rubbles, and debris from it and make use of it as he pleases. The owner of land is not forced to keep the mosque in existence.

It is valid to hire anyone to carry dead body, or to take out blood, or human ordure from the place.

It is valid to hire anyone for teaching good manners to a slave, child, or mate. It is not objectionable to beat your slave or child to teach him good manners. However, it is not appropriate to beat one's parents or a stranger.

It is valid to hire a male female slave for rendering services and other things for ten days or fifteen days. Khalīl states this without making a distinction between two kinds of contract lease-hire: common lease-hire (*ajīr mushrak*) and particular lease-hire as did al-Qudūrī did. This kind of lease-hire is particular lease-hire in which person commits himself to serve for specified services.

The differed payment in the contract of lease-hire comprises in order of land, then house, then slave, then animal, and then cloth.

It is valid to rent land for thirty or forty years without cash payment, if it is reliable that the water is available.

It is valid to hire a sewer to sew cloth on the condition to return it on the day of beginning of week, month, or year. If with sewing other workmanship is combined such as restricting it to time and workmanship in one contract, it is not valid.

It is invalid to hire for suckling an animal which is forbidden to eat such as donkey for suckling it by female donkey.

If the washing of rage by wet nurse is not stipulated, then it is done as currently practiced among the people. It includes the suckling to an infant, fastening him in bed, anoint him, washing his body with warm water, and coloring the eyelids with kohl making him look beautiful.

It is invalid to hire wet nurse to breastfeed a child, if it is detriment to the child. According to Ibn Qāsim, if one hires wet nurse to breastfeed an infant, then it is not valid that she breast-feeds other children.

It is valid if the rightful owner sells wares such as for one hundred *dīnārs* on the condition that the seller sells it for him for one hundred *dīnārs* a year and the profit is for him only and he pays wages for the seller, since the purpose is to sell the property for one hundred *dīnārs*. If the seller does trade and buys and sells with one hundred *dīnārs* all some of the wares, it is valid according to the consensus, if it is stipulated in the contract that (even if) the price of all or some wares become reduced by continuing the trading for a year. If it is not stipulated, it is not valid because of the higher degree of uncertainty.

It is valid to hire an instructor for teaching *Qur'ān* for a known wage for each month, year, or week. If it is not described, it is pursued as in all times or on the condition of the memorization of whole of or a portion of it. It is repugnant to hire anyone for the recitation of *Qur'ān* with the appropriate nasal sonorous voice to tune with according to what is known in music. It is repugnant to hire anyone for teaching science of *fiqh* (*'ilm al-fiqh*), and teaching of the divine precept (*farā'iḍ*), and selling *fiqh* books.

It is valid to hire an Imam (prayer leader) to lead prayers, including the prayer calls; however, it is not valid to hire anyone for the performance of one's compulsory or supererogatory prayers.

It is forbidden to hire a mute person for teaching and a blind person guarding and killing any innocent person or cut parts of his body or cleaning mosque.

It is repugnant that a Muslim hires a slave to an unbeliever in the valid workmanship such as construction and tailoring and in the invalid workmanship such as wine and guarding pigs.

It is repugnant to build mosque for renting it. It is not permitted because of the forbiddance.

It is valid to rent house with the fruits of Dahlia plants or palm trees for which no more than one-third is retained from the rent for watering them and other related services.

Chapter 7 deals with the difference of opinions among the jurists described in the classical *fiqh* literature under the title "Differences of Opinion among the Jurists" (*Ikhtilāf al-Fuqhā'*). These differences of opinion among the jurists generally came to be understood because of the different tenets of schools of law rather than considering that they are because of the different hermeneutical interpretations in the process of the formation of Islamic law.

NOTES

1. Husain Kassim, "Possibility of Applying *Autopoisis* Theory," p. 6; See also for a detailed account of it, Husain Kassim, *Islamicate Societies* (Lehman: Lexington Books, 2012), Chapter Five, pp. 87–98.
2. Niklas Luhman, "Operational Closure and Structural Coupling: The Differentiation of Legal System in *Cordozo Law Review*, 13, 1992, p. 1423.
3. Husain Kassim, "Law of Contract and Obligaton: Accommodating Civil and Commercial Law with the *Sharīʿa*," *Islamic Quarterly*, vol. 58, no. 3, 2014, p. 210.
4. Kassim, "Law of Contract and Obligation," vol. 58, no, 3, p. 211.
5. Kassim, "Law of Contract and Obligation: vol. 58, no. 3, p. 216; See also J. N. D. Anderson, "Sharīʿa and Civil Law" in *The Islamic Quarterly*, 1954.
6. Kassim, "Law of Contract and Obligation," vol. 58, no. 3, p. 216; George N. Sfeir, *Modernization of the Law in Arab States* (San Francisco, 1988), p. 97.
7. Kassim, "Law of Contract and Obligation," vol. 58, no.3, p. 216; See also J. N. D. Anderson, "Sharīʿa and Civil Law" in *The Islamic Quarterly*, 1954.
8. Kassim, "Law of Contract and Obligation, vol. 58, no. 3, p. 216; George N. Sfeir, *Modernization of the Law in Arab States* (San Francisco: Bethsda, 1988), p. 97.
9. Norman Calder, *Studies in Early Muslim Jurisprudence* (Oxford: Clarendon, 1993), p. 245.
10. See for further elucidation Robert Gleave, *Islam and Literalism* (Edinburgh: Edinburgh University Press, 2012).
11. David R. Vishanoff, *The Formation of Islamic Hermeneutics* (New Haven, CT, 2012), p. 18.

Part I

ISLAMIC LEGAL HERMENEUTICS, AND THE GENRE OF *MUKHTAṢAR*

Chapter 1

Al-Shāfi'ī's Concept of Hermeneutics

The Risāla *and the Role it has played in the Formation of Islamic Law*

In this brief sketch of the *Risāla* of Muḥammad ibn al-Shāfi'ī (204/820), we shall discuss in a very broad outline the nature and purpose of a hermeneutical approach. This approach is unlike the great detail one finds in *Early Islamic Legal Theory: The Risāla of Muhammad ibn Idrīs al-Shāfi'ī* by Joseph Lowry[1] and, in some respects, in *The Formation of Islamic Hermeneutics: How Sunni Legal Theorists Imagined a Revealed Laws* by David R. Vishanoff.[2] We shall mostly refer to these two sources to the extent needed.

It can be asserted that al-Shāfi'ī in his *Risāla* planted seeds of a hermeneutical approach in the formation of Islamic law. It is this hermeneutical approach with its further development by the Muslim jurists in succeeding generations that Islamic law took the form of a comprehensive legal system.[3] Thus, in a very broad sense, one can characterize the entire legal discourse as the hermeneutics. "The originality of *Risāla* lies in its departure from the previous approach in the study of Islamic law."[4] Al-Shāfi'ī defined the methodology in which legal reasoning was restricted within the framework of revealed sources provided in the *Qur'ān* and the prophetic *Ḥadīth* reports. Al-Shāfi'ī was the first jurist who laid down a hermeneutical methodology of Islamic law in its rudimentary form that confined legal reasoning within the parameter of the revealed sources.

Prior to al-Shāfi'ī, Islamic legal system does not appear to have hermeneutical theory. Al-Shāfi'ī's *Risāla*, discussing the matters of abstract theory, proceeds from its example problems. "It is through those individual example problems in applied legal reasoning that al-Shāfi'ī demonstrates the truth of theoretical claims."[5] In constructing his arguments by giving examples of legal and textual problems using hermeneutical technics for deriving legal rulings, al-Shāfi'ī provides the framework for the formation of the Islamic legal system.

AL-SHĀFI'Ī'S HERMENEUTICAL LEGAL SYSTEM

The purpose of al-Shāfi'ī's legal theory was to determine hermeneutically legal rulings in accordance with the revealed sources. For al-Shāfi'ī, the Islamic legal system is a comprehensive and coherent system of law in the sources revealed by God. In the environment in which al-Shāfi'ī constructs this hermeneutically Islamic legal system, neither the legal discourse of his day nor the *corpus* of the prophetic *Ḥadīth* reports were yet fixed as the canon.

According to Hallaq, "legal theory—the science of sources of law (*uṣūl al-fiqh*), epistemology, and hermeneutics—was not yet developed."[6] Nevertheless, by the end of the second/eighth century, there was already a broad consensus formed about the general ideas of Islamic law as well as established rules. Gradually, the discussions began to focus on subsidiary aspects within the parameter of the mainstream of positive law. What remained was to establish a methodology to systematize and unify comprehensively legal rulings of positive law within the revealed legal canons. Al-Shāfi'ī expounded it in the *Risāla* systematically. It is the only preserved work, which offers hermeneutically sustained treatment.[7] Al-Shāfi'ī's hermeneutics was designed to bring changes to the arbitrary way of applying the legal canons to the legal rulings in the Islamic legal system. When we are talking about bringing changes in the existing legal system, it is in the context al-Shāfi'ī intended to bring any radical changes in the existing legal system was out of question, since by the second/eighth century consensus was already formed of the main ideas of Islamic law. Thus, it was the question of justification for a slowly evolving legal discourse in which changes could be made to hermeneutically systematize and comprehensively unify the legal system. Al-Shāfi'ī demonstrates in the *Risāla* how one could hermeneutically co-relate the legal rulings to the revealed legal canons.

"At the heart of the *Risāla*," to use Lowry's phrase, "is al-Shāfi'ī's concept of *bayan*,"[8] which is the first primary legal theoretical concept explored in detail by al-Shāfi'ī around which the whole *Risāla* is organized and structured. According to al-Shāfi'ī, the entirety of law resides in two texts, the *Qur'ān* and the prophetic *Ḥadīth* reports and all the legal rulings are derived and expressed by one of the combinations

> (i) the *Qur'ān* alone, (ii) the *Qur'ān* and the prophetic *Ḥadīth* reports together, (iii) The *Qur'ān* and the prophetic *Ḥadīth* reports, when the prophetic *Ḥadīth* reports either explain or modify the meaning of the *Qur'ān*, (iv) the prophetic *Ḥadīth* reports standing alone, and (v) lastly, neither the *Qur'ān* nor the prophetic *Ḥadīth* reports, then one can exercise *qiyās* (analogical reasoning).[9]

They are epistemologically employed by al-Shāfi'ī' hermeneutically to systematize comprehensively the Islamic legal system. These are exclusively two sources of revealed sources of authority and does not include, for example, the *ijmā'* of the inhabitants of Medina that Mālik bin Anas claimed to employ.[10]

MODES OF THE BAYĀN

Al-Shāfi'ī lists four modes of the legislative statements of law:

First mode of the *bayān* is when the Qur'ānic text stands alone. The *Qur'ān* spells out an obligation in the form of explicit text such as to pray, give arms, perform pilgrimage, and observe fasting.[11]

Second legislative statement includes those obligations of which God has affirmed in the *Qur'ān* and then explained how they are performed through the prophetic *Ḥadīth* reports.[12]

Third mode of legislative statement is the practice established by the *Sunna* of Prophet and in respect to which God has provided no explicit text of rule, but He has imposed obligation to obey the Prophet and abide by his rulings.[13]

Fourth mode of legislative statement is when the vast *corpus* of the prophetic *Ḥadīth* reports is not sufficient to answer the legal question. Then, God has imposed on his obedient servants the obligation to engage in legal interpretation for arriving at a legal answer from the natural evidence, as opposed to from revelation. For example, God commands to pray facing toward the direction of the sacred mosque. If it is not possible to determine the direction, it is clarified by natural signs such as the stars indicating its direction to the rational faculty of human beings that enables one to know what direction the *Qur'ān* has commanded one to face.[14]

Al-Shāfi'ī attempts to ground the law in the *Qur'ān* and the prophetic *Ḥadīth* reports, but they belong to two different levels. The *Qur'ān,* to use Lowry's phrase, is ontologically different from the prophetic *Ḥadīth* reports. "The *Qur'ān* is ontologically primary and function of the prophetic *Ḥadīth* reports is to govern, classify, and make explicit the intended meaning of the Qur'ānic verses." However, as regards the prophetic *Ḥadīth* reports that are transmitted with the same degree of certainty as the *Qur'ān*, they have the same or greater epistemological function and status. In some cases, they are epistemologically considered more important in resolving the problem concerning the rulings. Therefore, the prophetic *Ḥadīth* reports become co-source of law with the *Qur'ān*. With this emerged the prophetic legal authority embodied in the textual form as the co-source along with the *Qur'ān.* In fact, when we would come to deal with the civil and commercial laws in the compositions of *Mukhtaṣar*, it would become obvious that the prophetic *Ḥadīth* reports govern the legal rulings and are employed more so than the *Qur'ān*, since the civil and commercial transactions deal with the worldly affairs (*aḥkām al-dunyā*) of human beings and their mutual relations (*mu'āmalāt*). They involve human utterances and fall under the analysis of human language in the varied ways of expressing the meanings and implications of the specific legal problems, affecting the contracts drawn in writing or expressed verbally. They are expressed by describing conditions of valid contracts by the seller and the purchaser stating price, quality, and quantity, and various kinds of contracts such as the *ṣarf* sale, *salam* sale, contracts involving *ribā*, and contracts of partnership (*shirka*), lease-hire (*ijāra*), etc.

> All transactions involving such matters are expressed in human language, indicating the intention and purpose of the contract. Besides such written words and verbal utterances, gestures and signs of indication are used such as nodding, pointing to the object of contract, and standing up during the meeting suggesting that the offer or acceptance is unacceptable.[15]

After describing the modalities of legislative statements, al-Shāfi'ī illustrates the following five kinds of interpretation through which the legal meaning of the *Qur'ān* can be made clear:

First kind of legislative statement in which the *Qur'ān* is made clear by a Qur'ānic verse is clear can be confirmed by another text. Al-Shāfi'ī illustrates it, for example, with Q 2:196, which prescribes fasting for three days during the major pilgrimage and followed by seven days after returning. This makes it ten days in all, which simply confirms without adding anything further to what was already clear.[16]

Second kind of legislative statement is in respect to the Qur'ānic text that seems clear but can be further elaborated or modified by another text. Al-Shāfi'ī illustrates, for example, that the Q 4: 11–12 prescribes a precise number of inheritance shares, but then specifies that these are distributed after bequests and debts, while the prophetic *Ḥadīth* report specifies further that bequest cannot exceed one-third.[17]

Third kind of legislative statement is concerning the Qur'ānic text that is not detailed, but which can be elaborated by another Qur'ānic text. For example, Q 4: 103 says, perform prayer, but it does not say when and the number of prayers. Its illustration is sought by the prophetic *Ḥadīth* reports which clarifies the number of prayers, their times, and specific practices concerning the prayers. Thus, the prophetic *Ḥadīth* reports clarify questions raised by the Qur'ānic text.[18]

Fourth kind of legislative statement is concerning the practices (*Sunna*) established by the Prophet for which we find no Qur'ānic verses. This is very overwhelming in dealing with the matters of the civil and commercial laws because of their epistemological functions. In such cases, it can be regarded as the elaboration of those Qur'ānic texts that urge general obedience to the Prophet, when the *Qur'ān* itself does not address legal problems.[19]

Fifth kind of legislative statement is when neither the *Qur'ān* nor the *corpus* of prophetic *Ḥadīth* reports address a certain legal question, such as the natural evidence for the requirement to face toward the sacred mosque in prayer. This is accomplished by means of signs that God has furnished humans with the rational faculty to draw inferences from them.

Thus, these five kinds of intertextual classificatory relations described as the legislative statements follow from al-Shāfi'ī's four ways of hermeneutical modes in which the *Qur'ān* reveals law. The four ways of modalities are an expression that all laws are provided in the revealed sources, whereas the five kinds of legislative statements provide the structure.

After establishing the internal textual relationships for the justification of interpretation, al-Shāfi'ī describes five conditions one must know that the *Qur'ān* is entirely revealed in Arabic language. He makes this basis for the assertion of the ambiguous nature of the revealed text. He does not distinguish terminologically between logical ambiguity and ambiguity arising from any other causes. He recognizes both as existing in the revealed text and refers to them.[20] Al-Shāfi'ī makes it the ground and precondition of all classification by enumerating several characteristic ambiguities of Arabic speech (*kalām*) that affect the hermeneutical concepts of generality (*'āmm*) and particularity (*khāṣṣ*), transgressive (*majāz*), indirect reference or context (*qarā'in*) and verbal implication, synonymy, and homonymy.

God addressed Arabs in his book in a way consistent with what they knew about the semantic features of their language. These semantic features are as follows:

i. Among those semantic features of their language that were familiar to Arabs was its broad scope (*ittisā'*). It is, moreover, in the language that it can be used to address people in a way what is revealed in the Qur'ān as general or unrestricted (*'āmm*) with an apparent (*ẓāhir*) meaning, which is in fact intended as unrestricted and in its apparent sense; the beginning of such a statement can obviate the need for recourse to its ending.
ii. There are also statements whose sense seems unrestricted and apparent, but in which an unrestricted sense together with a partly restricted sense (*khāṣṣ*) is intended, so that one must make an inference based on part of what is contained in such an address.
iii. There are also unrestricted statements whose apparent meaning is seemingly intended, but it is understood as restricted.
iv. Then, there are also statements which are understood from the context (*siyāq*) to mean something other than their apparent meaning.
v. Arabs may speak about something known in meaning without expressing it verbally, just as a gesture can make something known.[21]

These five kinds of ambiguities as described above al-Shāfi'ī exploits in the *Risāla*. These semantic features of Arabic language are known to Arabs.

Al-Shāfi'ī defends the Qur'ānic language by asserting that despite all its ambiguities, Arabic language is perfectly clear in stating the entire law. Thus, by asserting the Qur'ānic ambiguities as legitimate features of Arabic language, he makes them the ground and precondition of the text of clarification that he uses hermeneutically to co-relate the legal rulings with the revealed legal canons.

AL-SHĀFI'Ī'S HERMENEUTICAL RUBRIC

The specific forms of ambiguities that al-Shafi'ī discussed under the general (*'āmm*) and particular (*khāṣṣ*) represents the first hermeneutical rubric of three rubrics along with the summary speech (*jumla*) and abrogation (*naskh*) that illustrate the function of the mode of *bayān* in which the *Qur'ān* and the prophetic *Ḥadīth* reports together hermeneutically relate the legal rules to the legal revealed canons.

Concerning the terms the texts that appear general or unrestricted in the *Qur'ān* can be in the general sense as it appears or it can mean to refer to particular as it is stated in the text applies to the entirety of a class, it is called *'āmm*. When the rule appears (*ẓāhir*) to apply for the entirety of a class, but in fact it applies only to a subset of the class, it is called restricted or particular (*khāṣṣ*). All texts appear at first to be *'āmm*, but some are in fact *'āmm* at one level, but some others are then shown to refer to be *khāṣṣ*. Al-Shāfi'ī uses these terms to resolve an ambiguity or a potential contradiction. In elaborating types of classification, al-Shāfi'ī states how the prophetic *Ḥadīth* reports particularize, modify, and extend the legal meaning. They are second only to the *Qur'ān*. But relating the legal rules to the legal canons epistemologically, they serve effectively as a co-source along with the *Qur'ān* and play a greater epistemological role in the hermeneutical interpretative process.

AL-SHĀFI'Ī'S HERMENEUTICS AND THE EPISTEMOLOGICAL FUNCTIONS OF PROPHETIC ḤADĪTH REPORTS

Since our investigation is mainly concerned with the civil and commercial laws in the genre of *Mukhtaṣar* where most of the rulings are based on the prophetic *Ḥadīth* reports for their epistemological functions and relevance, we shall expound on hermeneutical rubric in general relating it specifically to the prophetic *Ḥadīth* reports rather than analyze it in detail as does Lowry in his *Early Islamic Legal Theory*.

Al-Shāfiʿī discusses how the prophetic *Ḥadīth* reports can extend the authority of *Qur'ān* not mentioned in the *Qur'ān* itself. This is discussed in the *Risāla* at great length,[22] the brief account of which follows below:

Al-Shāfiʿī gives example of the *'āmm/khāṣṣ* rubric and shows that class involved that could in principle be restricted by the prophetic *Ḥadīth* report which states that God's Emissary passes his hands over his footwear in performing the ablution, an act interpreted to mean that one's feet were already in the state of ritual purity, then a simple pass over with his hands over the footwear could satisfy the requirement of washing feet during ablution. Thus, al-Shāfiʿī harmonizes two potentially contradictory reports by showing that the rules contained in the *Qur'ān* and the prophetic *Ḥadīth* reports are complementary to each other and how the *Qur'ān* and the prophetic *Ḥadīth* reports function together. Lowry comments concerning the *'āmm/khāṣṣ* rubric as discussed by al-Shāfiʿī in the *Risāla* that overall "it is only the *Qur'ān* that is *'āmm* or *khāṣṣ* and the prophetic *Ḥadīth* reports is neither, functioning instead merely as an indicator of which quality characterizes a given passage from the *Qur'ān*."[23]

Al-Shāfiʿī discusses also how the prophetic *Ḥadīth* reports can help in determining which Qur'ānic verses abrogate which other Qur'ānic verses, though they cannot abrogate the Qur'ānic verses. Only the practice of God's Emissary may abrogate it.[24] Al-Shāfiʿī's reason for neither can abrogate each other is as Lowry says that "they are ontologically distinct, despite their shared divine origin. Both these sources have their own specific complimentary role to play."[25]

Al-Shāfiʿī illustrates how the prophetic *Ḥadīth* reports can elaborate summary requirements (*jumla al-farā'id*) with the Qur'ānic verse, "prayers are prescribed at fixed times for the believer." God clarified how to perform those obligations using words of the Prophet. "God's Emissary let it be known that the number of the obligatory prayers are five, and that number of bowings for the noon, afternoon, and evening prayers was four, and four again if one was in settlement, that the sunset prayer was three and dawn prayer two."[26] This is a major hermeneutical device that allows all kinds of clarification. For instance, a word with two possible meanings constitutes summary speech (*jumla*) in the sense that it lacks detail as to which meaning it intends. Al-Shāfiʿī gives the example of Q 2:220, "which says that a divorced woman cannot remarry her former husband until after she has been married to a second husband."[27] It could mean either that the contract of marrying with the second husband must be concluded or it could mean that the marriage must have been concluded and she had sexual intercourse with her second husband. The intended meaning is sought through the prophetic *Ḥadīth* report. The Prophet did not allow to remarry a woman to her first husband until she had intercourse with the second husband and had been divorced from him.

The concept of summary speech is al-Shāfiʻī's principal innovation in the analysis of language, which was pursed and subsequently developed and applied by later jurists in all the four Sunni school of law.[28] They used the term *mujammal* (summarized speech) and not *jumla*. For classical jurists, as for al-Shāfiʻī, the analysis of ambiguity in the language of revealed sources served to principally ground the relationships of clarification of the texts in the hermeneutical interpretations. The classical jurists subsequently gave a more systematic account to al-Shāfiʻī's rudimentary form of analysis of ambiguity.

The prophetic *Ḥadīth* reports can also particularize the *Qur'ān*. Several Qur'ānic verses, for example, Q 2: 180–181 assign inheritance shares to the parents, siblings, spouses, and children without restrictions, but al-Shāfiʻī states that the prophetic *Ḥadīth* report restricts it to the non-Muslims, murderer of the deceased, or a slave. Further, he stated that bequests were restricted to one-third of the state and no more, and that the heirs take the remaining two-thirds and the debts should be satisfied before bequests and inheritance shares are divided.[29] The *juml: naṣṣ* overlaps to some degree with *'āmm: khāṣṣ* rubric as they are used by al-Shāfiʻī synonymously.

If there are no relevant legislative provisions provided in the *Qur'ān,* the prophetic *Ḥadīth* reports can validly function alone. In chapter 2 of *Risāla*, al-Shāfiʻī discusses the conflicts between the prophetic *Ḥadīth* reports and shows how to define intertextual relationships between them. In such a case, one can claim that the text in one prophetic *Ḥadīth* report abrogates the text in other prophetic *Ḥadīth* report or one can argue that one prophetic *Ḥadīth* report is not reliably transmitted or it is not sound. For instance, as when we would come to analyze the case of *ribā*. All jurists agree that the *ribā* is forbidden in all transactions, but another prophetic *Ḥadīth* report states that *ribā* occurs only when there is a delay in payment. Al-Shāfiʻī explains that this might have been when the transmitter failed to report that in all exchanges including the unequal exchange of like goods which were permitted so long as there was no delay in payment.[30] This shows that some of the prophetic *Ḥadīth* reports might not fully describe their contents and, consequently, they might have no legal signification. One prophetic *Ḥadīth* can also be declared ambiguous and reinterpreted based on another prophetic *Ḥadīth* report. Al-Shāfiʻī maintains that the conflicting prophetic *Ḥadīth* reports must be reconciled with reason so that neither is discounted.[31]

Al-Shāfiʻī did not use the term *majāz* (transgressive) in the *Risāla*, but he allowed certain transgressive usage of expression, for instance, Jacob's son telling him in the Q: 12:82 that to confirm their story "he should ask the town they were in" meaning "he should ask the people of the town." This core idea though not used by al-Shāfiʻī in a technical sense was coined subsequently by the jurists in later generations as the technique or category.

Al-Shāfi'ī used the term general (*'umm*) very loosely and held that general expressions should be interpreted as general by default in the absence of particularizing evidence, but that can virtually be particularized by any kind of evidence, whether rational, contextual, the Qur'ānic verse or from the prophetic *Ḥadīth* reports.[32]

Concerning the statements of prohibitions of legal values, al-Shāfi'ī analyzes them as a special class of speech for resolving apparent conflicts between prohibitions and evidence of permissibility, thereby, interpreting some prohibitions as entailing less than absolute prohibitions or some prohibitions are particularized by others. For instance, concerning the Friday prayer Prophet's commands were accompanied by a separate obligation, but this command was only a recommendation. Al-Shāfi'ī approves the negative implication such as in the case of tax on free grazing live stocks implies that stable-fed livestock is exempt from the tax. These ideas are further developed in conjunction with the ambiguous nature of Arabic language, wherein it is discussed that in fact all obligations can be considered recommendations by some jurists in succeeding generations.

The significance of this brief account of al-Shāfi'ī's rudimentary form of hermeneutics lies in the fact that hermeneutical formation of the Islamic legal system first began with al-Shāfi'ī, whether he could be called the Master architect of the Islamic legal system or not.[33] With the gradual acceptance of al-Shāfi'ī's hermeneutics in all four Sunni schools of law, the jurists in succeeding generations attempted to subsequently further develop and apply it hermeneutically in the formation of Islamic law. Thus, one can characterize the entire *corpus* of the Islamic legal system as the hermeneutical development of Islamic law.

To conclude, the significance of al-Shāfi'ī's concept of hermeneutics lies in the fact that it was continually employed in the formation of the Islamic legal system in the four Sunni schools of law. In the classical *fiqh* works what is discussed as the "Differences of Opinion among Jurists" (*Ikhtilāf al-Fuqhā'*) are per se not the differences of opinion because of the different school tenets. These juristic different interpretations are more relevantly to be viewed as the result of hermeneutical interpretations from the jurists from one generation to the next generation in the four Sunni Islamic schools of law. We would expound on this aspect further in chapter 7.

NOTES

1. Joseph E. Lowry, Early Islamic Legal Theory, *Risāla of Muḥammad Idrīs al-Shāfi'ī* (Leiden: Brill, 2007).

2. Vishanoff, *The Formation of Islamic Hermeneutics* (New Haven, CT, 2001).

3. See chapter 2 for the elucidation of the term *comprehensive* in the sense in which it is used in this text.

4. Majīd Khadduri, *Islamic Jurisprudence: Shāfi'ī's Risāla* translated with an Introduction, Notes, and Appendices (Baltimore: The John Hopkins Press, 1961), p. 41.

5. Joseph E. Lowry, *Early Islamic Legal Theory* (Brill: Leiden and Boston, 2007), p. 17.

6. Weal Hallaq, *Origins and Evolution of Islamic Law* (Cambridge: Cambridge University Press, 1997), p. 22.

7. Vishanoff, *Formation of Islamic Hermeneutics*, p. 1.

8. Lowry, *Early Islamic Legal Theory,* p. 19.

9. Lowry, *Early Islamic Legal Theory*, p. 45.

10. See, Lowry, *Early Islamic Legal Theory*, p. 33, note 13.

11. Throughout this section, we are using Joseph Lowry's translation of al-Shāfi'ī *Risāla*, *The Epistle on Legal Theory* (New York: New York University Press, 2013), p. 15, para # 19). Lowry's translation is based on Shākir's edition supplemented with 'Abd al-Muṭṭalib's edition.

12. Lowry, *Epistle*, p. 20, para # 15.

13. Lowry, *Epistle*, p. 15, para # 21.

14. Lowry, *Epistle*, pp. 17–18, para # 23–25.

15. Vishanoff, *Formation of Islamic Hermeneutics*, p. 9.

16. Lowry, *Epistle*, p. 19, para # 29.

17. Lowry, *Epistle*, pp. 23–25, para # 36, 37.

18. Lowry, *Epistle*, p. 25, para # 38.

19. Lowry, *Epistle*, p. 27, para # 39, 40, and 41.

20. Lowry, *Early Islamic Legal Theory*, p. 66.

21. Lowry, *Epistle*, p. 45.

22. See, Lowry, *Epistle*, pp. 63–69; para # 98–125.

23. Lowry, *Early Islamic Legal Theory*, p. 85.

24. Lowry, *Epistle,* pp. 81–111, para, # 126–182.

25. Lowry, *Early Islamic Legal Theory*, p. 90.

26. Lowry, *Epistle*, pp. 129–131, para # 210–211.

27. Lowry, *Early Islamic Legal Theory*, pp. 113–14.

28. See chapter 2 for the subsequent development of al-Shāfi'ī's Concept of Hermeneutics.

29. Lowry, *Epistle*, p. 57, para # 57.

30. Lowry, *The Epistle*, pp. 205–207, para # 339–342.

31. Lowry, *Epistle*, p. 209, para # 209.

32. Lowry, *Epistle*, pp. 45–63, para # 72–97.

33. Hallaq, Weal B., "Was al-Shāfi'ī the Master Architect of Islamic Jurisprudence" in *International Journal of Middle East Study*, 4, 1993.

Chapter 2

The Nature of the Compositions of *Mukhtaṣar* and the Formation of Islamic Legal System

In general, the word "*mukhtaṣar*" is literally translated as "abridgment" or "summary." This literal translation, though correct, fails to convey the real nature of compositions of *Mukhtaṣar*, their main contention and purpose for which they were really composed. This gives, somewhat, a false impression to the extent that it could lead to a misunderstanding of their real nature in the hermeneutical formation of Islamic law.

Whether al-Shāfi'ī was the master architect of Islamic jurisprudence or not,[1] it is most certainly true that al-Shāfi'ī was the first jurist to use the hermeneutical approach to systematize the Islamic legal system in a comprehensive manner. Viewed from this perspective and in that context, the compositions of *Mukhtaṣar* are products and reproductions of the hermeneutical formation of Islamic law. Thus, the compositions of *Mukhtaṣar* are not to be understood as the reproductions of legal rulings of the eponyms of schools of law in an abridged form. Rather the authors of compositions of *Mukhtaṣar* comprehensively systematize Islamic legal system in the hermeneutical interpretative process relating the legal rulings to the legal canons as intended by al-Shāfi'ī'*s* hermeneutics.

Muḥammad bin Muḥammad al-Ḥaṭṭāb (954/1547) in the *Kitāb Mawāhib al-Jalīl li Sharḥ Mukhtaṣar* describes the complex nature of compositions of *Mukhtaṣar* as follows:[2] Haṭṭāb explains juristically the "*real*" (*ḥaqīqa*) nature of the compositions of *Mukhtaṣar a*s the shortening or abridgment of statement in which one thing is united with another thing. With this, the jurists mean replacing a longer statement with a shorter statement, which entails comprehensively all the essential expanded additional elements included in the longer statement. According to Khalīl (774/1374), the author of the composition of *Mukhtaṣar*, it is called abridgment when a shorter statement indicates the meaning contained in its entirety in a longer statement, permitting (a jurist) to convey hermeneutically the meaning of legal ruling in consistency with the legal norms as laid down in the revealed sources.[3] This shows that the word *mukhtaṣar*, when it is translated just as shortening or abridgment fails to convey the "*real*" nature of it. It conveys only one aspect and that also partially without even suggesting that the shorter statement in the compositions of *Mukhtaṣar* should cover complete meaning. In fact, the "*real*" nature and purpose for which these compositions of *Mukhtaṣar* were composed is very complex that reflects varied manifold aspects in the hermeneutical interpretative process. The most important aspect of these compositions is that they are continuity of the hermeneutical approach in which the jurist draws together, incorporating all expanded additional elements that have been developed over the course of time. It is the continuity of al-Shāfi'ī's hermeneutical approach culminating in the compositions of *Mukhtaṣar*. Thus, the best way to describe the nature of compositions of *Mukhtaṣar* would be that they are hermeneutically comprehensive legal treaties. For this purpose, Khalīīl brings all *mashhūr* legal opinions together incorporated hermeneutically additional expanded elements that have been developed over the course of time, regardless of which individual jurists or schools of law.

"These compositions of *Mukhtaṣar*", as described by Norman Calder, "are authored texts composed by individual jurists."[4] They claim independently to personal hermeneutically interpretations in producing them. Calder and al-Ḥaṭṭāb both do not further expound that these compositions of *Mukhtaṣar* are the continuous process of hermeneutical interpretations of legal rulings relating them to the legal canons of revealed sources.

The characteristic text of the composition of *Mukhtaṣar* of the formative period represents itself as mostly relating the legal rulings to the legal canons[5] incorporating a few expanded additional elements, but gradually this hermeneutical interpretive process develops incorporating more expanded additional elements not necessarily adhering to the legal opinions of the eponyms of school.

Our investigation focuses on these juristic writings. For this purpose, following compositions of *Mukhtaṣar* from four Sunni schools of law are selected in our investigation. Some of these compositions do not bear the title *Mukhtaṣar*, but as for their contents, they technically belong to the genre of *Mukhtaṣar*. These compositions are as follows:

COMPOSITIONS OF *MUKHTAṢAR* IN THE SHĀFI'Ī SCHOOL OF LAW

(1) Al-Muzanī (264/878), Abū Ibrāhīm Ismā'īl ibn Yaḥyā, *al-Mukhtaṣar Kitāb al-Umm fī al-Fiqh*, edited by Ḥusayn 'Abd al-Ḥamīd Nīl, vol. III

& IV (Cairo: Dār al-Arqam); *Mukhtaṣar al-Muzanī*, edited by Maḥmūd Muṭrajī (Beirut: Dār al-Kutab al-'Ilmīya), 1993.

(2) Al-Shīrāzī (399/1003), Abū Isḥāq Ibrāhīm ibn 'Alī ibn Yūsuf, *al-Tanbīh* Cairo, 1951.

COMPOSITIONS OF *MUKHTAṢAR* IN THE ḤANAFĪ SCHOOL OF LAW

(3) Al-Ṭaḥāwī (264/878), Abū Ja'far Aḥmad ibn Muḥammad ibn Salāma, *Mukhtaṣar al-Ṭaḥāwī*, edited by Abū al-Wafā' al-Afghānī (Cairo: Dār al-Kitāb al-'Arabī), 1992.

(4) Al-Ḥakīm al-Shahīd Muḥammad ibn Aḥmad al-Marwazī (333/945), *Mukhtaṣar* contained in al-Sarakhsī's *Mabsūṭ*, vol. 11, 12, 14, and 15 (Cairo: Dār al-Ma'rif, 1906–1912).

(5) Al-Qudūrī (392/1037), Abū al-Ḥasan Aḥmad ibn Aḥmad ibn Ja'far, *Mukhtaṣar al-Qudūrī*, edited by Muḥammad al-Badawī (Lebanon: Beirut), 1997.

(6) Al-Marghīnānī, Burhan al-Dīn 'Alī Abū Bakar (593/1197), Cairo, 2000.

COMPOSITIONS OF *MUKHTAṢAR* IN THE MĀLIKĪ SCHOOL OF LAW

(7) Khalīl ibn Isḥāq (179/795), *Mukhtaṣar Khalīl*, edited by Ṭāhir Aḥmad al-Zāwī (Cairo: Dār al-Aḥyā' Kutab al-'Arabīya), 1980; *Manḥ al-Jalīl Sharḥ 'alā Mukhtaṣar 'Allāma Khalīl* by Muḥammad bin Aḥmad bin 'Ulaysh, vol. iv, v, vi, vii, and viii (Beirut: Dār al-Fikr, 1989).

COMPOSITION OF *MUKHTAṢAR* IN THE HANBALĪ SCHOOL OF LAW

(8) Al-Khiraqī (324/946), 'Omar ibn al-Husayn, *al-Mukhtaṣar al-Fiqh* (Lebanon, Beirut: Dār al-Nawādir), 1429. This is the only *Mukhtaṣar* composed in the Ḥanbalī school of law.

SIGNIFICANCE AND EMERGENCE OF THE COMPOSITIONS OF *MUKHTAṢAR*

Before expounding on the emergence of the phenomenon of writings of the genre *Mukhtaṣar*, we shall briefly state that the compositions of genre

Mukhtaṣar are highly significant in unfolding its varied aspects. First, the compositions of *Mukhtaṣar* are not simply and necessarily "abridgment" as it is traditionally understood. Besides embodying abridgment, they manifest many other features. They incorporate hermeneutically entailed expanded additional elements that have been developed over the course of time in the formation of Islamic legal system comprehensively. This tendency becomes increasingly more over the course of time with the jurists from the earlier generations to the next generations. Secondly, the authors of compositions of *Mukhtaṣar* can exercise their own independent juristic opinions different from their eponym, not necessarily reproducing his legal opinions. Thirdly, the authors of compositions of *Mukhtaṣar* can and do bring information not contained in the writings of their eponyms and provide additional information from other sources. In fact, when one examines the nature and contents of these compositions of *Mukhtaṣar,* especially concerning the civil and commercial law, one finds that in the writings of school eponyms (except al-Shāfi'ī), one does not find an application of the hermeneutics comprehensively and employment of its techniques. Moreover, the authors of compositions of *Mukhtaṣar* can include occasionally more than one juristic opinion, which should have been developed concerning an issue over the course of time. This would become obvious when we would deal later with these compositions. This phenomenon becomes more prevalent with the jurists of later generations. Fourthly, in the process of developing hermeneutically the Islamic legal system in a compressive manner, the authors of compositions of *Mukhtaṣar* hermeneutically systematize the legal rulings according to the legal canons in a comprehensive manner. In this way, there was a continuity of the hermeneutical interpretations in the formation of the Islamic legal system from one generation to the next. Fifthly, the authors of compositions of *Mukhtaṣar* try to articulate their statements in general and abstract forms that entail all the essential elements in the ruling. In that sense, they provide a gist of the matter comprehensively in an easy, clear, and concise form. This shows a great progress in the refinement, articulation, and diction in the writings of *Mukhtaṣar*. Lastly, the hermeneutical approach also gives a greater flexibility, especially in the matters of civil and commercial law, to the jurists in interpreting the legal rulings in accordance and consistent with the revealed sources, integrating all the expanded additional elements. This keeps not only the continuity of hermeneutical approach in the formation of Islamic legal system, but also, at the same time, broadens the scope of Islamic law.

These features and trends will be shown when we explore and analyze the contents of the contract (*'aqd*), contract of sale (*'aqd al-bay'*), *ribā*, partnership (*shirka*), and lease-hire (*ijāra*) in the above-selected compositions of *Mukhtaṣar* in the four Sunni schools of law.

The phenomenon of composing legal compositions of *Mukhtaṣar* emerged in the seventh/thirteenth century. They are "*Horned Books,*" *which contain the most basic and fundamental rules*.[6] The authors of these compositions of *Mukhtaṣar* are primarily concerned with determining hermeneutically the legal rules in accordance with the legal canons in response to the ongoing problems (*masā'il*). This hermeneutical task was supposed to accomplish the articulation of the abstract statements within the scope of hermeneutical interpretative process. After the evaluation of the various existing compositions of *Mukhtaṣar* at a time, only one was recognized as the most authoritative text of the legal rulings. This implies that such hermeneutically rulings were considered *mashhūr* (well accepted). It functioned as the textbook and made part of the curricula in the *madrasas* and higher learning institutions. They were designed to teach under the guidance of a man of knowledge in the *fiqh*, who instructs students and average persons what the statement entails by explaining, so to say, "decoding" it.

In the beginning of the formation of Islamic law, we find in the writings of the eponyms of school there is no systematic employment of hermeneutical approach. Most likely, as pointed out by Calder, Melchert, and others, these writings ascribed to the eponyms underwent several redactions to acquire their final forms. Viewing it from the perspective of hermeneutics, the formation of the Islamic legal system from its very inception reflects the continuation of hermeneutical development in the compositions of *Mukhtaṣar* as in the entire formation of Islamic law.

In general, the authors of compositions of *Mukhtaṣar* try to retain the most essential elements for the justification of the view asserted in the statement, though in some cases, the authors of the compositions of *Mukhtaṣar* do also go into details when it comes to include some expanded additional elements not previously transmitted. In the beginning, this hermeneutical interpretative process was slow. To make an abstract and general rule in a statement was a slow and long process. It gradually develops and culminates in the compositions of *Mukhtaṣar*. Thus, these compositions of *Mukhtaṣar* are not in their literal sense just "abridgment" or "summary" transmitting the legal opinions of the eponyms of the school of law.

In general, the idea of hermeneutical interpretation in the compositions of *Mukhtaṣar* of Shāfi'ī, Ḥanafī, Mālikī, and Ḥanbalī schools of law concerning the matters of civil and commercial laws consisted epistemologically relating the legal ruling to the prophetic *Ḥadīth* reports. This is because the civil and commercial law generally deal with the human utterances and expressions. But, when we would deal with Khalīl's *Mukhtaṣar* in Mālikī school of law, we would find that Khalīl brings in all *mashhūr* (well-accepted) legal opinions together, denoting them comprehensively in an abridged form. These *mashhūr* legal rulings have been developed by various jurists over the course time from the time of Mālik, Saḥnūn and earlier jurists until the time Khalīl composed the *Mukhtaṣar*.

NOTES

1. Al-Hallaq, "Was al-Shāfi'ī the Master Architect of Islamic Jurisprudence," *International Journal of Middle East Study*, 4, 1993, pp. 587–605.

2. Muḥammad bin Muḥammad al-Ḥaṭṭāb, *Kitāb Mawāhib al-Jalīl li Sharḥ Mukhtaṣar*, vol i (Beirut: Dār al-Fikr, 1992), p. 24.

3. Al-Ḥaṭṭāb, *Kitāb Mawāhib al-Jalīl lī Sharḥ Mukhtaṣar*, vol. I (Beirut: Dār al-Fikr, 1992), p. 24.

4. Norman Calder, *Studies,* p. 245.

5. Calder, *Studies*, p. 245.

6. Khaled Abu El Fadl, *Speaking in God's Name* (Oxford: One World, 2005), p. 16.

Part II

CONTINUITY OF HERMENEUTICS IN THE COMPOSITIONS OF *MUKHTAṢAR* WITH TRANSLATION OF ARABIC TEXTS

Chapter 3

Shāfi'ī School of Law

Hermeneutics as Reflected in the K al-Umm, *al-Muzanī's* Mukhtaṣar, *and al-Shīrāzī's* Tanbīh

Civil and commercial law deals, in general, with the worldly affairs (*aḥkām al-dunyā*) of human beings and not religious affairs (*aḥkām al-dīn*). This aspect falls under the analysis of human language and its varied ways of expressing the meanings and implications of the specific legal problems that involve human utterances. As already mentioned, these human utterances affect the contracts drawn in writing or expressed verbally such as conditions of valid contracts, offer and acceptance of the contract by both parties stating the price, quality, quantity of the commodity, etc., and other contracts of sales such as the *ṣarf* sale, *salam* sale, *ribā*, partnership (*shirka*), lease-hire (*ijāra*), etc. "All the transactions involving such matters are stated in human language, expressing the intention and purpose of the contract. Besides, such written words and verbal utterances, the gestures, and signs of indication are used, such as nodding, pointing to the object of contract, and standing up during the meeting, suggesting that the deal is unacceptable, acceptable, and so forth."[1]

A BRIEF BIOGRAPHICAL ACCOUNT OF AL-SHĀFI'Ī

Muḥammad bin Idrīs bin al-Shāfi'ī was born in 150/820, the year in which Abū Ḥanīfa died. He was born in Ghāza 'Asqalān, Palestine. Due to poverty, he was unable to pay tuition fees to his teachers, but he soon caught up with acquiring knowledge. The teachers, finding him keen and ambitious, did not ask for tuition fees. He completed his studies of the *Qur'ān* at the age of seven and then committed the *Aḥādīth* (sing. *Ḥadīth*) to memory. Among his teachers were Mālik bin Anas, Muslim bin Khālid, Wakī' bin Jarāḥ bin Malīḥ al-Kūfī, and others.

Al-Shāfi'ī recited Mālik's *al-Muwaṭṭa'* after committing it to memory. Al-Shāfi'ī stayed in Medina until Mālik died in the year 179/795.[2]

Al-Shāfi'ī came to Egypt in the year 199/814–815 and, then, came to Baghdad and stayed there until he died in 204/819–820. In the later years of his life, he suffered from chronic hemorrhoids.

HERMENEUTICS AND AL-SHĀFI'Ī AS AN EPONYM OF THE SCHOOL OF LAW AND HIS CHAPTER *AL-BUYŪ'* OF HIS *K AL-UMM*

The *K al-Umm*, which is associated with al-Shāfi'ī's name as its author, deals with all aspects of law including religious laws (*aḥkām al-dīn)* as well as non-religious laws (*aḥkām al-dunyā*); the chapter *al-Buyū'* of the *K al-Umm* forms one part of the latter and covers all the topics of our investigation mentioned in the last chapter.

It is not certain whether al-Shāfi'ī was actually the author of *K al-Umm*, especially the chapter *al-Buyū'*, as it went through several redactions,[3] but it appears that al-Shāfi'ī was of the view that some of the aspects of law cannot cover all matters, especially those which deal with worldly affairs (*aḥkām al-dunyā*) among human beings.[4] Thus, it is doubtful whether he analyzed such matters completely dealing with them with a formal legal hermeneutics.

A BRIEF BIOGRAPHICAL ACCOUNT OF ISMĀ'ĪL IBN YĀḤYA AL-MUZANĪ

Ismā'īl ibn Yāḥya al-Muzanī (264/878), a student of al-Shāfi'ī and the champion of the Shāfi'ī' school of law, compiled a celebrated composition of *Mukhtaṣar* of the writings and lectures of his teacher.[5] When al-Shāfi'ī came to Egypt, al-Muzanī was already twenty-three-years old and had already completed his studies. A well-known Ḥanafī scholar Abū Ja'far Aḥmad ibn Muhammad ibn Salāma al-Ṭaḥāwī (321/933) was one of his students. It is said that al-Ṭaḥāwī in the composition of his own *Mukhtaṣar* followed the patterns of al-Muzani's composition of *Mukhtaṣar* as well as transmitted collection of the prophetic *Ḥadīth* reports of al-Shāfi'ī.

Al-Muzanī's composition of *Mukhtaṣar* was the literary basis of the Shāfi'ī's school of law founded in the next century. He was one of the leading transmitters and by far the most important representative of al-Shāfi'ī teachings. Al-Muzanī says in the very beginning of his *Mukhtaṣar* that he is presenting al-Shāfi'ī's teachings very faithfully.[6] It purports to derive its material from the extant written works of al-Shāfi'ī and partly from al-Muzanī's own memory of the sessions with al-Shāfi'ī. Al-Muzanī occasionally differs in his views from his master on some points. Most probably, because of this reason Norman Calder remarks that al-Muzani's *Mukhtaṣar* should not be taken in the usual sense of the term *Mukhtaṣar*.[7] Calder does not explain why it cannot be considered *Mukhtaṣar*. In fact, al-Muzanī in the composition of his *Mukhtaṣar* follows al-Shāfi'ī's concept of hermeneutics and is concerned with its hermeneutical contention of systematizing comprehensively legal rulings in accordance with legal canons as provided in the text. Considering the nature of *Mukhtaṣar* provided by al-Ḥaṭṭāb as discussed in chapter 2, al-Muzanī's *Mukhtaṣar content wise* belongs to the genre of *Mukhtaṣar*.

A BRIEF BIOGRAPHICAL ACCOUNT OF ABŪ ISḤĀQ IBRĀHĪM AL-SHĪRĀZĪ

Abū Isḥāq Ibrāhīm al-Shīrāzī, a Shāfi'ī jurist, was born in Firawzābād in 399/1003. Al-Shrāzī went to Shirāz to study *fiqh*, then to Baṣra and reached Baghdad where he completed his studies in the *Uṣūl* with Abū Ḥātim al-Quzwānī and in *fiqh* with Abū al-Ṭayyīb.[8] He belonged to an eminent group of scholars. He began to teach in Baghdad. The fame of his learning soon became so great that students came from all over the Muslim world. The vizier Nizām al-Mulk appointed him to open the first public *madarasa* founded by him in Baghdad. He taught there until his death in 479/1083. Al-Shīrāzī's *al-Tanbīh* is generally classified under the title *mutūn* (basic tenants), but it is shorter and more concise than all the *Mukhtaṣars* listed in chapter 2.

To al-Shīrāzī's credit are the works *Kitāb al-Tanbīh fī al-Fiqh* written in (1060), a legal compendium in the genre of *Mukhtaṣar*, which is selected here for our investigation, *Kitāb al-Mudhdhab fī al-Mudhhab,* composed in 1069, and *Tadhkirāt al-Mu'lūlin*, which is the *Ikhtilāf* work.

AL-MUZANĪ'S *MUKHTAṢAR* AND AL-SHĪRĀZĪ'S *TANBĪH*

In al-Muzanī's composition of *Mukhtaṣar*, we find two chapters one under the chapter *al-Bay'*[9] and the other under *al-Buyū'*.[10] In his chapter *al-Bay'*, al-Muzanī discusses transactions dealing strictly with the contract of sale and does not discuss the subject of partnership (*shirka)* and hire-rent (*ijāra*). It is mainly an abridgment whereas al-Muzanī in the chapter *al-Buyū'* does not narrate all the prophetic *Ḥadīth* reports with full chain of narrations. He suffices by stating what al-Shāfi'ī said.

As already mentioned, al-Shīrāzī's *al-Tanbīh*[11] is generally listed under the title *mutūn*, but in fact it is more of an abridgment. Al-Shīrāzī neither cites the Qur'ānic verses nor does he, like al-Muzanī who meticulously adheres to al-Shāfi'ī's hermeneutics, cite the prophetic *Ḥadīth* reports. Furthermore, al-Shīrāzī neither follows al-Shāfi'ī's ordering of the chapters and subchapters nor does he use wordings of al-Shāfi'ī as al-Muzanī does especially in the chapter *al-Buyū'*. In al-Shīrāzī's *al-Tanbīh*, the topic of right of option of seeing in the contract of sale is missing, as in al-Muzanī's *Mukhtaṣar* no discussion of hire-rent (*ijāra*) is found.

The authors of compositions of *Mukhtaṣar* are more concerned relating hermeneutically the legal ruling to the legal cannons comprehensively rather than simple abridgment. It was a continuing process of hermeneutical interpretations of producing and reproducing the compositions of *Mukhtaṣar*. In general, the authors of these compositions of *Mukhtaṣar* attempt to present material with clarity and in a concise and comprehensive form, incorporating expanded additional elements that have been developed over the course of time.

HERMENEUTICAL GENERAL FEATURES AS REFLECTED IN AL-MUZANĪ'S CONTRACT OF SALE

In Islamic law, the word used for any kind of legal contract between two parties is called "*'aqd*." It is a legal instrument and becomes binding between the parties upon concluding the contract. The contract of sale (*'aqd al-bay'*) refers to any kind of transactions concerning civil and commercial laws.

Al-Shāfi'ī, as well as al-Muzanī, both declare transactions (*tijāra*) lawful (*ḥalāl*) as sanctioned by the Qur'ānic verse (4:29) and supported by the prophetic *Ḥadīth* reports. The transactions in which one article of exchange is in excess (*ribā*) of another article of exchange are declared unlawful (*ḥarām*).[12] Al-Shāfi'ī, according to the hermeneutical contention of the *Risāla*, and al-Muzanī following it, cite the Qur'ānic verse and prophetic *Ḥadīth* reports, although al-Muzanī cites only one or two prophetic *Ḥadīth* reports without full chain of narrations in comparison to al-Shāfi'ī, who cites several traditions and with full chain of narrations, which he had at his disposal at the time.

As already mentioned, al-Muzanī discusses the theme of contract, one in chapter *al-Buyū'* and other in chapter *al-Bay'*, which deals with all themes regarding only the nature of contract and contract of sale, whereas the chapter *al-Bay'* contains those transactions which are concerning the contract of sale, right of option, right of option of seeing, *ṣarf* sale, and *salam* sale. It does not include partnership and lease-hire, though they fall under the species (*aṣnāf*, pl. of *ṣanf*) of the contract of sale. In general, al-Muzanī's chapter *al-Buyū'* reproduces *verbatim* from al-Shāfi'ī' chapter *al-Buyū'* of his *K. al-Umm* without any significant changes either in the wordings or in arrangement of topics and subtopics. Al-Muzanī's account of the contract of sale in chapter *al-Bay'* uses his own wordings and adds some information which he might have heard verbally from al-Shāfi'ī. Al-Muzanī also brings his own opinion as we will find in the contents of chapter *al-Bay.*[13]

THE CONTENTS OF AL-SHĀFI'Ī'S CONTRACT OF SALE IN THE *K aL-UMM*[14] AS REFLECTED IN AL-MUZANĪ'S CONTRACT OF SALE IN THE COMPOSITION OF *MUKHTAṢAR*

According to al-Shāfi'ī and al-Muzanī, a contract is valid when both parties to the contract agree to the stipulations of the contract. Upon the contract being concluded, it becomes binding for both parties, except when a defect is found in the article of sale. The article of sale must be according to the description, be in existence, and be capable of delivery. The contract is concluded without breaking meeting (*majlis*), and parties separating from each other and from leaving the place where contract is concluded. The right of option is valid for three days.

In al-Shāfi'ī's chapter *al-Buyū'*, we find that it is narrated on the authority of Sulaymān al-Rabī'[15] that "al-Shāfi'ī said": the right of seeing (*khiyār al-ru'ya*) is permitted, but at the other place he said that it is not permitted. Al-Muzanī, as a clarification, adds that the latter statement is found in older writings of al-Shāfi'ī while he was staying in Iraq, and the former statement is found in his writings during his stay in Egypt.[16] Al-Muzanī's clarification of the issue shows that he tries to bring hermeneutically the legal rulings consistent with the legal canons.

Hermeneutical General Features as Reflected in al-Shīrāzī's Contract of Sale in the *Tanbīh*[17]

Al-Shīrāzī comes almost after more than one hundred and fifty years than al-Muzanī. His composition of *al-Tanbīh* is marked by clarity, precision, and refined articulation of statements. By this time, the authors of juristic compositions have become more conscious of the style, diction, and language. It seems by this time, many interactions taking place among the jurists of four Sunni schools of law. As we will see in the next chapter, al-Shīrāzī's description of the contract of sale shows great similarities with the contract of sale of Ḥanafī jurist Abū Husayn Aḥmad al-Qudūrī (428/973) and 'Alī Abū Bakr al-Jalīl al-Farghīnānī al-Marghīnānī (593/1135) in stating thoroughly all essential characteristics and stipulations of the contract of sale.

Al-Shīrāzī discusses contract of sale under the title "The Completion of the Contract of Sale in General." Al-Shīrāzī, unlike Muzanī, in his discussion of contract of sale includes partnership and lease-hire.

Al-Shīrāzī, unlike al-Shāfi'ī or al-Muzanī, does not cite in the entire chapter *al-Buyū'* of the *Tanbīh* any Qur'ānic verses or the prophetic *Ḥadīth* reports.

Al-Shīrāzī, like al-Qudūrī, introduces in his contract of sale the wordings of offer by the seller and its acceptance by the purchaser, and the different ways of indication which is used as one of the hermeneutical techniques in al-Shāfi'ī's concept of hermeneutics.

Al-Shīrāzī's discussion of the usufruct (*taṣarruf*) of the exchange of articles of sales specifies that in the contract of sale no extraneous conditions are allowed attached to it. Both parties to the contract have absolute right of usufruct to the articles of exchange. He also discusses when the purchaser and the seller can make usufruct of them and the consequences of it, if it is destroyed.

Al-Shīrāzī allows the extension of three days option regarding the esculent articles (*ṭa'ām*).[18]

Unlike al-Muzanī, al-Shīrāzī in his contract of sale describes two juristic opinions (*qawlān*).[19] They should have been developed later by the jurists over the course of time. This is like what we find in the Ḥanafī school of law and, particularly, more so in the Mālikī school of law as we would find it when we discuss it in chapter 4 and chapter 6 respectively.

In some ways, al-Shīrāzī's discussion of the contract of sale is more extensive than that of al-Muzanī and some of the discussions regarding the usufruct and possession are incorporated in the contract of sale, which we find scattered in al-Shāfi'ī's discussion of it in chapter *al-Buyū'*.

THE CONTENTS OF AL-SHĀFI'Ī'S CONTRACT OF SALE AS REFLECTED IN AL-SHĪRĀZĪ'S CONTRACT OF SALE OF THE *TANBĪH*

In the valid contract of sale, both the purchaser and the seller have absolute right of usufruct of articles of exchange without any restriction and extraneous conditions.[20] This is implicit in al-Muzani's concept of the contract of sale, which is narrated in al-Shāfi'ī's *K al-Umm* at different places regarding several individual items and instances. Al-Shīrāzī brings them together in a general statement applicable to all instances of the contract sale.

The contract of sale is valid only when the seller makes offer and the purchaser accepts it. This can be expressed by indicating in several ways such as the seller says that "I offer it to you" and the purchaser says that "I accept it or something similar." It can be expressed by gesture, nodding, or pointing out the article itself. Here al-Shīrāzī uses one of the techniques of al-Shāfi'ī's hermeneutics.[21]

Upon the conclusion of the contract, both parties have right of option either to accept it or reject it, so long as they have not separated from each other without breaking meeting. The right of option is valid only for three days and no more except in case of esculent articles. The right of option for three days is determined according to one juristic opinion (*qawl*) from the day the contract is concluded. According to another juristic opinion, it is determined upon the separation of parties from each other and the sold article is transferred as stipulated in the contract. Al-Shīrāzī very often states two juristic opinions, whereas neither al-Shāfi'ī nor al-Muzanī cites two juristic opinions as al-Shīrāzī does. This shows that different juristic opinions should have developed later over the course of time because of the hermeneutical different interpretations.

Following additional information in al-Shīrāzī's chapter *al-Buyū'* of *al-Tanbīh* is found neither in al-Shāfi'ī's *K al-Umm* nor in al-Muzanī's chapters of *al-Buyū'* and *al-Bay'*.

After the expiration of three days, the right of option is terminated according to one juristic opinion, but according to another juristic opinion, it can be deferred.

If the article of sale is not transferred from the possession of each party to the contract, then neither the purchaser nor the seller becomes proprietor of it and can make usufruct of it, unless the right of option has expired, and the article of sale in exchange is taken into possession, then the usufruct of article of exchange is legally not affected.[22]

In case, the right of option of the purchaser expires and he has taken the article of sale in exchange into his possession, then it becomes his responsibility (*dhimma*). In regard to the usufruct of article before the expiration of right of option, there are two juristic opinions: according to one juristic opinion, the usufruct of it is valid, and, according to the other juristic opinion, it is not valid as the article of sale has yet not entered into the responsibility of purchaser, unless the right of option has expired and the article has been taken into his possession, and his proprietorship of it has become established.

If the article of sale is destroyed before the purchaser has taken it into his possession, the contract becomes canceled. If it is destroyed while it was taken into possession by the purchaser, he is responsible for its price and it becomes incumbent upon him. If it is destroyed by a third person (*ajnabī*), there are two juristic opinions: according to one of the juristic opinions, the contract of sale becomes canceled and according to other juristic opinion, it does not become canceled, but the purchaser has right of option to cancel it or the price becomes incumbent on the third person. In case, the article of sale to the purchaser is destroyed by the seller, contract of sale becomes void and the purchaser is considered a stranger, regardless if the price of the article of sale has been transferred to the seller and received by him.

RIGHT OF OPTION

Hermeneutical General Features of Right of Option as Reflected in al-Muzanī's Right of Option in the *Mukhtaṣar*[23]

In al-Shāfi'ī's chapter of the Right of Option of *al-Buyū'*, one finds several prophetic *Ḥadīth* reports with complete chain of narrations as it is usually the case in every chapter *al-Buyū'* in the *K al-Umm*, whereas al-Muzanī here cites a few narrations relevant to the contents. In al-Shāfi'ī's chapter of Right of Option, one observes the absence of any Qur'ānic verses. It is entirely based on the prophetic *Ḥadīth* reports. As already mentioned in chapter 1, according to al-Shāfi'ī's hermeneutics of *Risāla* the prophetic *Ḥadīth* reports are the co-source of legislation. It can be used to provide epistemologically necessary details or explain the ruling of the *Qur'ān* or in the absence of any ruling in the *Qur'ān*, the prophetic *Ḥadīth* reports can be used independently as the source of legislation as it is the case here. Al-Shāfi'ī also uses the narrations from early Muslims such as Abū al-Wāṣī sold a horse to a person going for military expedition, thereupon, the Prophet said: "The purchaser and the seller both have right of option either to accept or reject it, so long as they have not separated from each other without breaking meeting."[24] One also finds that al-Shāfi'ī as well as al-Muzanī acknowledge custom as it was practiced by the residents of Ḥijāz as a source of legislation, because they were also recognized in the *Qur'ān* and by the Prophet.[25]

In al-Muzanī's chapter of *al-Bay'*, one finds two cases of interest in his presentation of the right of option. One is regarding the use of *qiyās* as it would be discussed in the contents of right of option and the other is regarding the right of option of three days which in Shāfi'ī school of law is generally observed, but according to al-Shāfi'ī and al-Muzanī, it is valid if one party lets the other party to have right of option after the conclusion of contract.[26] According to al-Shāfi'ī[27] and al-Muzanī, the right of option of three days is to be observed, since it is based on the prophetic *Ḥadīth* report, but in case one party to the contract permits the other party the right of option after the conclusion of the contract, it is allowed.

THE CONTENTS OF AL-SHĀFI'Ī'S RIGHT OF OPTION IN HIS KITAB *al-UMM* REFLECTED IN AL-MUZANĪ'S RIGHT OF OPTION IN HIS *MUKHTAR*[28]

Based on the prophetic *Ḥadīth* report al-Muzanī, like al-Shāfi'ī, declares in chapter *al-Bay'*, as well as in chapter *al-Buyū'*, that both parties to the contract have the right of option either to accept or reject it so long as they have not separated from each other. Al-Muzanī's account in chapter *al-Buyū'* brings together what is described by al-Shāfi'ī at different places in his *K al-Umm*. Al-Muzanī, in the very beginning of discussion, declares by integration that in the contracts of *ṣarf* sale, *salam* sale, or debt both parties have right of option of accepting or rejecting the contract so long as they have not separated from each other, for these contracts are the species (*aṣnāf*) of the contract of sale. This integration shows that al-Muzanī tries to state in general statement applicable to all the cases rather than describing it in each case separately such as in the *ṣarf* sale, *salam* sale, or debt.

Except if the parties to these contracts separate from each other after taking the possession of each other's merchandise and one of them permits the other party after the right of option has expired, it is valid.

In case, the merchandise becomes destroyed in the hands of purchaser after concluding the contract and after taking its possession, but before breaking meeting or prior to having exercised right of option, he becomes responsible for the price as it was under the contract that has not yet ended.

One purchases a female slave and emancipates her before breaking meeting, or prior to exercising his right of option, the seller can cancel the contract of sale. The emancipation by the purchaser of the female slave becomes void as she is considered still the property of the seller, so long as the right of option has not expired. Thus, if the seller cancels it, it is valid.

Likewise, if the purchaser hastens to perform the cardinal intercourse with female slave because of the neglect (of not knowing), the seller has an option to cancel the contract and it becomes incumbent upon the purchaser to pay to the seller an equivalent amount of the price which is payable in the *mahr* (dowry). If he makes the female slave pregnant, the seller has an option to cancel the contract and she becomes his property. In this case, it is incumbent on the purchaser to pay the amount of the price equivalent to that which is payable in the *mahr* as well as the price for the child born in semblance. Al-Muzanī bases this contention on the analogy (*qiyās*) of the evidence regarding a person who gives divorce to one of his wives and had the cardinal intercourse with her in semblance. Al-Muzanī exercises here his own *qiyās* to justify this juristic opinion. This shows that al-Muzanī tries to incorporate such possible elements so that no uncertainty is left in any transactions. This is contrary to what is assumed in general that the authors of the compositions of *Mukhtaṣar* just present legal opinions of the eponyms of the school in an abridged form.

If one of the parties to the contract dies prior to separating from each other before breaking meeting, then the inheritor takes his place as his representative and can exercise the right of option in the contract of sale.

If one of the parties to the contract dies prior to the separation, and the animal gives birth to an offspring, it belongs to the purchaser and the contract as it was originally *(aṣl)* stipulated remains valid as in all other stipulations in the contract. It is not objectionable to stipulate right of option in the contract of sale, but no more than three days as according to the prophetic *Ḥadīth* report concerning the animal left un-milked for some days.

In al-Shāfi'ī's chapter *al-Buyō'* and al-Muzanī's chapter *al-Buyō'* a case is described that is not found in al-Muzanī's chapter *al-Bay'*. It is if of one of parties to the contract becomes mute or madness takes over him prior to separating from each other, then the ruler (*Ḥākim*) takes over the case and the decision is left over to him.

Al-Muzanī's account of the right of option in chapter *al-Buyō'* does not essentially differ from that of his chapter *al-Bay'* as well as that of al-Shāfi'ī. Al-Muzanī renders it faithfully in conformity with al-Shāfi'ī's presentation of it, only instead of citing full chain of narrations of the prophetic *Ḥadīth* reports *verbatim*, al-Muzanī suffices by stating that "al-Shāfi'ī said," whereas in the chapter *al-Bay'*, al-Muzanī cites only a few prophetic *Ḥadīth* reports.

RIBĀ

Hermeneutical General Features of *Ribā* as Reflected in al-Muzani's Chapters *al-Bay'*[29] and *al-Buyū'*[30] of his *Mukhtaṣar*

The word *ribā* is used generally to refer to usury or what is nowadays called interest, but its use is not confined to this meaning alone. In fact, any kind of excess in exchange of one article for another article is considered *ribā* and unlawful.

In al-Shāfi'ī's *K al-Umm*, we find its discussion under the title *Bāb al-Ribā fī al-Ṭa'ām* (Usury concerning the Articles of Esculent Nature). Al-Muzanī' discusses it under the more precise title *Bāb al-Ribā wa mā yajōzaw b'aḍhu bi b'aḍhu Mutafāḍula wa lā Mu'ajalā wa Ṣarf* (Usury and Invalidity of the Exchange of Articles of the same Species (*jins*) at an unequal rate, Suspension of Payment to a Future specified time, and *Ṣarf* sale in which *ribā* can be involved and comprehensively brings them together, whereas in Shāfi'ī's *K al-Umm* each of them are discussed separately such as the *Bāb al-Raṭab bi*

Tamar,[31] *Bāb al-'Urūḍ*,[32] *Bāb al-Ṭa'ām bi al-Ṭa'ām* (Exchange of Esculent Articles),[33] *Bāb al-Makīl wa Wazn* (Articles of Measurement and Weight),[34] *Bāb al-Laḥam bi al-Laḥm*),[35] (*Bāb al-Ṣarf*),[36] Suspension of Payment to a Future specified time, and the list goes on.

Al-Shāfi'ī in the *K al-Umm* discusses the classification of the articles into genus (*jins*), species (*ṣanf*), and kind (*nau'*) in which *ribā* can be involved. Al-Muzanī, without discussing al-Shāfi'ī's classification itself, brings them comprehensively together.

Al-Muzanī in chapter *al-Buyū'*, in contrast to chapter *al-Bay'*, follows the arrangement of the material from al-Shāfi'ī's *K al-Umm* that gives an account of *ribā* of each individual kinds of things falling into genus, species, and kinds, though using sparingly the prophetic *Ḥadīth* reports. In chapter *al-Bay'*, al-Muzanī integrates them comprehensively together, which is scattered in al-Shāfi'ī's *K al-Umm*.

Al-Muzanī' discusses in connection with *ribā*, the possession of articles of exchange by each party to the contract particularly in *ṣarf* sale. If one of them fails to hand over the article to other, then there is a possibility of *ribā* involved in it.[37] In such a case, for al-Muzanī and al-Shāfi'ī, there is an uncertainty besides *ribā* involved in it. Moreover, it is based on the prophetic *Ḥadīth* report that the articles of sale should be exchanged from hand to hand (*yadan fa yadan*).

In one place, we find al-Muzanī exercising *qiyās*. According to al-Shāfi'ī, the sale of moist meat in exchange for dry meat is invalid. From this, al-Muzanī goes further and deduces that the sale of moist meat is invalid altogether,[38] because one would not know the real quantity of meat in this case. Thus, there is an uncertainty and possibility of *ribā* involved in it.

We find in al-Muzanī's chapter *al-Buyū'* a statement that refers to the opinion of Abū Ḥanīfa and Abū Yūsuf that the sale of moist meat of all (*ḥalāl*) animals is valid, but Muḥammad al-Shaybānī disagrees with him.[39] This indicates that by the time of al-Muzanī increasingly more interactions taking place among the different Sunni schools of law.

Hermeneutical General Features of *Ribā* as Reflected in al-Shīrāzī's *Ribā* in the *Tanbīh*[40]

Al-Shīrāzī's account of *ribā* is thorough, lucid, and short. Al-Shīrāzī articulates his statement in the general form. This reflects the progression in the development of compositions of *Mukhtaṣar*.

Al-Muzanī shows greater awareness of al-Shāfi'ī's classification of the things into the genus, species, and kinds, and the validity and invalidity of the rulings applicable to them in the transactions of contract of sale as it is done by al-Shāfi'ī in the *K al-Umm*. This is clearly indicated by his use of al-Shāfi'ī's term *ism khāṣṣ*.

Al-Shīrāzī in several cases presents two juristic opinions which over the course of time should have been prevalent. This shows the development of hermeneutical differences of opinion among the jurists in Shāfi'ī school of law similar to what we find in the case of jurists in the Ḥanafī and Mālikī schools of law.

THE CONTENTS OF AL-SHĀFI'Ī'S *RIBĀ* AS REFLECTED IN AL-MUZANĪ'S *RIBĀ* IN THE *MUKHTAṢAR*

Al-Shāfi'ī's and al-Muzanī's account of *ribā* is based on the prophetic *Ḥadīth* report which states

> Do not sell gold in exchange for gold, silver in exchange for silver, land in exchange for land, barley in exchange for barley, fresh dates in exchange for fresh dates, and salt in exchange for salt for each other except equal in measurement and weight from hand to hand (*yadan fa yadan*), but you are at liberty to sell gold in exchange for silver, silver in exchange for gold, gold in exchange for barely, land in exchange for barely, barely in exchange for land, palm dates in exchange for salt, and salt in exchange for palm dates as you please.

This means that the exchange of articles under the same species should be at an equal rate, but the exchange of articles of different species can be sold at an unequal rate.

Thus, if an article of the exchange in the same species is found more in measurement or weight than the other article of the same species, then the quantity of more in measurement or weight is considered involving *ribā* in the contract of sale.

The suspension of payment to a future specified time in exchange of articles is not valid. In such a case, there is a possibility of involving *ribā*, because the suspension of payment to a future specified time can affect an unequal rate (*tafāḍul*) of cash money to the original price.

Al-Muzanī narrates other prophetic *Ḥadīth* reports including the narrations by early Muslims regarding the possession of the articles of exchange. The purchaser and the seller must take articles of sale into possession before breaking meeting, otherwise the contract is void as required originally (*aṣl*) by the stipulation in the contract itself.

There is no *ribā* except in case of exchange of gold, silver, and esculent articles. But, it is not valid to accept esculent articles of weight in exchange for *dīnārs* as it is not valid to accept silver in weight for *dīnārs*. There are different opinions among Muslims with respect to the acceptance of *dīnārs* and *dirhams* in exchange of anything as they constitute themselves measure by which the price of other things is determined.

In the exchange of *dīnārs* and *dirhams*, it is valid to accept *falūs* (currency in circulation). However, there is no tax (*zakāt*) levied on *falūs* and other raw metals (*tibar*) such as raw gold, silver etc., as they have no value (*thaman*) in themselves originally (by *aṣl*). Thus, there is no *ribā* involved in the exchange of raw metals.

The *salaf* sale (suspension of payment to a future specified time) in the esculent articles of measurement and weight is invalid, though the *salaf* sale is not objectionable if all the articles excluding the esculent articles, gold, and silver, are sold at an unequal rate with the suspension of payment to a future specified time, even if the articles are of the same species (*ṣanf*).

The *salaf* sale of one camel for two camels of the same species is not objectionable with or without the intention of slaughtering them or not. Likewise, the *salaf* sale is not objectionable of one *raṭl* of copper for two *raṭls* of copper and one article for two articles with the description of suspension of payment to a future specified time. But based on this juristic ruling (*qawl*), it is not appropriate to analogically infer from this that the *salaf* sale is not objectionable of one pomegranate in exchange for two pomegranates, either counted by number or by weight and, likewise, the *salaf* sale of one quince (a certain kind of fruit) in exchange for two quinces, one watermelon in exchange for two watermelons, and other such kinds (*naḥw*) of esculent things of the same species. But if they are of different species, the *salaf* sale of a thing of one species in exchange for a thing in other species at an unequal rate as well as by estimate (*juazāf*) is valid (*mubāḥ*). The same way, the *salaf* sale is not objectionable of one embolic fruit for two quince fruits as it is not objectionable of one *mudd*[41] of wheat in measurement for two *mudds* of dry dates in measurement.

The (*salaf*) sale of wheat and fresh dates by measurement or weight is not valid with the measurement of *ṣā'*,[42] as it can weigh more measured with the *ṣā'* than without it.

The (*salaf*) sale of the vinegar made from grapes in exchange for the vinegar made from olive is not valid (good, *lā khayra*), unless they are of two different species.

One *mudd* of dough in measurement and *dirham* for two *mudds* of dough in measurement is not objectionable as in sale of fresh dates in exchange for fresh dates.

The sale of all articles of the same species such as oil, grease, almonds, walnuts, seasoning seeds for food is not valid, except in equal measurement or weight. The sale of articles of two different species (at an unequal rate) is valid.

The (*salaf*) sale of the articles of same species such as cooked food in exchange for raw food is not valid, because of the lesser weight of cooked food than the weight of raw food. Likewise, the sale of honey in exchange for honey, except if they are of two different species (*aṣnāf*) such as the sale of honey by weight in exchange for the candles, because the weight of honey in the candle would not be known. Likewise, the sale of milk of sheep, goat, and milk of Arabian, *Gewāmīsa*, and *Mahraba* camels are considered sale of the same species. The sale of each of them is not valid (*lā khayra*) except in equal measurement or weight. However, if they are of two different species, it is not objectionable to sell animal milk of one species in exchange for animal milk of the other species at an unequal rate.

It is not valid (good) to sell butter made from the sheep's milk in exchange for the sheep's milk, nor is it valid to sell fat of sheep in exchange for sheep butter.

In the sale of *dīnārs* in exchange for *dirhams*, neither party to the contract is at liberty without breaking meeting to take article of exchange into possession. If the purchaser separates from the seller without taking the article of exchange into his possession and if it is destroyed, the seller cannot take the price from the purchaser. If it is destroyed in the hands of purchaser after taking the article of sale into his possession, he is liable for the price. If any defect is found either in *dīnārs* or *dirhams*, each party to the contract has right of option either to return them or keep them.

In the above account of *ribā* of al-Muzanī, one finds expanded additional elements comprehensively incorporated not found in al-Shāfi'ī's account of *ribā*.

THE CONTENTS OF AL-SHĀFI'Ī'S *RIBĀ* AS REFLECTED IN AL-SHĪRĀZĪ'S *RIBĀ* IN THE *TANBĪH*[43]

Ribā is unlawful regarding gold and silver, edibles articles and article of drinks.

The unlawfulness of *ribā* regarding gold and silver is based on the effective reasoning (*'illa*) as they both determine the price of all other things thus, they are considered of the same species. The unlawfulness of the exchange of edible articles and articles of drinks in measurement and weight at an unequal rate (*ribā*) is based upon the effective reasoning that they belong to the same species. It is also unlawful in such exchange the suspension of payment to a future specified time (*nisā'*), and the separation of the parties to the contract before taking the articles of exchange into possession.

The sale of an article in exchange for an article of different species, such as gold for silver, wheat for barley, at a different rate is valid, but with the suspension of payment to a future specified time and before taking it into possession is unlawful. However, the exchange of one article for another article at a different rate (*tafāḍul*) is considered lawful, if they are of the same species on the condition of the suspension of payment to a future specified time, and prior to taking the article of exchange into possession.

Any two things which share a proper name (*ism khāṣ*)[44] such as *'Aqalī* dates and *Barnī* dates are considered of the same species, but any two things which do not share the same proper name such as wheat and barley, meat and pappy fruit, liver and tail of buttock are considered two different species.

Regarding two kinds of meat and milk, there are two juristic opinions (*qawlān*): one juristic opinion is that they are of two different species and the sale of them at different rate is valid and the other juristic opinion is that if they are of the same species, it is not valid to sell meat of a cow in exchange for meat of a sheep at different rate.[45] If one of them makes its usufruct and after taking it into possession finds it with defect which it is not as specified by description (*ṣifa*) in the contract, he can return it and contract of sale is canceled. In this case, substituting it with another thing is not valid. However, if the substitute was stipulated as the responsibility of the seller, the purchaser can return it and ask for its substitute before or after the separation of both parties to the contract. In this case, there are also two juristic opinions (*qawlān*): according to one juristic opinion, he can return it and take the substitute for it, and according to another juristic opinion, he has the right of option either to keep it or return it as he pleases, and the contract of sale is canceled. The different rate of exchange is lawful of the articles equal in measurement, if one of them is measured by clay (*turāb*) vessel, which is less. However, the sale of the articles in exchange by weight is not valid unless they are equal in weight. If one of them is less measured by clay vessel, it is not valid.[46] Regarding the articles of exchange, which are neither measured nor weighed, there are two juristic opinions: according to one of them, it is not valid and according to another juristic opinion, is it is valid.

It is not valid to sell grains in exchange for flour, flour in exchange for flour, articles of cooked food in exchange for the articles of cooked food with the suspension of payment to a future specified time, and exchange of articles of pure juice in their origin (*aṣl*) for articles of pure juice, pure articles for mixed articles, mixed articles with mixed articles, moist articles for moist articles except as the *'ārya*, such as ripe dates in exchange for dates which are ripening on the palm tree, grapes in vineyard in exchange for raisin, which are of not more than five *awsāq* (pl. of *wasq*)[47] in weight by estimate.

The sale of two articles in exchange for two articles of the same species at a different price such as the sale of one *Qāṣānī dīnār* and one *Sābūrī dīnār* in exchange for two *Qāsānī* or *Sābūrī dīnārs* is valid.

The sale of milk of sheep in exchange for milk in her udder is not valid.[48]

The sale of edible animal meat in exchange for inedible animal meat is not valid.

ṢARF SALE

Defining Ṣarf Sale

The *ṣarf* sale is sale of price in exchange for price such as *dīnārs* and *dirhams*. In this mode of sale, it is a necessary condition (*sharṭ*) that such an exchange of articles takes place at a meeting in exchange of such as silver for silver and gold for gold from hand to hand on the spot (*yadan fa yadan*).

HERMENEUTICAL GENERAL FEATURES OF *ṢARF* SALE AS REFLECTED IN AL-MUZANĪ'S *ṢARF* SALE IN THE *MUKHTAṢAR*

Al-Muzanī in his presentation of al-Shāfi'ī's contents of *ṣarf* sale follows al-Shāfi'ī's concept of hermeneutics and bases it supported by the prophetic *Ḥadīth* reports. We find no Qur'ānic verses in the account of the *ṣarf* sale in al-Shāfi'ī's *K al-*Umm as well as in al-Muzanī's *Mukhtaṣar*. This is because of two reasons: one, the *ṣarf* sale is only one of the species of contract of sale. The distinguishing mark of it is the possession of the articles of exchange from hand to hand on the spot without breaking meeting. Since the *ṣarf* sale is one of the species of the contract of sale, it follows that one must observe all the stipulations of contact of sale such as the right of option of the purchaser and the seller, right of option in the case of defect in the article of sale, condition of three days etc. Two, the *Qur'ān* itself gives the authority to the Prophet. The prophetic *Ḥadīth* reports make it explicit what is intended by the *Qur'ān*. This shows also al-Shāfi'ī's contention of the hermeneutics in respect to the use of prophetic *Ḥadīth* reports as an independent source for legislating the rulings.

Al-Muzanī incorporates all the material concerning the *ṣarf* sale and tries to present it in general statements using less of descriptive statements in each case separately. Al-Muzanī also brings here the validity or invalidity of the *ṣarf* sale in relation to the contract of partnership (*shirka*), friendly partnership (*tawlīya*), and acceptance of *falūs* as a mode of exchange.

The Contents of al-Shāfi'ī's *Ṣarf* Sale as Reflected in al-Muzanī's *Ṣarf* Sale in the *Mukhtaṣar*[49]

For whatever reason, neither al-Muzanī's chapter *al-Bay'* nor al-Shīrāzī's *al-Tanbīh* contain an account of the *ṣarf* sale, but in chapter *al-Buyū'* al-Muzanī faithfully renders al-Shāfi'ī's contents of the *ṣarf* sale by presenting the material in a comprehensive form with only a few prophetic *Ḥadīth* reports. He suffices here by stating simply "al-Shāfi'ī said."

In the *ṣarf* sale, it is prerequisite that each party to the contract takes an article of exchange into possession prior to separating from each other, and without breaking meeting as it is prerequisite in all kinds of contracts of sale, since the *ṣarf* sale is one of the species (*ṣanf*) of contract of sale.[50]

In the *ṣarf* sale, the exchange of articles should be equivalent in weight with each other. This is based on the prophetic *Ḥadīth* report, which states:

> Do not sell gold in exchange for gold, silver in exchange for silver, and esculent articles of the same species except equal in weight. If they are exchanged in measurement, then exactly equal in measurement, but the *ṣarf* sale is not valid of the esculent articles of the same species by measurement in exchange for articles by weight."[51]

Likewise, the *ṣarf* sale of gold in exchange for gold in measurement is not valid, if they are different in weight.[52]

In the *ṣarf* sale, if a person purchases twenty *dirhams* in exchange for one *dīnār* and takes possession of nineteen of them and one *dirham* less to be received later, it is not valid that the parties to the contract separate from each other, unless the purchaser takes the remaining one *dirham* into his possession.[53]

In the *ṣarf* sale, if a person purchases one *dīnār* in exchange for twenty *dirhams* and two *dirhams* are found counterfeit that is not embellished as coin or it is bad silver, it is not objectionable that the purchaser accepts or returns it. If he returns it, the contract of sale is canceled, since it is the transaction in the contract of sale in which right of option of returning the thing is included.[54]

In the *ṣarf* sale, if a person having sold one *dīnār* in exchange for ten *dirhams* and if he should purchase a piece of cloth with them prior to taking them into his possession, the sale of cloth is invalid in that case, because it was incumbent on him to take into possession ten *dirhams*. Otherwise, the *ṣarf* sale would be usurious.[55]

In the *ṣarf* sale, it is not valid either to purchase or sell metals in their raw form, because in that case neither the purchaser nor the seller would know the quantity of metal without soil or dust in it.[56]

The *ṣarf* sale of *falūs* with the suspension of payment to a future time is not objectionable, as there is no *ribā* involved in it.

Regarding the partnership (*shirka*) and friendly partnership (*tawlīya*) what is considered valid or invalid in the *ṣarf* sale is considered valid or invalid in the partnership and friendly partnership.[57]

It is not valid that a person gives one hundred *dīnārs* to another person in Medina on the condition that he gives the same amount of *dīnārs* in Mecca with or without the suspension of payment to a future specified time. It is considered neither debt nor *ṣarf* sale.[58] In the same manner, if a person buys cloths for one *dīnār* at a certain month on the condition that he receives in exchange two *dirhams* for one *dīnār* after two months, it is invalid and unlawful.

SALAM SALE

Defining *Salam* Sale

The *salam* sale signifies a contract involving a prompt delivery in return for a distant delivery, causing an immediate payment of price by one party to the contract and admitting a delay in the delivery of articles by the other party to the contract.[59]

HERMENEUTICAL GENERAL FEATURES AS REFLECTED IN *SALAM* SALE IN AL-MUZANĪ'S *SALAM* SALE IN *MUKHTAṢAR*'[60] AND AL-SHĪRĀZĪ'S *TANBĪH*[61]

Al-Shāfi'ī's account of *salam* sale is scattered at various places. Al-Muzanī, following al-Shāfi'ī, bases his contention regarding the *salam* sale on the prophetic *Ḥadīth* reports whereas al-Shīrāzī nowhere cites any prophetic *Ḥadīth* reports. All three of them al-Shāfi'ī, al-Muzanī, and al-Shīrāzī do not cite any verses from the *Qur'ān*.

The *salam* sale is one of the species of the contract of sale like the *ṣarf* sale, lease-hire, and partnership. Their rulings are mostly based on prophetic *Ḥadīth* reports. Al-Shīrāzī's account of *salam* sale in comparison to al-Muzanī's account is much more concise, lucid, and juristically the most comprehensive covering all aspects of al-Shāfi'ī's account of *salam* sale.

Al-Shīrāzī's description of the contract sale includes the wording "*salam* sale" to indicate precisely that it is a contract of *salam* sale.

Al-Shīrāzī presents in the *salam* sale two juristic opinions which should have developed over the course of time.

Al-Muzanī presents material in an abridged form, but following al-Shāfi'ī, he narrates the rulings for different items and articles separately case by case and fails to articulate them in the form of a general statement whereas al-Shīrāzī packs them together in a statement.[62] This shows a great progression toward the formulations in a generalized form.

According to al-Shīrāzī, the *salam* sale in partnership (*shirka*) and friendly partnership (*tawlīya*) is not valid. Al-Shīrāzī does not provide any explanations for it. According to al-Shāfi'ī, partnership requires the property (*māl*) in *dīnārs* or *dirhams* at the time when the contract of partnership is concluded, whereas in the *salam* sale, it is required that the article to be delivered must be existing and must be in the possession at the time at the time of contracting *salam* sale.

THE CONTENTS OF AL-SHĀFIʿĪ'S *SALAM* SALE AS REFLECTED IN AL-SHĪRĀZĪ'S *SALAM* SALE IN THE *TANBĪH*[63] AND AL-MUZANĪ'S *MUKHTAṢAR*[64]

We shall follow al-Shīrāzī's account of *salam* sale, since it is from the juristic point of view comprehensive. His statements are in the general and abstract form. Here we will produce, in most part, al-Shīrāzī's account of the *salam* sale that includes extended additional elements, which are neither found in al-Shāfiʿī's account nor are they found in al-Muzanī's account. We shall introduce al-Muzanī's contents of the *salam* sale wherever it is relevant and needed.

Al-Muzanī, following al-Shāfiʿī's narration of prophetic *Ḥadīth* report, states it *verbatim*: "God permits *salam* sale and *rahan* (deposit) and forbids anyone from the sale of what is not in his possession, but authorizes *salam* sale as valid."[65]

Al-Shīrāzī declares in the very opening statement that the *salam* sale is one of the species (*ṣanf*) of sale and is contracted with the wordings that include the "*salam* sale," involving the establishment of the right of option of meeting, but no option of extraneous stipulations to the contract are permitted.[66] If one of them stipulates that the property (*rās al-māl*) is delivered in the meeting, then it is his responsibility to describe its quality and quantity. If it is already determined, it does not need to be described (by the wordings). This juristic opinion is more valid than the previous juristic opinion where it was mentioned that the description of quality and quantity of the property (*rās al-māl*) was necessary.[67] The *salam* sale is not valid except the possession of property in exchange is taken with its description such as the price, grains, flour (*al-adqa*), metals, animals, slave, meat, greenery (groceries), wool, barley, cotton, silk, cloths, lead, copper, iron, stones, essence (*'aṭar*), medicine, and other such things.[68] Al-Shāfiʿī and al-Muzanī tend to describe them separately case by case for each of these articles, whereas al-Shīrāzī packs them together in one statement.[69] The *salam* sale is not valid if the article of exchange differs in quality from what is specified in the contract and if it differs from the purpose for which it is sold as known in general.

It is not valid to renew the stipulation in a *salam* sale.

The *salam* sale of ornaments (jewelry), shells, animals carrying an offspring in the womb, the articles baked on fire such as loaf of bread, meat cooked on grill, and the different articles mixed with each other is not valid. Here again al-Shīrāzī appropriately puts them together in a general statement.[70]

The *salam* sale regarding the cotton cloth on the edge of which silk fabric is wrapped is valid. However, according to another juristic opinion it is not valid, if the wrapping is done outside the edging of cotton cloth.[71]

The *salam* sale of acid mixed with water is not valid,[72] though the *salam* sale of cheese with diffusing odor or vinegar mixed water is valid.[73]

The *salam* sale of vessels of excellent, average, and lower qualities such as glittering vessels and pale metallic buckets with cramped necks is not valid.[74]

The *salam* sale of articles is not valid unless their quantity is specified. However, the articles which are counted numerically, but if they differ in weight such as eggs, walnuts, almonds, figs, and watermelons is not valid, except only by weight. It is said regarding the *salam* sale of the walnuts and almonds measured by *ṣāʿ* is valid.

The *salam* sale with the suspension of payment at a future time is not valid, except if the time is specified, but the *salam* sale with the suspension of payment in two installments at two specified future times is valid.

If the *salam* sale is concluded on the spot in a meeting, the description of the place of delivery is not needed. The requisite of the location of delivery is the place where the contract is concluded. However, if the place of delivery of the article of *salam* sale is to a specified at a future specified time, then it is incumbent that the place of delivery is described. If one of the parties to the contract claims that the place of delivery was incumbent and the other denies it, the *salam* sale is canceled, except if the place of delivery is cut off from reaching it for the delivery of the article.[75]

In the *salam* sale. it is not valid to stipulate any condition such as the fruits from a definite place, or from a certain tree, or of specified weight or measurement. According to al-Shīrāzī, such conditions are extraneous to the contract.

The article of *salam* sale to be delivered (*muslim fīh*) is not valid, unless it is (already) existing and is in the possession of the seller nor is the *salam* sale of it valid in the partnership (*shirka*) and friendly partnership (*tawlīya*).[76]

If the article of *salam* sale to be delivered is brought according to the description or better, it is incumbent on the purchaser to accept it.

In the *salam*, if it is claimed by the purchaser against the seller that one kind (*nauʿ*) of article is better than the article of another kind such as the fruits of *ʿAqalī* (palm) tree are better than the fruits of *Barnī* (palm) tree, it is not valid. It is not according to the description,[77] since it is extraneous to the contract as described above.

If the article of *salam* sale to be delivered to the purchaser is brought to him before the due date (*qabl maḥal*) and if there is no harm perceived in accepting it, then it is incumbent on the purchaser to accept it. If he takes the possession of the article to be delivered and claims against the seller that there was an error regarding the measurement or weight in the article, his word (without an oath) is not accepted against the word of seller (without an oath).[78]

If the seller delivers the article of *salam* sale to the purchaser by estimate and the purchaser claims that it was lesser than his right of share, his word (*qawl*) is accepted. If he finds the article of delivery with defect, he can return it and demand its substitute. If another defect occurs in the article while it is in his possession and demands the price (*irsh*) and the seller denies it by saying "I delivered it to you without any defect, his word is accepted (with an oath)."[79]

PARTNERSHIP

HERMENEUTICAL GENERAL FEATURES OF PARTNERSHIP AS REFLECTED IN AL-MUZANĪ'S *MUKHTAṢAR*[80] AND IN AL-SHĪRĀZĪ'S *TANBĪH*[81]

Al-Shāfi'ī's account of partnership is the shortest possible in the entire *K al-Umm* extending not more than five to six lines in one paragraph, containing barely the most essential elements.[82] In fact, al-Shāfi'ī's account is so short, in comparison to the account of partnership of al-Muzanī and al-Shīrāzī, that one can describe al-Shāfi'ī's account not comprehensive.

In al-Shāfi'īs account of partnership, there is no Qur'ānic verse or prophetic *Ḥadīth* report cited. It begins with "al-Rab'ī narrated that al-Shāfi'ī said."

Al-Shāfi'ī declares in the very opening statement, "I know not what partnership in reciprocity (*shirka mufāwada*) is. It is void (*bāṭil*)."[83] This suggests that the partnership of this description is not valid, because that may, according to him include the power of agency (*wakāla*) concerning the unknown subject. This might create uncertainty as it would be difficult to determine hermeneutically the legal ruling in accordance with the legal canon.[84]

Al-Shāfi'ī recognizes the other kinds of partnerships such as (i) the partnership in which only the capital (*māl*) consisting of *dīnārs* and *dirhams* is allowed, but no merchandize, (ii) the partnership of capital mixed with workmanship, (iii) the partnership in traffic (*shirka al-'aynān*) and (iv) the partnership in workmanship (*shirka abdān*). In all these partnerships, the profit (*ribḥ*) is to be divided between the partners as specified in the contract.[85] It is not permitted that any partner spends the capital from the partnership for personal needs such as food, clothing, and other things of such nature, except for business transactions. No partner has any share in the gift and inheritance received by the other partner.

Al-Muzanī in the chapter *al-Bay'* observes the contention of al-Shāfi'ī's hermeneutics and bases the validity of partnership on the prophetic *Ḥadīth* report regarding the property acquired in the battle as booty was shared by the participants in the battle,[86] though al-Shāfi'ī himself does not cite the prophetic *Ḥadīth* report justifying the validity of partnership. This shows that though al-Shāfi'ī does not provide any support by the prophetic *Ḥadīth* report, al-Muzanī following hermeneutical contention tries to base the rulings relating them to the revealed canons.

After giving the accounts of al-Shāfi'īs contents of partnership, al-Muzanī brings in following expanded additional elements related to the partnership.[87]

When one of the partners dissolves the partnership, then the other partner can neither purchase nor can he sell any property until the dissolution of the contract becomes effective.

If one of the partners dies, the partnership becomes dissolved and the distribution of the property is commissioned to an authorized guardian appointed by the deceased person. It is valid, if the inheritor is of full legal age and prefers to become shareholder in the place of his father.

If a partner purchases a slave and after taking her/his possession, should a defect befall the slave, he can return the slave, or the other partner can keep him, if he pleases.

If one of the partners makes purchase, the claim for the price lies against him and not against the other partner, because this kind of partnership comprehends only agency (*wakāla*) but not bail (*kafāla*), contrary to in the partnership in reciprocity, which is not recognized by al-Shāfi'ī.

Regarding treason (*khiyāna*), al-Shāfi'ī is silent in his account of partnership. Al-Muzanī says that if one of the partners commits any treason, then it is incumbent on the other partner to bring evidence against him. If the other partner denies it and refuses to bring evidence, he is considered liable for it.

Al-Shīrāzī's account of partnership is more specific expressing its offer by one party and its acceptance by the party in various ways, including gesture, pointing, and nodding.[88] This shows that al-Shīrāzī uses one of the techniques of al-Shāfi'ī's hermeneutics.

Al-Shīrāzī declares that the partnership is based on the *Sunna*.

Like al-Muzanī, al-Shīrāzī introduces additional expanded elements related to the ruling of partnership by stating that no partner should be in debt.[89] With this, he makes it very explicit that the partnership requires capital (money) such as *dīnārs* and *dirhams*. It seems also that by the time of al-Shīrāzī, the interactions among the jurists of different schools of law were taking place as al-Shīrāzī's comments on partnership on credit, which is recognized by Abū Ḥanīfa and his disciples.

The Contents of al-Shāfi'ī's Partnership as Reflected in al-Muzanī's Partnership in the *Mukhtaṣar* in Chapter *al-Bay'*[90] and Chapter *al-Buyū'*[91]

Al-Muzanī's account of partnership in chapter *al-Buyū'* is not more than of four lines basically saying the partnership in reciprocity is void (*bāṭil*), but not providing hermeneutically any comprehensive account of the partnership.[92] In fact, it is even shorter than al-Shāfi'ī's account of his *K al-Umm*. However, al-Muzanī's account of it in chapter *al-Bay'* is much more detailed and extensive in comparison to al-Shāfi'ī's account of it in the *K al-Umm*. Therefore, we shall discuss the contents of partnership first from al-Muzanī's chapter *al-Bay'*.

Contrary to the usual procedure of his hermeneutics, al-Shāfiʻī in this case does not cite any Qur'ānic verse or the prophetic *Ḥadīth* reports. Al-Muzanī, following al-Shāfiʻī's hermeneutics, bases the validity of partnership on the prophetic *Ḥadīth* report regarding the booty acquired in the battle of Khaybar. The Prophet considered it the property in partnership and distributed it in five parts, four parts for those who took part in the battle and one part for the Muslim treasury (*bayt al-māl*).[93]

The partnership in property consists of *dīnārs* and *dirhams*. No other merchandise or wares (*'urūd*), and merchandise, or wares mixed with *dīnārs,* or *dirhams* constituting the property in partnership is allowed.[94]

There is no objection if the partnership is contracted in which one person contributes the capital (*māl*) and the other partner workmanship and the profit is divided between them as stipulated in the contract.[95]

The partners are not permitted to spend on themselves from the property of partnership except for the traffic or lease-hire.[96] In the same manner, regarding the gift or inheritance received by one partner, the other partner does not have any share in it.[97]

In case, two persons intend to join in partnership having no property (*māl*) except the merchandise, then each partner can sell his merchandise in the amount of half and half in value so that each become the proprietor having equal share in the partnership. They become partners in selling and holding the merchandise, and the share of one partner is not to exceed the share of another partner.[98]

It is not valid for one partner to sell the property of the other partner without his consent.[99] Each partner trades for the other in all transactions and both share the equal amount in profit or loss.

If one partner dissolves the partnership, then the other partner neither purchases nor does he sell any property in partnership, until the dissolution of the partnership becomes established.

If one of the partners dies, the partnership becomes dissolved and his share in the distribution of partnership is commissioned to an authorized agent or a guardian. However, it is valid if his inheritor is of full legal age and prefers to become shareholder in the partnership in the place of his father.[100]

If a partner purchases a slave and after taking possession of her/him a defect befalls her/him, he can return the slave, or the other partner can keep him, if he pleases. If one of the partners (in traffic) makes a purchase, then the claim for the price is against him, and not against the other partner.[101] This is because such a contract of partnership comprehends only agency (*wakāla*) and not bail (*kafāla*), contrary to the partnership in reciprocity, which al-Shāfiʻī does not acknowledge.

If one of the partners claims that the other partner has committed treason, then it is incumbent on the other partner to bring evidence against him. In case the other partner denies it and refuses to take an oath, he is considered liable for it.[102]

If the property is destroyed in the hands of one of the partners, then it is considered loss in the partnership as in such a kind of partnership, the partners are considered only custodians of the property in partnership.[103]

The Contents of *a*l-Shāfi'ī's Partnership as Reflected in the Contents of Partnership in al-Shīrāzī's *Tanbīh*[104]

According to al-Shīrāzī, the contract of valid partnership is based on the clear textual evidence (*naṣṣ*) in all articles of usufruct and price (*thaman*).[105]

The partnership is valid on the condition that the property in partnership is of the same description (*ṣifa*) such as one partner has *dīnārs* and the other has *dirhams* or both have the same, the *dīnārs* or the *dirhams*.[106]

The contract of partnership is not valid if one of the partners is in debt.[107]

Al-Shīrāzī, as al-Muzanī, following al-Shāfi'ī maintains that if two persons having no capital (*māl* i.e., *dīnārs* or *dirhams*) intend to join in partnership, they can raise capital by each contributing his merchandise in an equal amount consisting of half and half of each in value in partnership. Each partner is permitted the profit (*ribḥ*) and loss as stipulated in the contract.[108]

It is not valid if the property in partnership is stipulated in an equal amount, but the profit at different rates (*tafāḍul*), or the property at different rate, but the profit at an equal rate. It is valid, if the distribution of the profit is stipulated according to the amount of the property in partnership and each partner pays the wages for the work performed by the other from his property.

The contract of partnership in manual work (*shirka al-abdān*) is valid in which each partner earns wages for the performance of his (manual) work and each takes his wages for the work he performs.[109]

Regarding the partnership in reciprocity (*shirka mufāwaḍa*), al-Shīrāzī first explains it as follows:

> The partnership in reciprocity constitutes the property and wages for the work each partner performs. Each one of them is responsible for the other in liability for the usurpation, or invalid sales, or any liability against the property. But at the end, al-Shīrāzī declares it invalid as al-Shāfi'ī does.[110]

Al-Shīrāzī, unlike al-Shāfi'ī and al-Muzanī, shows the awareness in respect to the partnership on credit (*shirka wujūh*) which is permitted by Abū Ḥanīfa and his disciples, but in the end he declares it to be invalid, though he describes the nature of such a partnership, which consists of when two persons share the profit in what they purchase on the credit of each of them and each one of them permits the other to purchase a specific thing, then in such a purchase of the thing and profit earned on it, each partner is considered only a custodian, if it is destroyed or there is a claim of treason against him.[111]

But to my mind, al-Shīrāzī's primary reason for its rejection is the question of having property in cash (*māl*) such as *dīnārs* and *dirhams* and neither one of them has it in his possession. Such a kind of partnership can cause many concerns.

This also shows that al-Shāfi'ī' does not provide the comprehensive account as it becomes evident here in this case. It is the later jurists who, over the course of time, incorporate the expanded additional elements in the formation of Islamic legal system comprehensively.

LEASE-HIRE

Al-Shāfi'ī's account of lease-hire in the *K al-Umm* is found scattered under the chapters *Ijārāt*[112] (Lease-Hire), *Kirā' al-Dawāb*[113] (Hire of Animals), *Ijārāt wa Kirā' al-Arḍ*[114] (Lease-Hire of Land), *al-Musāqāt*[115] (Hire-Lease of Plantation), and *Kirā'al-Arḍ al-Bayḍā'*[116] (Lease-Hire of Uncultivated Land). They describe the nature of lease-hire of different kinds of lands and the purposes for which they are leased-hired such as the lease-hire of residential place, workshops, lease-hire of manual labor, animals, and other such things.

As a mark of his hermeneutics, al-Shāfi'ī justifies the validity of the lease-hire based on the Qur'ānic verse (65:6). "If they suckle our offspring, give them their recompense."[117] In this verse, one finds the validity of contract of lease-hire of a wet nurse to feed milk to an offspring and she is paid wages as a recompense for it. Thus, the usufruct is the subject of the thing contracted, because lease-hire is considered one of the species of the contract of sale. Therefore, what is valid in the contract of sale is also valid in the contract of lease-hire, in which the parties to the contract have right to the usufruct of the articles of exchange.

According to al-Shāfi'ī, the contract of lease-hire becomes immediately effective upon being concluded.

Al-Muzanī discusses it in neither chapter *al-Bay'* nor in chapter *al-Buyō'*. Only we find the topic of lease-hire in al-Shīrāzī's *al-Tanbīh*.

Hermeneutical General Features of Lease-Hire as Reflected in al-Shīrāzī's *Tanbīh*

The most important aspect of the account of lease-hire is that al-Shīrāzī in this chapter cites very frequently more than one legal opinion. It shows that even within a school of law, there can be different legal opinions because of the hermeneutical interpretations. This is also the case regarding the differences of juristic opinion in different schools of law. It is traditionally understood that the differences of opinion among the jurists are because of the tenets of school of law, rather than considering that they are because of the hermeneutical interpretations even among the jurists in the same school of law. Otherwise it would undermine completely the significance and import of al-Shāfi'ī's concept of hermeneutics. This would become increasingly more obvious, as we would see when we would deal with the compositions of *Mukhtaṣar* of other Sunni schools of law.

Al-Shīrāzī's account covers all aspects and elements found in al-Shāfi'ī's account of lease-hire and brings them together at one place. In fact, it is very extensive and as lengthy as al-Shāfi'ī's account of lease-hire. For that reason, it cannot be characterized just abridgment. The authors of the compositions of *Mukhtaṣar* are as much concerned as the eponyms of the school of law with the comprehensive systematization of the legal system and certainty of the legal rules to be applied in accordance with the legal canons.

Al-Shīrāzī presents especially here two juristic rulings regarding the certain aspects of the lease-hire. They should have been known to be held by different jurists as valid and they should have developed because of different hermeneutical interpretations.

Al-Shīrāzī's account provides a complete picture of the lease-hire covering all the aspects related to it.

According to al-Shīrāzī, the contract of lease-hire should include the word "lease-hire" clearly expressed and specified the usufruct of the thing leased-hired, and the wages for it as a recompense for its validity (*mubāḥ*). Al-Shīrāzī's cautious use of the word "*mubāḥ*" indicates that such transactions belong to the worldly matters and not strictly to the religious affairs, though their validity or invalidity is determined by the canons consisting of the Qur'ānic injunctions and the prophetic *Ḥadīth* reports.

The Contents of al-Shāfi'ī's Lease-Hire as Reflected in al-Shīrāzī's *Tanbīh*

According to al-Shīrāzī, it is not valid to lease-hire (*isti'jār*) a dog for hunting, a male camel for riding on the female camel, *dīnārs* and *dirhams*, singing girls and musicians for entertainment, and porter of wine.[118] As to the exchange of *dīnārs* and *dirhams* al-Shāfi'ī considers it simply borrowing.[119]

The lease-hire of a house, wet nurse for suckling a child, person for performing pilgrimage, lease-hire of animal for riding on it, lease-hire of person to purchase and sell merchandise are all valid.[120]

The attainment of the purpose or the work is the responsibility of the lessor (*mu'ajjir*).[121]

The lease-hire of an article is not valid except if its usufruct is possible.[122] Thus, it is not valid if a person leases-hires land for the purpose of cultivation when the water is cut off reaching it from the stream, or it is covered with rugged stones, or snow or water flowing from the mountain.[123] Likewise, it is not valid if it is in the city, unless it is possible to cultivate that land.[124] Al-Shāfi'ī discusses the lease-hire of lands and describes or rather repeats all the stipulations which are already included in the contract of sale itself.[125] In this chapter, al-Shāfi'ī also narrates that if a Muslim leases land for cultivation to the *dhimmī*, the land tax (*kharāj*) is levied upon him, but not the tithe (*'ushr*).[126]

The hire-lease of land is not valid except the purpose for which it is specified, inspected, and the wages for it are specified, such as in the case of a hire-lease of an immovable property. If it is not possible to determine the wages, then it is determined after the performance of the work, such as in the performance of pilgrimage and riding of an animal to a place. Concerning the place of residence, suckling of a child, or brick-laying, the wages are determined for the period for which services are rendered. The wages for the dressmaker and builder are determined according to the work they perform.[127]

There are two juristic opinions (*qawlān*) regarding the validity of duration of lease-hire: according to one juristic opinion, it is terminated by the end of each year and according to the other juristic opinion, it is terminated at the end of every three years.[128] Again, this case can be attributed to the result of hermeneutical differences of opinion in the interpretation of the legal ruling.

If the lessor asks for the rent for the entire period of lease, it is invalid. It is said that the contract of lease-hire is valid for the first month and not valid (for remaining period), unless the usufruct (wages) and the description (*ṣifa*, i.e., the purpose for which it is leased-hired) is specified. It can be specified by custom such as the place of residence and porter of cloth. If the description cannot be specified of things such as carrying load of iron, cotton, building material, plaster (whitewash), backed brick, potter's clay, and milk, then it is determined according to the custom. If it is not specified because of the great difference in the description, such as carrying of load, riding, suckling of the child, the lease-hire is not valid, unless it is inspected.[129]

If the contract of lease-hire is not for a specified duration, the stipulation of the right of option and meeting in it are valid. The contract of lease-hire is not valid except for the work for which wages are deferred (namely, payment after the completion of the work).[130]

The contract of lease-hire is not valid except if the wages, quantity, and quality (*ṣift*) are specified.

The lease-hire of food and clothing is not valid. It is to be noted that the lease-hire of cloth is valid in the Ḥanafī school of law.

The contract of lease-hire concerning the property (*māl*) by estimate is valid. If one leases-hires an article for its usufruct in exchange of another thing for its usufruct, there are two juristic opinions: one, it is valid and becomes obligatory on concluding the contract itself and the other juristic opinion is that if the suspension of the payment to a future specified time is stipulated, the payment becomes obligatory at that future specified time. The wages become incumbent at the place of delivery of the article as in the *salam* sale.[131]

If the contract was of the article of *salam* sale to be delivered, or the work to be completed by a certain time expires, but in the meanwhile the delivery of the article or the work to be completed becomes feasible, then the wages become obligatory on the delivery of the article or the work being completed.[132]

If the contract is canceled, the establishment of wages as recompense also becomes canceled.

There is no need to establish the usufruct regarding the objects such as house key, camel halter, girdle, and hump when they are let on lease. They are the responsibility of the lessor (*mustā'jir*).[133]

Regarding the cleansing of pimples or cleaning sewer, there is no need to establish wages, though as custom Muslims pay for such services. Likewise, the lessee pays for the usufructs as custom such as for lowering down the camel to sit on it to enable him to ride on it.[134]

If a person leases land to cultivate wheat, he can cultivate anything of its kind and if he leases animal for riding, he can ride on it for the similar purposes such as bringing the animal to drink water, food for the animal and load on it. In case, the animal eats more food at one stage of the journey to the pilgrimage than the other stage, it is valid that the lessee receives the substitute for it from the owner.[135]

If a person leases-hires an animal to ride on it to a certain place, it is obligatory to specify the place and the wages. If he rides on it and travels a longer distance than stipulated and the animal is destroyed, then he becomes responsible for its price. If there was a co-rider with him, then there are two legal opinions: according to one legal opinion, the co-rider becomes responsible for half of the price and according to another juristic opinion, the co-rider is responsible for it only in part.[136]

If a person leases-hires an article after taking it into possession, it is not valid for him to sublease it to someone else. This is one of the (more) valid juristic opinion of the two. According to another legal opinion, it is considered valid.[137] It is to be noted that in the Ḥanafī school of law subleasing is permitted.

If the article of lease-hire is destroyed, the lessee dissolves the contract of lease for the remaining time of lease. Concerning the remaining time of lease, there are two juristic opinions. If he finds any defect in it or the defect befalls it, he has an option of dissolving it. If he dissolves or not dissolve it, the wages/rent is obligatory for the period of lease which is passed.[138]

If it is a residential place and it is destroyed, or it is a land for cultivation to which the water becomes cut off, there are two juristic opinions: according to one juristic opinion, the contract of lease-hire becomes dissolved and according to the other juristic opinion, the lessor has an option to dissolve it.[139]

If the leased-hired thing is usurped until the time of the lease expires, it is considered as the thing in the contract of sale is destroyed before it has been taken into possession.[140]

If the lessor dies and the contract of lease-hire happens to pass to a minor not of full legal age, then according to one juristic opinion, the contract is dissolved, according to the other juristic opinion, it is not dissolved. It is valid if both the lessor (minor) and lessee agree that the third person (*ajnabī*) takes over it in the place of minor. If they dwindle in the matter, the contract of lease-hire is dissolved.[141]

If the hireling going to perform pilgrimage for the lessee dies or becomes restrained from the performance of the state of ritual of consecration (*iḥrām*), he is not entitled to any wages.

If the hireling dies after the performance of the essential rituals of pilgrimage, he is entitled to the wages, but the blood is not on him (namely, the lessee is not responsible for his death). If he dies and some of the essential rituals remain to be performed, then the wages are paid in proportion for the rituals he has already performed. The lessee can recommence it afresh.[142]

If the hireling deserts the hired property (*makarī*) and the contract was for its usufruct, then the lessee has an option between dissolving the lease or keep it continuing.

If the lease-hire was for a certain time and if it is dissolved for the remaining time, it is considered not dissolved for the time already passed. If the lease-hire was for the performance of work, it is considered not dissolved, if the lessee has power over the lessor to demand that he completes the work.[143]

If the camel runs away and the lessee leaves it, then the price plus the expenses (of the journey) involve in it are incumbent on him. If the expenses exceed the price, it is considered a loan against him, if the judge commissions the lessor to give it to the lessee as loan.[144]

If one of them dies under distress, then the lease-hire is not void (*bāṭil*), in respect to the existing leased-hired property of the lessor. If the property of the lessor becomes destroyed without any enmity while it was in the hands of the lessee, he is not responsible for it. If the lease-hire is expired, it is incumbent on the lessee to return the property and the provisions given to him. If there is a difference of opinion in respect to the claim against the lessor that it was incumbent on him, the word of the lessor is accepted.[145]

If the property which is given to perform work on it becomes destroyed while it is in the hands of the hireling and the property belongs to the lessor or someone else, and the lessor testifies of it, the hireling is not responsible for it. However, if the property belongs to someone else, there are two juristic opinions: according to one juristic opinion, the hireling is not responsible for it and he is entitled to any wages for the work he has performed, and according to the other juristic opinion, he is not entitled to wages for the work he has performed.[146]

If the lessor sells the property under lease to the lessee, the lease is not terminated, but he must fulfill the contract of lease-hire as stipulated. If he sells it to someone, it is considered not valid according to one juristic opinion. According to the other juristic opinion, it is valid, but he must fulfill the remaining time of the lease as stipulated in the contract. If the purchaser had no knowledge of it, he has the right of option to accept it or leave it.[147]

If the owner emancipates a slave (under the contract for freedom in lieu of price) and has (already) emancipated him, then the owner is obligated to reduce the wages and the expenses of his maintenance from the price for his emancipation.[148]

If the time of the lease-hire has passed and the seedling is left behind in the soil by the negligence of the tenant, then it is valid to force him to cut it and level off the soil. If he does not cut it, there are two juristic opinions: either he is forced to do it or the wages for the performance of the work becomes the responsibility of the lessee. It is valid that the wages for the work performed is taken from the rent which was paid in advance.[149]

If the animal under lease runs away (for example, camel), the lessor on that ground or excuse (*'udhr*) has an option either to terminate the lease-hire or wait until camel is found.

NOTES

1. Vishanoff, *The Formation of Islamic Hermeneutics*, p. 28.
2. Ḥusayn 'Abd al-Ḥamīd Nīl (edit), *Mukhtaṣar Kitāb al-Umm fī al-Fiqh*, vol. I, (Beirut: Dār *al-Arqam*), pp. 7–12.
3. Aḥmad El Shamsy strongly rejects Calder's contention and maintains that al-Shāfi'ī' was the author of *K. al-Umm* by analyzing critically the text. See, Aḥmad El Shamsy, "Al-Shāfi'ī's written corpus: a sourcecritical study," in *Journal of the American Oriental Society*, 132/2 (2012), 199–220.
4. Vishanoff, *The Formation of Islamic Hermeneutics*, p. 27.
5. W. Heffening, First Encyclopaedia of Islam, vol. vii (Leiden: E. J. Brill, 1993), p. 822; Jonathan E. Brockopp, "Early Islamic Jurisprudence in Egypt: Two Scholars and their Mukhtaṣars" in *Journal of Middle East Studies*, Cambridge University Press, 1988, pp. 173–175.
6. Brockopp, "Early Islamic Jurisprudence in Egypt: Two Scholars and their Mukhtaṣars," p. 173.
7. Norman Calder, *Study in Early Muslim Jurisprudence*, pp. 246–247.

8. W. Heffening, First Encyclopaedia of Islam, vol. viii (Leiden: E. J. Brill, 1993), p. 377; Muḥayī al-Dīn Yaḥyā al-Nūrī (edit), *al-Tanbīh* (Egypt, 1951), pp. 3–4.

9. Ismā'īl ibn al-Muzanī, *Mukhtaṣar*, chapter *al-Bay'*, vol. I (Cairo: Dār al-Arqam), pp. 119–175.

10. Al-Muzanī, *Mukhtaṣar*, vol. III, chapter *al-Buyū'*, pp. 491–625.

11. Abū Isḥāq, Ibrāhīm bin 'Alī ibn Yūsuf al-Shīrāzī, *al-Tanbīh* (Cairo, Sharka Maktaba, 1951), pp. 1–166.

12. Al-Shāfi'ī, Muḥammad ibn Idrīs, *K al-Umm*, chapter *al-Buyū'*, vol. III (Cairo: Bulaq, Kitāb al-Shu'ab, 1968), pp. 2–3; al-Muzanī, chapter al-Buyū', p. 491 and chapter *al-Bay'*, p. 119; Al-Shāfi'ī, *K. al-Umm*, vol. III (Beirut: Dār al-Kutab al-Ilmīya, 1993), p. 3.

13. Al-Muzanī, *al-Mukhtaṣar*, chapter *al-Bay'*, p.119.

14. Al-Shāfi'ī, *K al-Umm,* pp. 2–3; al-Muzanī, chapter *al-Buyū'*, p. 491; Al-Shāfi'ī, *K. al-Umm*, vol. III (Cairo: Bulaq, 1968), pp. 3–4.

15. Christopher Melchert, *The Formation of the Sunni Schools of Law* (Leiden: Brill, 1997), pp. 80–81. Al-Rabī' Sulaymān Murādī was one of the disciples of al-Shāfi'ī. He has been credited with compiling the basic collection of al-Shāfi'ī writings.

16. Al-Muzanī, *Mukhtaṣar*, chapter *al-Bay'*, p. 119.

17. Al-Shīrāzī, *al-Tanbīh*, chapter *al-Buyū'*, p. 62.

18. Al-Shīrāzī, *al-Tanbīh,* chapter *al-Buyū'*, p. 62.

19. Al-Shīrāzī, *al-Tanbīh,* chapter *al-Buyū'*, p. 62.

20. Al-Shīrāzī, *al-Tanbīh,* chapter *al-Buyū'*, p. 62. Al-Shīrāzī makes it quite explicit that no extra conditions or restrictions can be attached to the contract. Once the article has been taken into the ownership of the purchaser, he has an absolute right to its usufruct.

21. Al-Shīrāzī, *al-Tanbīh*, chapter *al-Buyū'*, p. 62.

22. According to al-Shīrāzī, if the price to the usufruct of the seller does not affect in the canceled contract, it is valid as it was stipulated in the contract.

23. Al-Muzanī, *Mukhtaṣar*, chapter *al-Bay'*, pp. 119–121

24. Al-Muzanī, *Mukhtaṣar*, chapter *al-Bay'*, p. 119.

25. Al-Shāfi'ī, *K al-Umm,* chapter *al-Buyū'*, p. 3; Al-Shāfi'ī, *K. al-Umm*, vol. III, p. 5.

26. Al-Muzanī, *Mukhtaṣar*, chapter *al-Buyū'*, p. 492.

27. Al-Shāfi'ī, *K. al-Umm*, p. 3; Al-Shāfi'ī, *K. al-Umm*, vol. III, p. 3.

28. Al-Muzanī, *Mukhtaṣar,* chapter *al-Buyū'*, pp. 492–493, and chapter *al-Bay'*, *Mukhtaṣar,* chapter *al-Bay'*, pp. 119–121.

29. Al-Muzanī, *Mukhtaṣar*, chapter *al-Bay'*, pp. 124–127.

30. Al-Muzanī, *Mukhtaṣar*, chapter *al*-Buyū', pp. 499–517.

31. Al-Shāfi'ī, *K al-Umm*, vol. iii, p. 31, al-Muzanī, *Mukhtaṣar*, chapter *al-Buyū'*, 502, p. 504; Al-Shāfi'ī, *K. al-Umm*, vol. III, pp. 28, 34.

32. Al-Shāfi'ī, *K al-Umm*, vol. III, p. 12, al-Muzanī, chapter *al-Buyū'*, pp. 499–501; Al-Shāfi'ī, *K. al-Umm*, vol. III, p. 43.

33. Al-Shāfi'ī, *K al-Umm,* p. 16, al-Muzanī, chapter *al-Buyū'*, p. 501; Al-Shāfi'ī, *K. al-Umm,* vol. III, pp. 24, 31–32.

34. Al-Shāfi'ī, *K al-Umm*, pp. 21–23, al-Muzanī, chapter *al-Buyū'*, pp. 504–505; Al-Shāfi'ī, *K. al-Umm,* vol. III, pp. 27–28.

35. Al-Shāfi'ī, *K al-Umm*, vol. III, p. 25, al-Muzanī, chapter *al-Buyū'*, p. 506; Al-Shāfi'ī, *K. al-Umm*, vol. III, p. 32.

36. Al-Shāfi'ī, *K al-Umm*, vol. III, p. 38; Al-Shāfi'ī, *K. al-Umm*, vol. III, pp. 43–49.

37. Al-Muzanī's title under Ribā' itself include the invalidity of the exchange of articles at an equal rate.

38. Al-Muzanī, *Mukhtaṣar*, chapter *al-Bay'*, p. 124.

39. Al-Muzanī, *Mukhtaṣar*, chapter *al-Bay'*, p. 125.

40. See al-Muzanī's *Mukhtaṣar, al-Bay'*, pp. 121–127 and chapter *al-Buyū'*, pp. 499–517.

41. *Mudd* is a kind of dry measure.

42. It is a cubic measure of varying magnitudes.

43. Al-Shīrāzī, *al-Tanbīh*, pp. 64–65.

44. Al-Shīrāzī's use of the term *ism al-khāṣ* is from al-Shāfi'ī's classification of things into genus, species, and kinds.

45. Al-Shīrāzī, *al-Tanbīh*, p. 64. Some articles are considered the same species such as in the Shāfi'ī school of law, but in the Ḥanafī school of law they are considered two different species.

46. Al-Shīrāzī, *al-Tanbīh*, p. 64.

47. *Wasq* (pl. *Awsāq*), cargo, load.

48. Al-Shīrāzī's discussion shows extreme cautiousness that there should remain no doubt that *ribā* is involved in the transaction in any form.

49. Al-Muzanī, *Mukhtaṣar*, chapter *al-Buyū'*, pp. 507–510.

50. Al-Muzanī, *Mukhtaṣar*, chapter *al-Buyū'*, p. 507.

51. Al-Muzanī, *Mukhtaṣar*, chapter *al-Buyū'*, p. 507.

52. Al-Muzanī, *Mukhtaṣar*, chapter *al-Buyū'*, pp. 507–508.

53. Al-Muzanī, *Mukhtaṣar,* chapter *al-Buyū'*, p. 510.

54. Al-Muzanī, *Mukhtaṣar*, chapter *al-Buyū'*, p. 508.

55. Al-Muzanī, *Mukhtaṣar*, chapter *al-Buyū'*, p. 508

56. Al-Muzanī, *Mukhtaṣar*, chapter *al-Buyū'*, p. 509.

57. Al-Muzanī, *Mukhtaṣar*, chapter *al-Buyū'*, p. 509.

58. Al-Muzanī, *Mukhtaṣar*, chapter *al-Buyū'*, p. 509.

59. Charles Hamilton, *The Hidāya: Commentary on Islamic Law*, vol. II (Karachi: Darul Ishhat), p. 677.

60. Bāb al-Salam is found neither in al-Muzanī's in chapter *al-Bay'* nor in the chapter *al-Buyū'* of the *Mukhtaṣar* of Cairo edition. However, it is contained in al-Muzanī's *Mukhtaṣar*, vol. IX, edited by Maḥmūd Maṭarajī (Beirut: Dār al-Kūtab al-'Īlmīya, 1993), pp. 100–102.

61. Al-Shīrāzī, *al-Tanbīh*, pp. 68–70.

62. Al-Shīrāzī, *al-Tanbīh,* pp. 68–70.

63. Al-Muzanī, chapter, *al-Bay'*, pp. 100–102

64. Al-Muzanī, *Mukhtaṣar*, chapter *al-Bay'*, pp. 100.

65. Al-Muzanī, *Mukhtaṣar,* chapter *al-Bay'*, p. 100.

66. Al-Shīrāzī, *al-Tanbīh*, p. 68.
67. Al-Shīrāzī, *al-Tanbīh*, p. 68.
68. Al-Shīrāzī, *al-Tanbīh,* p. 68.
69. Al-Shīrāzī, *al-Tanbīh*, pp. 68–69.
70. Al-Shīrāzī, *al-Tanbīh*, p. 69.
71. Al-Shīrāzī, *al-Tanbīh*, p. 69.
72. Al-Shīrāzī, *al-Tanbīh*, p. 69.
73. Al-Shīrāzī, *al-Tanbīh*, p. 69
74. Al-Shīrāzī, *al-Tanbīh*, p. 69.
75. Al-Shīrāzī, *al-Tanbīh*, p. 69.
76. Al-Shīrāzī, *al-Tanbīh*, p. 69.
77. Al-Shīrāzī, a*l-Tanbīh,* p. 70.
78. Al-Shīrāzī, *al-Tanbīh*, p. 70.
79. Al-Shīrāzī, *al-Tanbīh*, p. 70.
80. Al-Muzani, *Mukhtaṣar*, chapter *al-Bay'*, pp. 170–171.
81. Al-Shīrāzī, *al-Tanbīh*, pp. 75–76.
82. Al-Shāfi'ī, *K al-Umm*, vol. III, p. 206; Al-Shāfi'ī, *K. al-Umm*, vol. III, p. 265.
83. Al-Shāfi'ī, *K al-Umm*, vol. III, p. 206; Al-Shāfi'ī, *K. al-Umm*, vol. III, p. 265.
84. Hamilton, *The Hidāya, Commentary on the Islamic Laws*, vol. II, p. 542.
85. Al-Shāfi'ī, *K al-Umm*, vol. III, p. 206; Al-Shāfi'ī, *K. al-Umm*, vol. III, p. 265.
86. Al-Muzanī, *Mukhtaṣar*, chapter *al-Bay'*, p. 170.
87. Al-Muzanī, *Mukhtaṣar*, chapter *al-Bay'*, pp. 170–171. This additional information contains the cases such as the partnership is dissolved, if one of the partner dies, the other partner is allowed neither to make any purchases nor sale any articles from the property in partnership, and if the inheritor of the deceased can h old the share in that partnership etc.
88. Al-Shīrāzī, *al-Tanbīh*, p. 75.
89. Al-Shīrāzī, *al-Tanbīh*, p. 75.
90. Al-Muzanī, *Mukhtaṣar*, chapter *al-Bay'*, pp. 170–171, chapter *al-Buyū'*, p. 623.
91. Al-Muzanī, chapter *al-Buyū'*, p. 623.
92. Al-Muzanī, *Mukhtaṣar*, chapter *al-Buyū'*, p. 623.
93. Al-Muzanī, *Mukhtaṣar*, chapter *al-Bay'*, p. 170.
94. Al-Muzanī, *Mukhtaṣar*, chapter *al-Bay'*, p. 170.
95. Al-Muzanī, *Mukhtaṣar*, chapter *al-Bay'*, p. 170.
96. Al-Muzanī, *Mukhtaṣar,* chapter *al-Bay'*, p. 170.
97. Al-Muzanī, *Mukhtaṣar*, chapter *al-Bay'*, p. 170.
98. Al-Muzanī, *Mukhtaṣar*, chapter *al-Bay'*, p. 170.
99. Al-Muzanī, *Mukhtaṣar*, chapter *al-Bay'*, p. 170.
100. Al-Muzanī, *Mukhtaṣar*, chapter *al-Bay'*, p. 170.
101. Al-Muzanī, *Mukhtaṣar*, chapter *al-Bay'*, p. 170.
102. Al-Muzanī. *Mukhtaṣar*, chapter *al-Bay'*, p. 171.
103. Al-Muzanī, *Mukhtaṣar*, chapter *al-Bay'*, p. 171.
104. Al-Shīrāzī, *al-Tanbīh,* pp. 75–76.
105. Al-Shīrāzī, *al-Tanbīh*, p. 75.

106. Al-Shīrāzī, *al-Tanbīh*, p. 75.
107. Al-Shīrāzī, *al-Tanbīh*, p. 75.
108. Al-Shīrāzī, *al-Tanbīh*, p. 75.
109. Al-Shīrāzī, *al-Tanbīh*, p. 75.
110. Al-Shīrāzī, *al-Tanbīh*, p. 75.
111. Al-Shīrāzī, *al-Tanbīh*, pp. 75–76.
112. Al-Shāfi'ī, *K al-Umm*, vol. IV, pp. 250–253; Al-Shāfi'ī, *K. al-Umm*, vol. IV, p. 29.
113. Al-Shāfi'ī, K al-Umm, vol. IV, p. 250; Al-Shāfi'ī, *K. al-Umm*, vol. IV, p. 29.
114. Al-Shāfi'ī, *K al-Umm*, vol. IV, pp. 240–241; Al-Shāfi'ī, *K. al-Umm*, vol. IV, pp. 16–17.
115. Al-Shāfi'ī, *K al-Umm*, vol. IV, p. 237; Al-Shāfi'ī, *K. al-Umm*, vol. IV, pp. 11–13.
116. Al-Shāfi'ī, *K al-Um*m, vol. IV, P.241; Al-Shāfi'ī, *K. al-Umm*, vol. IV, p. 18.
117. Al-Shāfi'ī, *K al-Umm*, vol. IV, p. 250; Al-Shāfi'ī, *K. al-Umm*, vol. IV, p. 29.
118. Al-Shīrāzī, *al-Tanbīh*, p. 84.
119. Al-Shāfi'ī, *K al-Umm*, pp. 249, 253.
120. Al-Shīrāzī, *al-Tanbīh,* p. 84.
121. Al-Shīrāzī, *al-Tanbīh*, p. 84.
122. Al-Shīrāzī, *al-Tanbīh*, p. 84.
123. Al-Shīrāzī, *al-Tanbīh*, p. 84.
124. Al-Shīrāzī, *al-Tanbīh*, p. 84.
125. Al-Shāfi'ī, *K. al-Umm*, vol. IV, p. 240.
126. Al-Shāfi'ī, *K al-Umm*, vol. IV, p. 240.
127. Al-Shīrāzī, *al-Tanbīh*, p. 84.
128. Al-Shīrāzī, *al-Tanbīh*, p. 84.
129. Al-Shīrāzī, *al-Tanbīh*, p. 84.
130. Al-Shīrāzī, *al-Tanbīh*, p. 84.
131. Al-Shīrāzī, *al-Tanbīh*, p. 85.
132. Al-Shīrāzī, *al-Tanbīh*, p. 85.
133. Al-Shīrāzī, *al-Tanbīh*, p. 84.
134. Al-Shīrāzī, *al-Tanbīh*, p. 85.
135. Al-Shīrāzī, *al-Tanbīh*, p. 85.
136. Al-Shīrāzī, *al-Tanbīh*, p. 85.
137. Al-Shīrāzī, *al-Tanbīh*, p. 85.
138. Al-Shīrāzī, *al-Tanbīh*, p. 85.
139. Al-Shīrāzī, *al-Tanbīh*, p. 85.
140. Al-Shīrāzī, *al-Tanbīh*, p. 85.
141. Al-Shīrāzī, *al-Tanbīh*, p. 85.
142. Al-Shīrāzī, *al-Tanbīh,* p. 85.
143. Al-Shīrāzī, *al-Tanbīh*, p. 85.
144. Al-Shīrāzī, *al-Tanbīh*, p. 85.
145. Al-Shīrāzī, *al-Tanbīh*, p. 85.
146. Al-Shīrāzī, *al-Tanbīh*, p. 85.
147. Al-Shīrāzī, *al-Tanbīh*, p. 85.
148. Al-Shīrāzī, *al-Tanbīh*, p. 85.
149. Al-Shīrāzī, *al-Tanbīh*, pp. 85–86.

Chapter 4

Ḥanafī School of Law

Hermeneutics as Reflected in al-Ṭaḥāwī's Mukhtaṣar, *al-Shīrāzi's* Tanbīh *Supplemented with al-Marghīnānī's* Hidāya *in Reference*

PIONEERS OF THE ḤANAFĪ SCHOOL OF LAW

The pioneers of the Ḥanafī school of law are Nu'mān ibn Thābit Abū Ḥanīfa (150/767), Abū Yūsuf Y'aqūb bin Ibrāhim (182/798), and Muḥammad al-Shaybānī (189/804). All these three figures constitute the great authorities on the Ḥanafī *fiqh* tradition.[1] Abū Ḥanīfa is considered founder of the Ḥanafī school of law but left no significant writings behind. His views were later transmitted in the works composed by Abū Yūsuf and Muḥammad al-Shaybānī. All these three figures might have been not aware of the significance of al-Shāfi'ī's hermeneutics and its employment methodologically to relate the legal rules in accordance with the revealed legal canons.

Abū Ḥanīfa was reproached for exercising personal opinion of juristic reasoning (*ra'y*). As a result of al-Shāfi'ī's critical stand on the *ra'y*, it acquired a negative connotation, though *ra'y* originally meant "sound opinion" and was used as an element of human reasoning, whether strictly referring to the *qiyās* (doctrine of systematic reasoning) or the more personal opinion of juristic reasoning known as the *istiḥsān* (doctrine of juristic preference).[2] Al-Shāfi'ī's attack was launched on a methodic ground and not merely upon whether the prophetic *Ḥadīth* reports are used or not. For al-Shāfi'ī, the *Qur'ān* and the prophetic *Ḥadīth* reports as a hermeneutical method only the sources for legislating the legal rules in accordance to the legal cannons provided from them.

It is true that Muḥammad al-Shaybānī in his *Jāmi' al-Ṣaghīr* practically cites no prophetic *Ḥadīth* reports, but later jurists in all four Sunni schools of law do cite or refer to the Qur'ānic verses and prophetic *Ḥadīth* reports as al-Shāfi'ī's hermeneutics was gradually accepted in all four Sunni schools of law. Nonetheless, prior to al-Shāfi'ī, the Islamic legal system does not appear to have a proper hermeneutical theory. There was, however, as Vishanoff suggests, one form of early discourse in the Ḥanafī school of law that might be considered a kind of theoretical analysis of legal language of oaths, bequests, and matters concerning the transactions in contract sale. The Ḥanafī compilations of legal theory sometimes cite the view of Abū Ḥanīfa and his disciples Abū Yūsuf, and Muḥammad al-Shaybānī on specific hypothetical questions as evidence that they took positions on some of the questions, but there is no evidence that they developed a formal legal concept of hermeneutics for the interpretation of revealed language. It was only confined to positive law, but they did not deal as such with hermeneutical legal theory. One finds that they took position on specific problems involving interpretation of human utterance. They were concerned in a kind of theoretical discourse about some of the issues that would become central to the classical language with respect to human rather than revealed language.[3] Nonetheless, Abū Ḥanīfa and his two disciples did not themselves formulate classical hermeneutical techniques as al-Shāfi'ī did in the *Risāla*. They show very little awareness of hermeneutical approach. For example, they did not clearly formulate the concept of general (*'amm*) and particular (*khāṣṣ*) and the importance of their uses. They also did not discuss the issue of clarity (*ẓāhir*) and ambiguity (*bāṭin, mubham*), which al-Shāfi'ī employs under the terms *naṣṣ* and *jumla* to determine, for example, the Qur'ānic verse "cut off the hands of thieves, male or female" (Q 5: 38), by which individual thieves were not intended, which the Ḥanafī jurists decided arbitrarily, in contrast to it al-Shāfi'ī in the *Risāla* subjects the instances of positive law to hermeneutical procedures and techniques for establishing hermeneutically legal rules in accordance with the legal canons from the authoritative revealed sources.

However, with the general acceptance of al-Shāfi'ī's concept of hermeneutics, the Ḥanafī jurists in succeeding generations integrated it into the Islamic legal system. It can be said that the eponyms of the Ḥanafī school of law explicitly did not use the revealed sources. Our investigation is specifically concerned with the theoretical analysis of the legal discourse of human nontheological matters on specific problems involving human utterances, affecting the transactions of civil and commercial laws. The early Ḥanafī jurists were concerned with the legal effects of human speech and they may have not use the same terminology as al-Shāfi'ī did, nonetheless they were concerned with the theoretical discussion of human speech.[4]

A BRIEF BIBLIOGRAPHICAL ACCOUNT OF ABŪ ḤANĪFA

Abū Ḥanīfa (150/767) was the founder of the Ḥanafī school of law. Not much is known about his life. His grandfather was brought to Kūfa from Persia as slave by the Muslim conquers and received his freedom, thereby, becoming a client (*mawlā*) of the tribe Ta'im Allah to which his liberator belonged. His father Thābit belonged to 'Alide party for it is narrated that 'Alī blessed him and his descendants. Abū Ḥanīfa did not leave behind him any writings; his views were later compiled in the writings of Abū Yūsuf and Muḥammad al-Shaybānī which formed the basis of the Ḥanafī school of law.[5]

ABŪ YŪSUF Y'AQŪB BIN IBRĀHIM AL-ANṢĀRĪ

Abū Yūsuf (182/798) was a prominent jurist and one of the founders of the Ḥanafī school of law. He studied science of *Ḥadīth* and *fiqh* in Kūfa and Medina under Abū Ḥanīfa, Mālik bin Anas al-Lyth, and others. He lived in Kūfa until he was appointed *Qāḍī* in Baghdad, the office which he held until his death. He is more dependent on the prophetic *Ḥadīth* reports than Abū Ḥanīfa.

It is maintained in the classical *fiqh* that Abū Yūsuf and Muḥammad al-Shaybānī in some cases differ in their legal opinions from that of Abū Ḥanīfa. In case, there are different opinions among three of them, it is a general consensus in the Ḥanafī school of law that if the opinion of two of them is same, then it is accepted as legal ruling such as when the opinion of Abū Ḥanīfa and the opinion of Abū Yūsuf agree and Muḥammad al-Shaybānī's differ from it, then the opinion of Abū Ḥanīfa and Abū Yūsuf is accepted. If both disciples agree and differ from their teacher's opinion, the opinion of two disciples would be accepted. Thus, when two of them agree in their opinion, it is considered official ruling of the Ḥanafī school of law.

But, in the succeeding generations, as the hermeneutical approach was adopted in four Sunni schools of law, one finds that increasingly more differences of opinion have developed over the course of time, because of the hermeneutics and its application as a method. It seems that the jurists in the Ḥanafī school of law were yet not quite aware of al-Shāfi'ī's hermeneutics. As already mentioned, these eponyms of the Ḥanafi school neither had theory of hermeneutics, nor had they had clear idea of the concepts involved in it by which the rulings are determined in accordance to the revealed sources.

In the classical *fiqh* works such differences of opinion are, in general, discussed under the heading "Differences of Opinon among the Jurists" (*Ikhtilāf al-Fuqhā'*) and understood that such differences of opinion are because of the different tenets of four Sunni schools of law. These differences of opinion are, in fact, due to hermeneutically different interpretations as our investigation would show.

A BRIEF BIOGRAPHICAL ACCOUNT OF MUḤAMMAD AL-SHAYBĀNĪ

Abū 'Abd Allah Muḥammad al-Shaybānī (189/804) was born in Wāsit and was brought up in Kūfa. He studied under Abū Ḥanīfa and devoted himself to *ra'y*. He acquired his knowledge of *Ḥadīth* under Sufyān al-Thawrī and Mālik ibn Anas, whose lectures he attended in Medina. The Caliph Harūn al-Rashīd made him the *Qāḍī* of Raqqa, the new capital of his empire. He belonged to the moderate school of *ra'y*.[6] The distinction between *ahl al-ḥadīth* and *ahl-ra'y* is artificial. As we know, Muḥammad al-Shaybānī had also acquired his knowledge of the prophetic *Ḥadīth* reports. He did not use them in his *Jāmi' al-Ṣaghīr* as al-Shāfi'ī does in the *Risāla* and the *K al-Umm*, though the differences in legal opinion between them is not because al-Shaybānī did not make use revealed sources. These differences are mostly because of the hermeneutically interpretative process of relating legal rulings to the legal canons and secondly, there are some differences of opinion because of al-Shaybānī's employment of the doctrine of juristic preference (*istiḥsān*) against which his notable student al-Shāfi'ī wrote a polemic against him in the *K al-Radd 'ala Muḥammad bin Aḥmad al-Shaybānī*[7]and *Ibṭāl al-Istiḥsān*[8] on the methodic and formal grounds. According to al-Shāfi'ī, use of the doctrine of *istiḥsān* might open the doors for arbitrary personal opinions. Al-Shāfi'ī's main contention of his hermeneutics is that the rulings must be based on the revealed sources and not according to *ra'y* even though the ruling based on it is consistent with the revealed sources.

However, al-Shaybānī was writing his works as the jurist, and so was the case with Abū Yūsuf, and not as the *muḥaddīth* (Traditionists). Their concern as jurists was to compile legal rulings of the jurisprudence, though based on the revealed sources, but not explicitly cited from them in their writings. Such is the case with al-Shāfi'ī's account of *shirka*, al-Muzanī's account of *ribā*, and for that matter, in the entire al-Shīrāzī's *Tanbīh* we find that no Qur'ānic verses or prophetic *Ḥadīth* reports are cited. As we go further over the course of time, we find no jurists citing any prophetic *Ḥadīth* reports, except those who are aware of al-Shāfi'ī's contention of hermeneutics such as Ḥanafī jurist Muḥammad bin Aḥmad al-Sarakhsī (483/1090) in his *Mabsūṭ*, which is the *Sharaḥ al-Mukhtaṣar of Kāfī* by al-Ḥakīm al-Shahīd Muḥammad ibn Aḥmad al-Marwazī (333/945) that al-Marwazī dictated rulings based on al-Shaybānī's *Jāmi' al-Ṣaghīr* and *Jāmi' al-Kabīr*, which al-Sarakhsī supplemented with the Qur'ānic verses and prophetic *Ḥadīth* reports[9] and Marghīnānī, who in the *Hidāya* cites revealed sources in support of the rulings. This shows that al-Shaybāni had the knowledge of prophetic *Ḥadīth* reports on which he based the rulings, but he did not cite them *verbatim* in his writings, like al-Shāfi'ī. As we further over the course of time, we find that Ḥanafī jurists had become increasing more aware of al-Shāfi'ī's objections which he raised on the methodic grounds and based legal rulings by citing the Qur'ānic verses and the prophetic *Ḥadīth* reports. Thus, with the acceptance of al-Shāfi'ī's concept of hermeneutics, the authors of compositions of *Mukhtaṣar* in Ḥanafī school of law continued al-Shāfi'ī hermeneutical approach in the formation of Islamic law.

HERMENEUTICAL GENERAL FEATURES AS REFLECTED IN MUḤAMMAD AL-SHAYBĀNĪ'S CHAPTER *AL-BUYŪ'* OF *JĀMĪ' AL-ṢAGHĪR*

Al-Shaybānī's chapter *al-Buyū'* in comparison to that of al-Shāfi'ī's *K al-Umm* is not systematic. It seems at first sight that there is an absence of any methodology by which al-Shaybānī develops his legal system as we find al-Shāfi'ī does using the hermeneutical approach and its various techniques as developed in the *Risāla*. For al-Shāfi'ī, the importance of using them lies on the methodic grounds and not simply whether al-Shaybānī explicitly uses the prophetic *Ḥadīth* reports or not. Al-Shāfi'ī's stand, as a jurist, is on the methodic ground.

Viewing from this aspect, it is true that in al-Shaybānī's chapter *al-Buyū'* of *Jāmī' al-Ṣaghīr*, we find no Qur'ānic verses or the prophetic *Ḥadīth* reports cited *verbatim* and directly, but when one examines closely al-Shaybānī's works content wise, the rulings are based on the revealed sources and they are consistent with the legal canons provided in the *Qur'ān* and the prophetic *Ḥadīth* reports. If there are differences of opinion between al-Shāfi'ī and al-Shaybānī, they are not on that ground, but it was mainly due to either hermeneutically interpretative differences on the part of jurists or specifically the doctrinal difference of using the doctrine of *istiḥsān*, which al-Shāfi' outright rejected.

All three pioneers of the Ḥanafī school of law Abū Ḥanīfa, Abū Yūsuf, and Muḥammad al-Shaybānī consider doctrine of *istiḥsān* a kind of *qiyās* and claim that its extension is based, like *qiyās*, on deductive reasoning. The doctrine of *istiḥsān* is used for the facilitation of transactions, specially, concerning the civil and commercial matters in the hermeneutically formation of Islamic legal system.[10] Thus, the Ḥanafī jurists do not consider *ra'y* in a negative sense. As already mentioned in the forgoing chapter 3, that although the jurists in the Ḥanafī school of law do not use the hermeneutical concepts and techniques of al-Shāfi'ī's *Risāla,* but when one examines content wise, they follow formally what is required by al-Shāfi'ī''s hermeneutics.

THE GENRE OF *MUKHTAṢAR* AND ITS EMERGENCE IN ḤANAFĪ SCHOOL OF LAW

Whether al-Shāfi'ī can be considered the Master architect[11] of the Islamic legal system or not, he was certainly one of the first jurists to systematize it by the hermeneutical approach. This hermeneutical approach continued in the emergence of the genre of *Mukhtaṣar* in the Shāfi'ī school of law, beginning first with Shāfi'ī jurist al-Muzanī and followed by his student al-Ṭaḥāwī of Ḥanafī school of law. With the gradual acceptance of al-Shāfi'ī's hermeneutics, the Ḥanafī jurists were more active in producing and reproducing more compositions of *Mukhtaṣar* than the jurists of all the other Sunni schools of law.

Here we shall examine the subject matters of chapter *al-Buyū'* in al-Ṭaḥāwī's *Mukhtaṣar*, al-Qudūrī's *Mukhtaṣar* supplemented with al-Marghīnānī's *Hidāya* in reference, which is generally classified under the title *mutūn* as al-Shīrāzī's *Tanbīh.*

A BRIEF BIOGRAPHICAL ACCOUNT OF AL-ṬAḤĀWĪ

Abū Ja'far Aḥmad Muḥammad bin Salāma al-Ṭaḥāwī was born in the village Ṭāḥā in Upper Egypt in the year 321/933. He was one of the greatest jurists of his time and received his early education from his uncle al-Muzanī who, as already mentioned in chapter 3, composed *Mukhtaṣar* following al-Shāfi'ī's hermeneutics. Among the Ḥanafī jurists, al-Ṭaḥāwī was the first to compose his *Mukhtaṣar*. It is patterned after al-Muzanī's *Mukhtaṣar*. As mentioned by Abū al-Wafā al-Afghānī, there were about fifteen compositions of *Mukhtaṣar* written after him by various Ḥanafī jurists, including such figures as Abū al-Ḥasan al-Karkhi, Abū Bakr bin 'Alī al-Jaṣṣāṣ, Abū al-Ḥusayn Aḥmad bin Muḥammad al-Qudūrī, Abū Barkāt 'Abdallah bin Aḥmad al-Nasafī and many others.[12]

It is said that on one occasion al-Muzanī "made a remark that he (al-Ṭaḥāwī) would never make a name." Thereupon al-Ṭaḥāwī took up the study of Ḥanafī *fiqh* under Abū Ja'far bin Abī Imrān. Al-Ṭaḥāwī was never appointed as the Qāḍī, but he was continually employed by the chief judges for his skill in drawing valid contracts, though the prophetic *Ḥadīth* reports was not his cup of tea.[13]

In the later years, al-Ṭaḥāwī devoted himself to numerous works besides *Fatwās al-Ṭaḥāwī*. Al-Ṭaḥāwī worked on al-Shaybānī's *Jāmi' al-Ṣaghīr* under the title *Mukhtaṣar*. It is said that he did not contribute a great amount of additional information.[14] This is not quite true. Al-Ṭaḥāwī incorporates in his *Mukhtaṣar* some expanded additional elements in the hermeneutical formation of Islamic law.

In al-Ṭaḥāwī's *Mukhtaṣar*, the topics are arranged after al-Muzanī's *Mukhtaṣar* and in its patterns they are like it. Al-Ṭaḥāwī, like al-Shaybānī, does not cite Qur'ānic verses or prophetic *Ḥadīth* reports except at one or two places he uses the word "*Sunna*" concerning the contract,[15] though his later works abound the prophetic *Ḥadīth* reports.

A BRIEF BIOGRAPHICAL ACCOUNT OF AL-QUDŪRĪ

Abū al-Ḥasan Aḥmad ibn Muḥammad bin Aḥmad ibn Ja'far bin Hamadān al-Qudūrī died in 392/1037.[16] Al-Qudūrī is an ascription to the selling of pots (*qudūr*). He studied *fiqh* under Abū 'Abdallah Muḥammad ibn Jurjānī, Abū Bakr al-Rāzī, Abū al-Ḥasan al-Karkhī, Muḥammad Ḥusayn al-Shaybānī, and many other important figures of *'ilm al-fiqh.*

Al-Qudūrī's most important works are *Sharḥ Mukhtaṣar al-Karkhī, al-Mukhtaṣar al-al-Tajrīd*. Al-Qudūrī's composition of *Mukhtaṣar* is to be characterized as highly organized in the arrangement of the topics in a systematic manner.[17]

A BRIEF BIOGRAPHICAL ACCOUNT OF AL-MARGHĪNĀNĪ

Burhān al-Dīn Abū al-Ḥasan 'Alī bin Abū Bakr bin 'Abd al-Jalīl al-Farghānī al-Marghīnānī died in 593/1197. He was an eminent jurist. He studied under Najm al-Dīn Abū Ḥafṣ 'Umar al-Nasfī, al-Ṣadr al-Shahī Ḥisām al-Dīn 'Umar bin 'Abīd al-'Azīz, and others. He is known for his compositions of *K Majmū' al-Nawazil, K al-Tajnīs, K Bidaya al-Mubtadī*, and others.[18]

HERMENEUTICAL GENERAL FEATURES OF CONTRACT AS REFLECTED IN AL-ṬAḤĀWĪ'S *MUKHTAṢAR*[19]

Al-Shaybānī does not use the word *'aqd* as the legal instrument to signify its legal import. He neither describes the nature of contract nor does he discuss the stipulations involved in the contract. In comparison to it, Al-Ṭaḥāwī's account of the contract comes closer to al-Shāfi'ī's and al-Muzanī's concept of contract and its description.

Al-Ṭaḥāwī refers to the *Sunna* of the Prophet in support for the validity of right of option, though he does not explicitly narrate the prophetic *Ḥadīth* report as al-Shāfi'ī and al-Muzanī do in describing the right of option.

Al-Ṭaḥāwī prefers the juristic opinion of the two disciples, Abū Yūsuf and Muḥammad al-Shaybānī, who based it on the ground of the doctrine of *istiḥsān* for facilitating the transactions as it will be shown later. This shows that the differences of opinion were developing from early on within the same school of law, which was due to the hermeneutical interpretative approach.

CONTENTS OF THE NATURE OF CONTRACT, ITS STIPULATIONS IN AL-ṬAḤĀWĪ'S *MUKHTAṢAR*[20]

Al-Shaybānī's account of contract does not explicitly use the word contract (*'aqd*) in chapter al-*Buyū'* of his *Jāmi' al-Ṣaghīr*. In fact, it begins with the *salam* sale and the arrangement of the topics is not systematic, rather it is haphazard. In contrast, al-Ṭaḥāwī's arrangement of the topics and patterns are comprehensively systematic and patterned after al-Muzanī's *Mukhtaṣar*.

According to al-Ṭaḥāwī, the contract between two parties is valid without right of option is stipulated in it. According to the *Sunna* of Prophet, the right of option is included between the parties to the contract, so long as they have not parted physically from each other. Upon the separation of each other without concluding contract, it is no longer accepted. It is valid for one party to the contract to accept it so long as no word or action is received (*akhaḍa minhu*) from the other party. However, in the next line it is said that the right of option is not to exceed more than three days, as maintained by Abū Ḥanīfa and al-Shāfi'ī. Al-Ṭaḥāwī, following Abū Yūsuf and Muḥammad al-Shaybānī, allows exceeding more than three days for the facilitation of the transactions. As we have seen in chapter 3, al-Shīrāzī, contrary to al-Shāfi'ī, allows the extension to more than three days in case of esculent articles (*ṭa'ām*), but without providing any justification. This might be because the esculent articles are necessity of life, thus al-Shīrāzī's extension to more than three days in esculent articles can be justified. This shows the impact of the Ḥanafī doctrine of the *istiḥsān* implicitly in the account of al-Shīrāzī.

The right of option for the emancipation (*'itāq*) of a slave by the purchaser is valid and the price of her/him becomes incumbent on him, and the right of option of the seller becomes void (*bāṭil*). If she/he dies while in the possession of purchaser, the price of her/him becomes incumbent on him. If the slave dies while he was into the possession of seller, then the seller is responsible for the price.

HERMENEUTICAL GENERAL FEATURES OF CONTRACT AS REFLECTED IN al-QUDŪRĪ'S *MUKHTAṢAR* SUPPLEMENTED WITH AL-MARGHĪNĀNĪ'S CONTRACT IN THE *HIDĀYA* IN REFERENCE

Al-Marghīnānī's *Hidāya* is mostly based *verbatim* on al-Qudūrī's *Mukhtaṣar*. Al-Marghīnānī, as already mentioned, improves upon al-Qudūrī's *Mukhtaṣar* by adding the Qur'ānic verses and the prophetic *Ḥadīth* reports in support of the juristic opinion as required by al-Shāfi'ī's concept of hermeneutics. Thus, one finds with al-Marghīnānī that Ḥanafī jurists explicitly adopt al-Shāfi'ī's concept of hermeneutics, which was previously implicit with al-Shaybānī, al-Ṭaḥāwī, and al-Qudūrī.

Al-Qudūrī under the chapter contract (without using any heading) not only deals with the nature of contract, stipulations, and other essential conditions for a valid contract, but also discusses its import and bearings on different aspects of the contract of sale such as weight and measurement of the articles of exchange, use of currency of the place where contract is concluded, right of option in the sale of articles of exchange as to being more or less in their quantity, weight, and measurement from each other, sale of trees, palm trees, fruits, sale of land, possession of the articles of exchange in the contract of sale, etc. This describes not only the nature of contract, but it also provides an overview of its bearing on the different aspects of contract of sale.

Al-Qudūrī's account of contract incorporates expanded additional elements not covered in the texts of al-Shaybānī and al-Ṭaḥāwī. Though Al-Qudūrī does not cite any Qur'ānic verses or prophetic *Ḥadīth* reports, his rulings are juristically consistent with them. This shortcoming is overcome in the al-Marghīnānī, as did al-Sarakhsī, supplements it in his text by citing the Quranic verses and the prophetic *Ḥadīth* reports at the appropriate places. This shows that Marghīnānī's text fully represents hermeneutically relating the legal rules with legal canons as provided in the revealed sources.

Furthermore, al-Qudūrī and al-Marghīnānī both use al-Shāfi'ī's hermeneutical technique in expressing the declaration and acceptance of the contract, which can be expressed not only by using specifically the wordings, but it can also be expressed by gesture, pointing to the article under consideration etc. If one of the parties stands up during the meeting, the contract becomes canceled.

THE CONTENTS OF CONTRACT IN al-QUDŪRĪ'S *MUKHTAṢAR* SUPPLEMENTED WITH MARGHĪNĀNĪ'S *HIDĀYA* IN REFERENCE

The sale is contracted by the declaration and the acceptance between two parties. It is expressed as a necessary condition in the present or preparative indicative sense or by any other wordings that express declaration and acceptance. If either of the parties offer to sell an article, the other party has right of option to accept it or reject it before breaking meeting (*majlis*). Al-Qudūrī does not support it with any prophetic *Ḥadīth* report. Al-Marghīnānī cites in its support: "The purchaser and the seller both have right of option until they separate from each other." If one of them stands up during the meeting before accepting offer, the contract is void (*bāṭil*). If the offer and the acceptance are attained or obtained, the contract becomes binding, except if the article of sale is found with defect. If the articles are specified by pointing them out, it is not necessary to describe their quality or quantity in the valid contract. Absolute (*muṭlaq*) price is not valid, unless the quality and quantity of the articles of exchange are known. The contract of sale is valid either for cash or with the suspension of payment at a future specified time. Al-Marghīnānī cites the Qur'ānic verse in support of it that "absolute sale is unlawful." This shows the jurist in the Ḥanafī school of law have completely adopted al-Shāfi'ī' hermeneutics by bringing the legal rule consistent with the revealed sources.

In absolute price in sale, the currency prominently used is of the place where the contract of sale is concluded. If they are different, the sale is void except with the currency used in that place.

The sale of grains and wheat by measurement or by estimate, and by measurement of particular vessel (*rānā'*) of which the exact capacity is not ascertained or by stone of which the exact weight is not ascertained is valid.

The sale of a heap of grains at the rate of one *dirham* for every *qafīz*[21] is valid for only one *qafīz* and void for remaining all other remaining *qafīz*. This is according to Abū Ḥanīfa. According Abū Yūsuf and Muḥammad al-Shaybānī, it is valid if it is specified for all *qafīz*. The sale of a flock of cattle at the rate of one *dirham* for each cattle is void, if it is not specified for all cattle. Likewise, the sale of piece of cloth each in measurement of one *dhara'a*[22] in exchange for one *dirham*, if not specified for all *dhara'a* is void.

If a person purchases a piece of cloth measured in *dhara'a* at the rate of one hundred *dirhams* and finds it less than one hundred *dhara'a* in measurement, he has right of option to take price for it in proportion to the remaining piece of cloth or cancel the contract of sale. If he finds it more than one hundred *dhara'a* in measurement, then the more of it in *dhara'a* belongs to the seller. If one purchases a piece of cloth at the rate of ten *dhara'a* for ten *dirhams* or land at the rate of one hundred *dhara'a* and finds it less than one hundred *dhara'a*, then the purchaser has right of option to accept it for the whole and if he pleases, he returns it and the seller has no right of option or recourse to it. If the seller claims that he sold it at the rate of one hundred *dhara'a* for one hundred *dirhams* and the purchaser finds it lesser (shorter), then he has right of option to accept it in proportion to its price or leave it. If he finds it more than one hundred *dhara'a*, then he has right of option to accept each *dhara'a* of piece of cloth for one *dirham* and if he pleases, he can cancel the contract of sale.

Al-Qudūrī and al-Ṭaḥāwī[23] state that a person sells land, tree or palm tree on which fruits are growing, they are included in the sale, but the seedling is not included in the sale of land. Mālik and al-Shāfi'ī maintained that the fruits growing on a palm tree and other trees belong to the seller as we have seen in chapter 3 that such was the case with al-Shāfi'ī. A person sells palm tree or tree on which fruits are growing, they belong to the seller, unless the purchaser has stipulated and have said to the seller to cut it and deliver it to him.

If a person purchases fruits before they have reached full growth or have (already) reached full growth, it is valid. In that case, it is incumbent on the purchaser to pluck them.[24] If the stipulation is made of leaving the fruits on palm tree, the sale is dissolved.[25]

Al-Ṭaḥāwī adds here following expanded additional elements concerning sales:

The sale of fruits measured by *ṣā'* is not valid, though the sale of portion of it is not objectionable.[26] The sale of fruits with the condition that certain amount of *riṭls* is exempted from it is not valid. After the property has been taken into possession, if the loss is caused either by natural calamity or by perpetration of a crime on it, it is considered property of the purchaser. If it is caused before it has been taken into possession, it is considered property of the seller and the sale is void. After the natural calamity, the purchaser can buy the remaining property in existence for the price in proportion to it.[27] The partnership (*shirka*), friendly partnership (*tawlīya*), and cancelation (*iqāla*) of contract of sale before the article of sale has been taken into possession is not valid.[28] If a person purchases an article without seeing it before and takes it into his possession, and thereafter, the purchaser and the seller separate from each other from the place where the contract is concluded, then the contract of sale is considered complete.[29]

According to al-Ṭaḥāwī and al-Qudūrī, the sale of grains in the ear or beans in the husk is valid. In the sale of house of which locks are of fixed kind (not hanging), the keys are considered included in the sale.

The wages of the measurer of the wares and the wages of the essayer of money is paid by the seller, the price for weighing them is paid by the purchaser.

In sale of goods in exchange for price or goods, both the purchaser and the seller deliver articles of exchange to each other at the same time.

Al-Qudūrī and al-Marghīnānī's account contains expanded additional elements that we do not find in the account of al-Shaybānī and al-Ṭaḥāwī. This shows that the authors of the compositions of *Mukhtaṣar* in the process of hermeneutical interpretation try to comprehensively systematize the legal system, incorporating all the expanded additional essential elements.

RIGHT OF OPTION OF SEEING AND RIGHT OF OPTION OF STIPULATIONS

Hermeneutical General Features of Right of Option of Seeing and Right of Option of Stipulations as Reflected in al-Shaybānī's *Jāmī' al-Ṣaghīr*, *al*-Qudūrī's *Mukhtaṣar* Supplemented with al-Marghīnānī's *Hidāya* in Reference.

As usual al-Shaybānī and al-Al-Qudūrī do not cite any verses from *Qur'ān* or prophetic *Ḥadīth* reports in support of their rulings, only later al-Marghīnānī does it. Al-Marghīnānī, in general, states rulings *verbatim* from al-Qudūrī's *Mukhtaṣar*, supporting them by the revealed sources.

THE CONTENTS OF RIGHT OF OPTION OF SEEING AND RIGHT OF OPTION OF STIPULATIONS IN AL-SHAYBĀNĪ'S *JĀMĪ' AL-ṢAGHĪR*[30] AND IN AL-QUDŪRĪ'S *MUKHTAṢAR*[31]

Al-Shaybānī's account of right of option of seeing and right of option of stipulations is in some ways richer and more detailed in contrast to al-Qudūrī whose account is shorter.

Though Muḥammad al-Shaybānī was accused of exercising *ra'y*, it is al-Qudūrī who uses the doctrine of *istiḥsān* and al-Marghīnānī makes use of it explicitly. Al-Qudūrī states in the beginning of this chapter that "the stipulation of a three days for the seller and the purchaser is valid and not to exceed more than three days." This is the opinion of Abū Ḥanīfa as it was the case with al-Shāfi'ī, who cites in support of this juristic opinion the prophetic *Ḥadīth* reports, though neither al-Shaybānī in his *Jāmī' al-Ṣaghīr* nor do al-Qudūrī in his *Mukhtaṣar* cite any prophetic *Ḥadīth* reports, but the legal opinions of both are same as that of al-Shāfi'ī.

However, according to Abū Yūsuf and Muḥammad, the stipulation of three days can be extended on the condition that the time is specified. This is, according to al-Marghīnānī, based on the doctrine of *istiḥsān* for the facilitation of the transactions.

Al-Qudūrī asserts in the next lines that in the exchange of articles, the purchaser and the seller must take the article into possession to complete the transaction. The three days of right of option does not relinquish the ownership of the article by the parties to the contract.

According to Muḥammad al-Shaybānī and al-Qudūrī, if the article of exchange is found with defect, it is valid to return it. Al-Shaybānī adds that even though the purchaser has agreed to buy article without seeing it and, thereafter, if he finds it with defect, then he has right of option to return it. In case, he appoints an agent to take the sold article into possession, he (the purchaser) has right of option to return it. According to Abū Yūsuf and Muḥammad al-Shaybānī, the agent is considered representative of the purchaser.

A person purchases a bundle of *zūṭī*[32] clothes without seeing them and afterward sells them or gives away some of it as a gift, it is not valid to return the remaining cloths, unless they prove to be defective. Likewise, in such a case the stipulation of right of option is annulled.

Al-Shaybānī,[33] al-Qudūrī, and al-Marghīnānī' maintain that the valid purchase and sale of an article made by a blind person can be determined by touching it, provided it is such that the nature of it can lead by touch to knowledge of it or by smell provided it is of that nature to be known by smell or by taste. Abū Yūsuf adds to this by stating that the blind person is considered as the man of sight. However, according to al-Qudūrī, the right of option of seeing it by a blind person is not determined in the purchase of immovable property (*'iqār*), unless the description of article is provided.

According to al-Qudūrī, in case an agent sells property without he has been commissioned by its owner, then the owner has right of option to permit the sale or cancel it. If the owner permits sale, the existing contract remains valid.

It is valid that a person having stipulated right of option for the period of three days and cancels the sale during that period without the presence of other party (i.e., without informing the other party to the contract), it is valid. If once the contract is canceled, it cannot be renewed, except if the other party is present.

A person having stipulated right of option for three days, the price becomes incumbent on him upon taking article into his possession.

A person having stipulated right of option for three days sells the article and, then, he dies during that period, then right of option is void, and the article of sale is not transferred to his inheritors.

A person sells slave on the condition that he has right of option or he has right of emancipation, it is not valid. In such a case, the purchaser has right of option to take it for the price or leave it.

RIGHT OF OPTION CONCERNING ARTICLES OF DEFECT

Al-Shaybānī discusses right of option regarding the articles with defect under chapter Bāb fī al-'Uyūb,[34] al-Qudūrī discusses it under chapter Bāb al-'Ayb,[35] and al-Ṭaḥāwī does not have separate chapter on it, though we find some short comments connected to it under the heading Bāb al-Muṣarra wa Ghayra[36] of which the references will be made.

HERMENEUTICAL GENERAL FEATURES OF RIGHT OF SEEING ARTICLES OF DEFECTS AS REFLECTED IN AL-SHAYBĀNĪ'S *JĀMI' AL-ṢAGHĪR* AND *AL-QUDŪRĪ'S MUKHTAṢAR* SUPPLEMENTED WITH AL-MARGHĪNĀNĪ'S *HIDĀYA* IN REFERENCE

Al-Shaybānī, al-Ṭaḥāwī, and al-Qudūrī neither refer to the Qur'ānic verses nor do they cite the prophetic *Ḥadīth* reports, though implicitly their rulings are based on these sources. Their legal opinions are, in most part, not much different from those of al-Shāfi'ī. Wherever the differences of opinion are found between them, they are not because of noncompliance with al-Shāfi'ī's hermeneutics or simply because of the different tenets of school of law. Rather, they are because of the hermeneutical different interpretations, or they are because of the doctrine of *istiḥsān* by the Ḥanafī jurists, which we would discuss separately in chapter 7 under the heading "Differences of Opinion according to the Doctrine of *Istiḥsān* and the Hermeneutical Interpretations."

Al-Shaybānī's and al-Qudūrī's account of defects are extensive. Besides discussing the cases common between them, they also bring to light different aspects in respect to the articles of defects. Thus, al-Qudūrī's account can not to be characterized simply as an abridgement. It is rather a full-fledged blown account of the articles with defects, covering some of the aspects not dealt with by al-Shaybānī. This suggests that the authors of the compositions of *Mukhtaṣar* are continually trying to hermeneutically relate legal rulings to the legal canons, incorporating hermeneutically expanded additional elements in the formation of Islamic legal system.

Al-Shaybānī's account is some ways descriptive in comparison to al-Qudūrī, who precisely defines what does constitute a defect in commercial language by stating that "whatever causes *(aujab)* diminishing price of the article due to the defect, it is considered defective according to the practices and customs of the merchants in the market."

Al-Shaybānī discusses regarding the claim of articles with defect for establishing its validity by testimony with an oath.

THE CONTENTS OF ARTICLES WITH DEFECT IN AL-SHAYBĀNĪ'S *JĀMI' AL-ṢAGHĪR* AND al-QUDŪRĪ'S *MUKHTAṢAR*

We shall first describe cases which are common in al-Shaybānī's and al-Qudūrī's accounts with only minor variations in their narrations. The cases which are narrated only by al-Shaybānī or only by al-Qudūrī are described in each case by mentioning according to al-Shaybānī or according to al-Qudūrī.

According to al-Shaybānī and al-Qudūrī, if the articles of exchange are found with defect after the possession of articles by the purchaser or the seller, then each has right of option to return them or keep them. According to al-Qudūrī, in case the article with defect is returned, there is no right of option to exact compensation for the loss on that account.

According to al-Shaybānī and al-Qudūrī, if a female slave does not menstruate or menstruate constantly, or she is found to be an adulterer, or *dhimmī*, or the male slave who is habituated to committing adultery or he is a runaway slave, or madness in a minor, or constant urination of a minor, they all are considered cases of defect. To this al-Qudūrī adds that in case, the slave urinates in bed or has committed theft in childhood, but after reaching puberty such defects reappear until afterward when the slave is in the hands of purchaser, then purchaser is at liberty to return him, because it is the same defect which existed before while the slave was in the possession of the seller.

According to al-Shaybānī and al-Qudūrī, lunacy and bad smell from breath or armpit in female slave, but not in male slave except when it becomes disease, adultery and bastardy in female slave are considered defects, but not in male slave. If such defects appear in a female slave, then the purchaser has right of option to return her because of the loss of price due to the defect.

According to al-Shaybānī, a person purchases slave and takes him into his possession and, thereafter, claims that the slave was with defect and the seller denies it with an oath, the purchaser cannot force him to return the price, unless the purchaser brings the evidence. If both are claiming against each other, and the purchaser says that his witness is in Syria and the seller takes oath that slave was not absolutely (*muṭlaq*) runaway slave, then the purchaser pays price.

According to al-Shaybānī, a person purchases female slave and takes her into his possession and, thereafter, he finds defect in her, but the seller claims that he sold her with other female slaves and the purchaser claims that he purchased her and only her, then word (*qawl*) rests with the purchaser.

According to al-Shaybānī, if a person purchases melon, or walnut, or cucumber and when he breaks them open finds them with defect so that they are not of any use, he can return all of it. If only some of them are found with defect, he returns some of them for the loss in price due to the defect.

According to al-Shaybānī and al-Qudūrī with some variations in their narrations, if a person purchases a piece of cloth, then cuts and sews it, or mixes it with oil and, thereafter, he finds it with defect, he can return it to the seller. The purchaser is entitled to the compensation for the loss.

According to al-Shaybānī and al-Qudūrī, a person purchases a piece of cloth and gives it to dye in red color and then finds it with defect, he can return it for the compensation of the loss in price.

According to al-Shaybānī and al-Qudūrī, if a person purchases a slave and emancipates him in exchange for the property *(māl)* and finds him with defect, he has no right of option to return it. Al-Qudūrī describes another similar case that a person purchases a slave from the seller and after having purchased it, he sells it to another person, who returns him because of the defect, then the first purchaser is not permitted to return it to the original seller.

According to al-Qudūrī, a person purchases slave and emancipates him, or slave dies in his possession and, thereafter, he comes to know of that the slave was with the defect, he is entitled to the compensation, because the slave was already having defect, when he was in the possession of the seller. According to al-Marghīnānī, this is based on the doctrine of *istiḥsān*, though it is against the doctrine of *qiyās*.[37] This can be further substantiated as Ḥanafī jurist al-Sarakhsī maintain that the *'illa* employed in this case is, according to the doctrine of *istiḥsān*, strong (*qawī*), although it is concealed (*khafī or jalīy)* as against the *'illa* used in the doctrine of *qiyās* which is apparent (*ẓāhir*), but weak (*ḍa'īf*).[38]

As already mentioned, al-Ṭaḥāwī in the composition of his *Mukhtaṣar* does not deal with defective articles specifically under a separate chapter. He discusses only the case of animal that has been left un-milked and a person purchases it and after milking it more than one times, he finds that the animal does not have enough milk in its udder, then he has right of option to return it. Similarly, a person purchases a slave and emancipates him and, thereafter, finds him defective, he can return the slave for the price, but if the purchaser kills him and, thereafter, comes to know of defect later, he has no right of option to take the price. This is according to Abū Ḥanīfa, whereas Abū Yūsuf and Muḥammad al-Shaybānī maintain that he has right of option to take the price for the loss of it because of the defect.

RIBĀ

Hermeneutical General Features of *Ribā* in al-Shaybānī's *Jāmī' al-Ṣaghīr*, al-Ṭaḥāwī's *Mukhtaṣar*, and al-Qudūrī's *Mukhtaṣar* Supplemented with al-Marghīnānī's *Hidāya* in Reference

Al-Shaybānī discusses *ribā* under the heading "Sale of Articles of Measurement and Weight" without using the words *ribā* or *tafādūl*, though its import is implicit. His account of *ribā* is in comparison to al-Ṭaḥāwī and al-Qudūrī's account of *ribā* is shorter and not covering all essential elements. It is descriptive rather than concisely articulated as we find it in al-Ṭaḥāwī's and al-Qudūrī's accounts, which cover expanded additional elements except in case of the invalidity of *ṣarf* sale of one *falūs* in exchange for two *falūs* as maintained by Abū Ḥanīfa, whereas according to Abū Yūsuf and Muḥammad al-Shaybānī, it is valid. Another important point which al-Ṭaḥāwī and al-Qudūrī do not mention is regarding the sale, when a person purchases an article of measurement, weight, or number and sells it without measuring, weighing, or counting it, it is considered void.

Al-Ṭaḥāwī's discusses *ribā* under the heading "*Ribā* and *Ṣarf* sale." It is clearly patterned after al-Muzanī's *Mukhtaṣar*. He incorporates al-Shāfi'ī classification concerning its bearing on the sale of articles of different species in measurement and weight very explicitly rather than as it is implicit in al-Shaybānī's account.

Al-Qudūrī's shows the awareness of al-Shāfi'ī's hermeneutics in his account of *ribā* and establishes the legal ruling based on the verse from the *Qur'ān* and the textual evidence (*naṣṣ*) by using the word *taḥrīm* (unlawfulness). He also uses the word *'illa* as the legal reasoning for considering the articles of measurement and weight having the same *'illa* for their belonging to the same species.

Al-Qudūrī acknowledges custom as one of the sources of the law, but it is inferior to the declarations based on the *Qur'ān* and the prophetic *Ḥadīth* reports, which can override the custom.

THE CONTENTS OF *RIBĀ* AND *ṢARF* SALE IN al-ṬAḤĀWĪ'S *MUKHTAṢAR*

The sale of gold in exchange for gold is not valid except like in exchange for like equal in weight and both parties must take the articles of exchange into possession at an equal rate before separating from each other. Likewise, in case of silver in exchange for silver.

The right of option in respect to the *ṣarf* sale is not valid.

The *ribā* enters in all articles of same species of measurement and weight, whether they are edible or not, their sale at an unequal rate is not valid. In all cases of sale, it is not valid for the parties to the contract to separate from each other from the place where the sale is contracted, except if the sale is of heterogeneous species, then it is not objectionable.

The sale of anything of measurement and weight of same species on credit (*nasī'a*) is invalid.

The suspension of payment at a future specified time is invalid.

Everything in which unlawfulness of excess (*tafāḍul)* of one article to the other article has been established by the textual evidence (*naṣṣ*) is considered forever as of that nature, no matter humankind forsakes this kind of mode of estimation, because the custom of people is of the inferior force to the textual evidence.

In *ṣarf* sale, the possession of articles belonging to same species must take place without breaking meeting.

Those articles in which *ribā* does not enter, the articles of exchange to be taken into possession is not a condition.

The sale of wheat in exchange for flour or meal (*sawīq*) is not valid, though flour may be sold in exchange for flour provided the quantities be equal in measurement, but not for meal.

According to Abū Ḥanīfa and Abū Yūsuf, the sale of flesh of animal for animal is valid. However, Muḥammad al-Shaybānī maintains that it is not valid, unless animal is more in weight than flesh.

The sale of fresh dates in exchange for dry dates is valid, but the sale of sesame for sesame oil, the sale of olive for raisin is not valid, unless sesame and raisin are more in quantity or measurement.

The sale of different kinds of flesh in exchange for each other, milk of a cow and milk of a goat, vinegar made from dates in exchange for vinegar made from grapes at different rate and the sale of bread for wheat and flour at different rate is valid.

The *ribā* is not allowed between the owner and his slave, nor between Muslim and non-Muslim in the enemy territory.

ṢARF SALE

Hermeneutical General Features of *Ṣarf* Sale as Reflected in al-Ṭaḥāwī's *Mukhtaṣar* and al-Qudūrī's *Mukhtaṣar* Supplemented with al-Marghīnānī's *Hidāya* in Reference.

The account *ṣarf* sale is not found in Muḥammad al-Shaybānī's in the printed manuscript of *Jāmi' al-Ṣaghīr*. Al-Sarakhsī discusses it under the *ṣarf* sale in his *Mabsūṭ*, presumably based on Muḥammad al-Shaybānī's account of *ṣarf* sale. Al-Sarakhsī's *Mabsūṭ* is a commentary based on al-Ḥakīm's *Mukhtaṣar* of Muḥammad al-Shaybānī's *Jāmi' al-Ṣaghīr*, al-Sarakhsī represents his views based on al-Ḥakīm's account.

Another possibility is that the *ṣarf* sale is based on the same prophetic *Ḥadīth* reports which are used in the *ribā*, the article of weight and measurements, and having the same stipulations in the contract, Muḥammad al-Shaybānī did not treat *ṣarf* sale separately in the *Jāmi' al-Ṣaghīr* as well as in his *Jāmi'al-Kabīr.*[39] This might have been also the reason for which al-Ṭaḥāwī also deals *ṣarf* sale with *ribā* and not in a separate chapter.

Although al-Ṭaḥāwī and al-Qudūrī do not cite any Qur'ānic verses and prophetic *Ḥadīth* reports, al-Sarakhsī who had committed to memory one thousand and three hundred prophetic reports with complete chain of narrations (*riwāya*), cites throughout his works Qur'ānic verses and prophetic *Ḥadīth* reports in support of the legal rulings. This shows that al-Sarakhsī's *Mabsūṭ*, which is a commentary on al-Ḥakīm's *Mukhtaṣar* based on Muḥammad al-Shaybānī's works, is the continuation of hermeneutical interpretations in the formation of Islamic legal system. Thus, later jurists such as al-Sarakhsī, whose *Mabsūṭ* is composed almost after one hundred years later than al-Shāfi'ī's and Muḥammad al-Shaybānī' works, fully accepts al-Shāfi'ī hermeneutics in the formation of Islamic legal system.

The Contents of *Ṣarf* Sale in al-Shaybānī's *Jāmi' al-Ṣaghīr* based on al-Sarakhsī's *Mabsūṭ*, al-Ṭaḥāwī's *Mukhtaṣar* and al-Qudūrī's *Ṣarf* Supplemented with al-Marghīnānī's *Hidāya* in Reference

According to al-Qudūrī, in *ṣarf* sale of gold in exchange for gold, silver in exchange for silver is permitted only when they are equal in weight, but one may be excellent and the other bullion. Al-Sarakhsī cites here what is narrated from 'Umar that the Prophet has said "gold in exchange for gold, silver in exchange for silver, like in exchange for like at an equal rate of article in exchange for another article".

The mutual possession of article of sale is requisite in the *ṣarf* sale prior to the separation of parties from each other. It is narrated that 'Umar said "If the other party during the meeting require leave to go to his house, you must not grant it."

According to al-Ṭaḥāwī[40] and al-Qudūrī,[41] the suspension of payment to a future specified time is unlawful in *ṣarf* sale. According to al-Ṭaḥāwī, right of option in *ṣarf* sale is unlawful.[42] Al-Sarakhsī expresses it by stating that "the right of option is not admitted in the contract of *ṣarf* sale."[43]

According to al-Qudūrī, it is valid that a person sells for one hundred *dirhams* a sword on which silver ornament attached amounts to fifty *dirhams* of price in prompt payment. In such a case, prompt payment made is considered price of silver attached to the sword, even if the seller may have not specified it. If the sword admits of separation of ornament attached to it, the sale is valid in respect to the sword, but not in respect to the ornament.[44] Al-Sarakhsī describes the same case and cites in support of this legal opinion narrated on the authority of Muḥammad bin Sīrin.[45]

In the following rulings one would notice that in general, al-Ṭaḥāwī, al-Qudūrī, and al-Marghīnānī do not cite any Qur'ānic verses or the prophetic

Ḥadīth reports, though their legal opinions are consistent with the revealed sources, except only al-Sarakhsī cites the prophetic *Ḥadīth* report in the following rulings either directly narrated on the authority of Prophet on the authority of early Muslims.

According to al-Qudūrī, the sale of gold in exchange for silver at an unequal rate is permitted in the *ṣarf* sale.[46] Al-Sarakhsī describes this on the authority of narration from Prophet Muḥammad who said, if there are articles of different species, sell them as you please, when the exchange of articles is from hand to hand (*yadan fa yadan*).[47]

According to al-Qudūrī, the articles of exchange in the *ṣarf* sale should be owned and it is possible to deliver it. Al-Sarakhsī expounds it with more clarity that the articles of exchange should be free from debt (*dayn*) or borrowing (*qarḍ*). Al-Qudūrī adds to this that in case a person sells to another person ingot (*nuqqara*) and afterward someone claims part of it, the purchaser can take the remaining of it in proportion to the payment of its price.

According to al-Qudūrī, the usufruct of articles of exchange in the *ṣarf* sale (prior to their possession) is not permitted.[48]

According al-Qudūrī, *dirhams* in which silver is predominant is considered silver as a rule and *dīnārs* in which gold is predominant is considered gold as a rule. The excess (*tafāāḍul*) of one to the other as in the case of pure (*juyūd*) *dirhams* and *dīnārs* is unlawful.

According to Abū Ḥanīfa, *dirhams* and *dīnārs* in which the base metal is predominant, they are, in effect, not considered *dirhams* and *dīnārs* and if people abandon them to use, the sale of wares in exchange of them is void. Abū Yūsuf maintains that it is incumbent on the seller to pay to the purchaser value which these *dirhams* and *dīnārs* bore on the day of sale, while Muḥammad al-Shaybānī alleges that the value which *dirhams* and *dīnārs* bore on the day they fell in disuse is incumbent on him. Likewise, with respect to *falūs* (currency in circulation) that fall in disuse prior to their possession.

SALAM SALE

Hermeneutical General Features of *Salam* Sale as Reflected in al-Shaybānī's *Jāmi' al-Ṣaghīr*, al-Ṭaḥāwī's *Mukhtaṣar,* and al-Qudūrī's *Mukhtaṣar* Supplemented with al-Marghīnānī's *Hidāya* in Reference.

The *salam* sale is discussed by Muḥammad al-Shaybānī which is, on the one hand, relatively larger and with more details, covering some of the aspects related to the *salam* sale which are not dealt with by al-Ṭaḥāwī and al-Qudūrī, but al-Ṭaḥāwī and al-Qudūrī bring in their account of *salam* sale some other expanded additional elements not covered by Muḥammad al-Shaybānī.

Al-Qudūrī summarily puts all stipulations together for the validity of the contract of *salam* sale. They are seven stipulations of the articles of exchange, which are described as follows: (i) description of the species (*jins*), (ii) kind (*nau'*), (iii) quality (*ṣifa*), (iv) weight (*wazan*), (v) measurement (*makīl*), (vi) specified time, and (vii) place of delivery.[49]

As already mentioned, the Ḥanafī jurists were most active in the development of the genre of *Mukhtaṣar* by incorporating expanded additional elements interpreted hermeneutically in the formation of Islamic legal system. This becomes evident by examining the contents of the *salam* sale in al-Ṭaḥāwī's *Mukhtaṣar* and al-Qudūrī's *Mukhtaṣar*.

Muḥammad al-Shaybānī, al-Ṭaḥāwī and al-Qudūrī all three of them do not cite any prophetic *Ḥadīth* reports. Al-Marghīnānī throughout his *Hidāya* is as meticulous as was in the Shāfi'ī school of law al-Muzanī, who cites the verses from the *Qur'ān* and the prophetic *Ḥadīth* reports on which the legal rulings should be based. Al-Marghīnānī's *Hidāya* is, in most part, *verbatim* reproduction of al-Qudūrī's *Mukhtaṣar* with added prophetic *Ḥadīth* reports and explanations. This shows that, in general, the earlier Ḥanafī jurists did not cite explicitly verses from the *Qur'ān* or the prophetic *Ḥadīth* reports. Al-Marghīnānī in compliance with al-Shāfi'ī's hermeneutical contention cites the prophetic *Ḥadīth* reports appropriately. From this it is to be concluded that al-Shāfi'ī's objection against the Ḥanafī jurists is not quite valid on that account. His criticism seems mainly directed against the use of *ra'y* and the doctrine of *istiḥsān* which the Ḥanafī jurists such as al-Sarakhsī and others defend.

The Contents of *Salam* Sale in al-Shaybānī's *Jāmi' al-Ṣaghīr*, al-Ṭaḥāwī's *Mukhtaṣar*, and al-Qudūrī's *Mukhtaṣar* Supplemented with Marghīnānī' *Hidāya* in Reference

Al-Marghīnānī in the very opening of the chapter declares that the *salam* sale is valid and cites in its support the prophetic *Ḥadīth* report "The Prophet prohibited anyone from the sale of what is not in his possession but authorizing the *salam* sale."[50]

A-Marghīnānī cites the prophetic *Ḥadīth* report that "whoever enters into the *salam* sale with you, let him stipulate a determinate weight, measurement, and a determinate period of delivery."[51] According to al-Ṭaḥāwī[52] and al-Qudūrī,[53] the *salam* sale in respect to the articles of measurement and the countable articles is valid. According to Muḥammad al-Shaybānī, if there is a dispute regarding it and the purchaser claims that there was a stipulation to return article, then the word rests with him. If the dispute arises regarding the appointed time and the purchaser claims that there was no such a stipulation, then the word rests with the owner (seller) of the property.[54]

Al-Ṭaḥāwī declares the invalidity of stipulating delay in the *salam* until the harvest, or plucking of the fruits until they are ripe, or until thrashing of grains.[55] Al-Marghīnānī quotes the prophetic *Ḥadīth* report, "You shall not sell fruit by way of *salam* sale until their ripeness is apparent."[56] Al-Ṭaḥāwī further includes invalidity of delaying article of exchange to the Christian day of fasting (Lent) or to delay until the Judiac Day of Atonement begins, because in all these cases the uncertainty of time is involved.[57] If it is known when the day of fasting begins, then the *salam* sale is valid.

According to Muḥammad al-Shaybānī,[58] al-Qudūrī,[59] and al-Ṭaḥāwī,[60] the *salam* sale is valid in which the articles of the same species do not differ in their units such as eggs, walnuts, and *falūs* sold by numbers and articles of longitudinal measurement, because it is possible to describe them by specifying quality and workmanship.

Muḥammad al-Shaybānī, al-Ṭaḥāwī, and al-Qudūrī maintain that the *salam* sale of animal flesh is not valid. The *salam* sale of animals and their parts such as head, feet, and skin are not valid.

According to al-Shaybānī, the *salam* sale of fresh fish is not valid, unless its weight is known at the time of its delivery.[61]

According to al-Ṭaḥāwī[62] and al-Qudūrī,[63] the usufruct of article of exchange in the *salam* sale prior to its being taken into possession is not valid. The *salam* sale in partnership (*shirka*) and friendly partnership (*tawlīya*) prior to taking article of exchange into possession is not valid.[64]

According to al-Ṭaḥāwī[65,66] and al-Qudūrī,[67] the *salam* sale is not valid, unless the seller receives or takes article of exchange (price) into his possession prior to the separation of the parties to the contract.

According to al-Ṭaḥāwī,[68] the article of exchange in the *salam* must be in existence at the time of conclusion of the contract and at the time of its delivery.

According al-Ṭaḥāwī[69] and al-Qudūrī,[70] if the article of *salam* sale does not require expense of porterage, it is not necessary to specify or fix the place of its delivery. Marghīnānī remarks that this is the rule laid down in Muḥammad al-Shaybānī's *Jāmi' al-Ṣaghīr* and *Mabsūṭ*.[71]

According al-Ṭaḥāwī, if the place of delivery is not specified, the purchaser is obligated to take article into possession from the seller at the place where the *salam* sale was contracted.[72]

According to al-Ṭaḥāwī, it is not appropriate in the *salam* sale to bargain or ask for increase in price.[73] It is to be noted that this prohibition of bargaining in any contract of sale is based on the prophetic *Ḥadīth* report.

According to al-Qudūrī,[74] the *salam* sale of swine or hawk or predatory animals is not valid. The *salam* of wine and swine is not valid. The *salam* sale of silkworm is not valid except with silk or bee except with beehive.[75]

In the purchase and sale of articles, *dhimmī are* considered like Muslims except in respect of wine and hog which is valid for *dhimmīs*. Wine and swine are for them just as hawk is like sheep for them and wine for them is like juice.[76]

Following some of the material from Muḥammad al-Shaybānī's *Jāmi' al-Ṣaghīr* is not covered by al-Ṭaḥāwī or al-Qudūrī, but al-Marghīnānī's in the *Hidāya* deals with it as follows:

According to Muḥammad al-Shaybānī[77] and al-Marghīnānī,[78] whosoever requests a worker to manufacture article has right of option either to accept or reject it, because it was purchased without seeing it.

According to al-Marghīnānī, the *salam* sale of small pearls or marine shells is unlawful, because their unities vary in their value.[79] This is not mentioned by Muḥammad al-Shaybānī, al-Ṭaḥāwī, or al-Qudūrī. Issues *(masā'ils)* in respect to such items might have arisen as a recent phenomenon at that time. Al-Marghīnānī includes it by exercising his own *qiyās* in the account of *salam* sale. This shows that it is an ongoing process of hermeneutical interpretation relating the legal rules in accordance with the legal canons.

According to Muḥammad al-Shaybānī[80] and al-Marghīnānī,[81] a person sells one *dīnār* in exchange for ten *dirhams* without taking them into his possession until he purchases with them cloth in exchange, then the sale of cloth is void.

According to Muḥammad al-Shaybānī and al-Marghīnānī, a person having purchased a *kūr*[82] of wheat by way of *salam* sale, should order the seller to measure it and the seller accordingly having measured it in the absence of purchaser delivers it, then the delivery of goods is not held to have taken place in this case, because in the *salam* sale the purchaser does not become the proprietor of article until its actual possession is taken by him after measuring it by himself.[83]

According to Muḥammad al-Shaybānī and Marghīnānī, a person purchases *kūr* of wheat making female slave as payment in advance for it and the seller takes her in his possession, then parties to the contract dissolve contract of sale. If she dies while she was in the possession of the seller, then the price of female slave is incumbent on him. Likewise, if the purchaser dissolves contract of sale after she dies while she was in his possession, price is incumbent on him. If a person having purchased slave should agree with the seller to dissolve contract of sale, and the slave afterward dies in his possession, the dissolution of contract is invalid (*bāṭil*).[84]

PARTNERSHIP

Hermeneutical General Features of Partnership as Reflected in al-Shaybānī's partnership in his *Jāmī'al-Ṣaghīr*, al-Ṭaḥāwī's partnership in his *Mukhtaṣar*, and al-Qudūrī's partnership in his *Mukhtaṣar* Supplemented with al-Marghīnānī's partnership in the *Hidāya* in Reference.

Muḥammad al-Shaybānī discusses partnership under the chapter *Muḍāraba* in which he deals with only the partnership in reciprocity (*shirka mufāwada*)[85] and that also very briefly. Al-Ṭaḥāwī's and al-Qudūrī's accounts under the partnership deal with all four kinds of partnerships. Al-Marghīnānī at the very outset states that the validity of partnership is based on the prophetic *Ḥadīth* report: "In the time of Allah's Messenger, men were accustomed to have transactions in partnership and he confirmed partnership in them."[86]

Al-Marghīnānī also bases the validity of partnership in reciprocity on the prophetic *Ḥadīth* report: "Enter into partnership by reciprocity, because in that there is a great advantage."[87] Al-Marghīnānī states that partnership in reciprocity is valid according to the doctrine of *istiḥsān*, though according to the doctrine of *qiyās* it is invalid. In fact, al-Marghīnānī does not need to justify that it is based on the doctrine of *istiḥsān* nor does he need to assert that it is not valid according to the doctrine of *qiyās*, since the validity of the partnership by his own narration is based on the prophetic *Ḥadīth* report. In this case, contrary to al-Shāfi'ī and Mālik, who consider partnership in reciprocity is invalid, Al-Marghīnānī cites the prophetic *Ḥadīth* report and the custom, which is recognized as one of the sources of Islamic law. From this, one can claim that al-Shāfi'ī was himself guilty of violating the contention of his own hermeneutics. Probably, al-Shāfi'ī's objection should have been based on the ground of uncertainty involved in such transactions of partnership. For al-Shāfi'ī, one of the objects for the employment of hermeneutics was to ascertain the certainty involved in the transactions. The Ḥanafī jurists here make use of the prophetic *Ḥadīth* report which, according to them, provides hermeneutical certainty.

Al-Qudūrī in the account of partnership covers many expanded additional elements in comparison to not only al-Ṭaḥāwī's account, but also al-Shāfi'ī's, al-Muzani's, and al-Shīrāzī's accounts of partnership.

The Contents of Partnership in al-Shaybānī's *Jāmi' al-Ṣaghīr*, al-Ṭaḥāwī's *Mukhtaṣar*, and al-Qudūrī's *Mukhtaṣar* Supplemented with Marghīnānī's Partnership in the *Hidāya* in Reference.

Al-Qudūrī first clarifies the distinction between partnerships of two kinds, partnership by right of property (*shirka milk*) and partnership by contracts (*shirk 'uqūd*). He explains that the partnership by right of property applies when two or more persons are the proprietor of a thing (*'ayn)* or it is of two natures, one optional, when two persons make a joint purchase of one specific thing, or the other compulsive, when it is presented to them jointly as gift in bequest. It is, however, not valid for either partner to make the usufruct of share of other partner without his permission. Both partners are considered to each other strangers with respect to the share in their property.

The partnership by contract is of four types: (i) partnership in reciprocity (*shirka mufāwaḍa*), (ii) partnership in traffic (*shirka 'aynān)*, (iii) partnership in workmanship (*shirka ṣan'a* also known as *shirka al-abdān* or *shirka al-taqabbal*), and (iv) partnership upon personal credit (*shirka wujūh*).

PARTNERSHIP IN RECIPROCITY

Muḥammad al-Shaybānī and al-Ṭaḥāwī neither define nor explain the nature of partnership in reciprocity. According to al-Qudūrī, partnership in reciprocity comprises where two parties to the contract are considered equal in respect to the property of each, its usufruct, and debt.[88]

According to al-Shaybānī,[89] al-Ṭaḥāwī,[90] and al-Qudūrī,[91] partnership in reciprocity is valid between two Muslims or two *dhimmīs* of legal age and free persons, since equality exists between them, but not between a free person and a slave, an adult and a minor, and a Muslim and an unbeliever. In respect to the owner and slave, al-Ṭaḥāwī allows slave with limited rights (*ma'ḍūn*) to trade. Al-Marghīnānī states that according to Abū Ḥanīfa, a contract of partnership in reciprocity is not valid between a Muslim and an unbeliever. Abū Yūsuf and Muḥammad al-Shaybānī allege that it is valid, because equality exists between them in respect to the power of agency (wakāla) and bail (*kafāla*).[92]

According to al-Qudūrī, partnership in reciprocity comprehends both in respect to agency and bail.[93]

According to al-Qudūrī, in the purchase of an article, both partners are considered partners except in purchase of esculent articles and clothing for a partner himself and his family. If the debt incurred by one of the partners for a purchase of thing in partnership, the other partner is also responsible for it.[94]

According to Muḥammad al-Shaybānī,[95] al-Ṭaḥāwī,[96] and al-Qudūrī,[97] a partnership in reciprocity cannot be contracted, except in *dirhams*, *dīnārs*, and *falūs*.

PARTNERSHIP IN TRAFFIC

Hermeneutical General Features of Partnership in Traffic in al-Ṭaḥāwī's *Mukhtaṣar* and al-Qudūrī's *Mukhtaṣar* supplemented with al-Marghīnānī's *Hidāya* in Reference.

Al-Ṭaḥāwī''s and al-Qudūrī's account of partnership is thorough covering all aspects of different kinds of partnerships. Al-Qudūri brings in the expanded additional elements regarding partnership on credit and regarding the invalidity to trade in hunt, wood, and such things.

Contents of Partnership in al-Ṭaḥāwī's *Mukhtaṣar* and al-Qudūrī's *Mukhtaṣar* Supplemented with al-Marghīnī's *Hidāya* in Reference

When two persons are desirous of entering into contract of partnership in goods and effects, each must sell one-half of the goods and effects (for *dīnārs* and *dirhams*) equal to one-half of the goods and effects (for *dīnārs* and *dirhams*) of other partner so that the partnership in traffic could be established with equal amount of *dīnārs* and *dirhams* between them.

The partnership in traffic comprehends mutual agency, but not mutual bail.[98]

If the property (*māl*) of one partner exceeds the property of other,[99] or the property of each partner is equal, and the profit is shared unequally, it is valid.[100] Al-Marghīnānī, cites prophetic *Ḥadīth* report in support of it: "The profit between them is according to their agreement and loss in proportion to the property of each."[101]

According to al-Qudūrī[102] and al-Ṭaḥāwī,[103] it is valid for two persons to engage in partnership in (traffic when the property of one consists of *dirhams* and that of the other *dīnārs*).

Al-Ṭaḥāwī maintains that the contract of partnership in traffic between Muslim and *dhimmī*, is valid, though it is repugnant if Muslim is in debt.[104]

For Al-Ṭaḥāwī, the partnership in traffic between an owner and his slave with limited rights as well as an adult and a minor are valid.[105]

According to al-Qudūrī, if a partner makes purchase in partnership in traffic, the demand for its price can only be claimed from the partner, who incurs it and make payment of it. The purchaser takes from the other partner portion of the price from his property. In case, if a partner has made a purchase from his property and it is destroyed, the loss is entirely upon him. If the entire property in partnership or the property of one partner is destroyed, then the contract of partnership is dissolved.[106]

A person in contract of partnership in traffic makes a purchase with his own property and afterward the property of other partner perishes before he has made any purchase with it, the thing purchased is considered in partnership.[107]

If in the partnership in traffic any specific some of profit (*ribḥ*) is stipulated for one of the partners, it is not valid.[108]

Each partner in respect to the contract of partnership in reciprocity or partnership in traffic is at liberty to give his property from the portion of his profit[109] and in the same manner to lodge it as deposit (*rahan*) or pledge it as security. Likewise, each partner is at liberty to give his property by appointing an agent on his behalf. He (the agent) may sell it for cash or on credit and the property in his hands is considered trust (*amāna*).[110]

PARTNERSHIP IN WORKMANSHIP

A partnership is valid where two persons join in partnership by agreement to work and share their earnings between them.

According to al-Ṭaḥāwī, the partnership in workmanship is valid in all what is valid in respect to power of agency and invalid what is invalid in respect to bail.[111]

According to al-Ṭaḥāwī, the partnership in workmanship between two males and two females and likewise, between a male and a female is valid, regardless whether they both engage in the same kind of workmanship or different.[112]

According to al-Ṭaḥāwī[113] and al-Qudūrī,[114] it is not valid that the profit of one partner exceeds the profit of other partner as in the partnership in traffic, however, al-Marghīnānī maintains that it admits an inequality of profit.[115]

PARTNERSHIP ON PERSONAL CREDIT

It is valid that two persons having no property become partners on their personal credit to purchase and sell and each partner may become both bail and agent for the other partner in respect to each partner to make the purchase of article with the stipulation that it shall be of equal shares and of equal profit or loss. After stating the validity of the partnership on personal credit, al-Qudūrī proceeds to describe the cases of invalid transactions.

A partnership upon credit is not valid in the articles of nature such as wood, dry grass, hunt.[116]

A partnership on personal credit is not valid when the means of acquiring them are different such as one partner possesses a mule and the other possesses means of drawing the water.[117]

In all cases of partnership, the profit is divided in proportion to the property (*rās al-māl*), if the profit is stipulated for either party in excess to the profit of other party, it is void (*bāṭil*).[118]

According al-Ṭaḥāwī[119] and al-Qudūrī,[120] in all cases of partnership, if one of the two partners dies (whether it is known by the other partner or not), or apostatize, or joins the non-Muslim territory (*dār al-ḥarb*), the contract of partnership becomes annulled, because in that case the appointment of agency would not be comprehended.

According to al-Ṭaḥāwī, if the contract of partnership has become annulled after the death of one partner, it is not valid for the other partner to make usufruct of the property in partnership.[121]

According al-Qudūrī, it is not valid for either of the partner to pay taxes (*ẓakāt*) for the portion of the property of other partner without his permission. If one partner permits to pay all taxes, other partner is responsible to pay the portion of taxes to him.[122]

LEASE-HIRE

Hermeneutical General Features of Lease-Hire as Reflected in al-Shaybānī's Lease-Hire in *Jāmi' al-Ṣaghīr*, al-Ṭaḥāwī's *Mukhtaṣar,* and al-Qudūrī's *Mukhtaṣar* Supplemented with al-Marghīnānī's *Hidāya* in Reference.

Although al-Shaybānī, al-Ṭaḥāwī and al-Qudūrī do not cite any Qur'anic verses and prophetic *Ḥadīth* reports, al-Marghīnānī cites them appropriately. In the accounts of all three of them, we do not find any significant differences, save some variations in minor details.

Al-Shaybānī's and al-Qudūrī's account of lease-hire is much more detailed comparable to that of al-Ṭaḥāwī. Al-Shaybānī discusses contract of lase-hire under the following subsections: (i) kind of excuses (*'udhar*) that annuls the contract of lease-hire, (ii) invalid contract of lease-hire, (iii) two conditions of lease-hire, (iv) hiring of a servant, (v) responsibility of lessee, (vi) fault (*jināya*) of lessee, and (vii) various *masā'ils*. Al-Ṭaḥāwī and al-Qudūrī discuss the contract of lease-hire without any subsections which essentially does not bring more or significant information. Most of the material of al-Shaybānī's contract of sale is covered in al-Ṭaḥāwī's and a-Qudūrī's contracts of lease-hire with additional expanded elements.

The contents of lease-hire show that al-Qudūrī hermeneutically incorporated all expanded additional elements and details not found in the writings of eponyms. His account of lease-hire is significantly larger than what we find in the writing of al-Shaybānī.

Al-Qudūrī uses prophetic *Ḥadīth* reports in support of the validity of lease-hire and al-Shāfi'ī's one of the techniques of hermeneutics for indicating the place by pointing out.

In al-Shaybānī's text, the doctrine of *istiḥsān* is employed.

The Contents of al-Shaybānī's Lease-Hire in *Jāmi' al-Ṣaghīr*, al-Ṭaḥāwī's *Mukhtaṣar*, and al-Qudūrī's *Mukhtaṣar* Supplemented with al-Marghīnānī's *Hidāya* in Reference.

We shall here present al-Shaybānī', al-Ṭaḥāwī' and al-Qudūrī accounts of lease-hire together which deal with the same aspects, albeit with some variations in their narrations.

Al-Qudūrī,[123] in contrast to al-Shaybānī and al-Ṭaḥāwī, first defines lease-hire as the profit (*munāfi'a*) in exchange for the usufruct of thing of lease-hire. A contract of lease-hire is not valid, unless both the usufruct and lease-hire are specified. Al-Marghīnānī cites prophetic *Ḥadīth* report in its support: "If a person hires another person, let him inform him of the wages he is to receive."[124]

Al-Qudūrī, unlike Al-Shaybānī and al-Ṭaḥāwī, clearly states that a contract of lease-hire is like contract of sale. Therefore, whatever is valid in the contract of sale is also valid in the contract of lease-hire.[125] From this, it becomes clear that the contract of lease-hire is one of species (*ṣanf*) of contract of sale; the usufruct may be specified as in the lease-hire of house, or land for the purpose of cultivation, or by specifying work when a person hires another person for to dyeing or sewing cloth, or animal for carrying certain load, or riding on it to go to a certain distance.[126] Furthermore, according to al-Qudūrī[127] the usufruct may be ascertained by pointing (*ishāra*) the place to bring the load.

As to the time, al-Marghīnānī[128] states that lease-hire does not become valid on concluding the contract, contrary to al-Shāfi'ī's opinion. The recompense can be claimed on one of the three grounds: (i) It can be claimed in advance, (ii) in virtue of the previous agreement, and (iii) in consequence of lease holder (hirer) obtaining the thing contracted. Al-Ṭaḥāwī[129] adds to this by stating that according to Abū Ḥanīfa and Abū Yūsuf, it is not valid for the lessor to demand rent unless at the time when it is due. If the lease is terminated before the lease-hire has expired, the lessor returns the rent in proportion to the remaining period of lease.

According to al-Ṭaḥāwī[130] and al-Qudūrī,[131] in case either one party to the contract dies, the contract of lease-hire is void.

According to al-Shaybānī, if a person leases-hires land for cultivating wheat in it and instead, cultivates fresh dates and there is a loss he is responsible for it and rent becomes incumbent on him.[132] According to al-Qudūrī, it is valid to lease-hire field to build structure on it or plant palm trees, or other kinds of trees. When the term of lease expires, the lessee is obliged to tear down the structure, cut down the trees, and deliver the field leveled. If the owner chooses to pay the price for the structure and trees, then he can become the owner of them or leave them as they are.[133]

According to al-Shaybānī, it is valid if a person hires (female) camel (*iblā'*) to travel with it, but instead travels riding male camel (*jamāl*, male of *nāqa*), it is not valid. If a person hires slave and then sells him, it is inexcusable (invalid).[134] According to al-Ṭaḥāwī[135] and al-Qudūrī,[136] it is valid to lease-hire animal for riding. According to al-Qudūrī, if it is an absolute lease, it is valid that the lessee can give it to anyone whomever he likes to ride on it. According to al-Ṭaḥāwī, if he leases-hires to ride on it to a certain place and if he passes by to travel to another place, then he is responsible for the additional distance he crossed. If the animal is damaged, he is responsible for its price. According to al-Shaybānī, if a person leases-hires an animal to go to Ḥīra and passes by Qādsīya and returns it to Ḥīra while it has been exhausted (destroyed), he is responsible for it.[137] According to al-Qudūrī,[138] It is valid if a person leases-hires cloth and gives it to someone else to wear it. But if it becomes ruined, he is responsible for it. Likewise, in all such things because of different kinds of users. In the same manner, it is valid if he leases-hires a house and gives it to someone to reside in it.

Al-Shaybānī and al-Ṭaḥāwī[139] discuss following some expanded additional elements in respect to the lease-hire of house:

According to al-Shaybānī, if a person rents house without mentioning anything, it is valid. But it is not valid for him to engage in it as an iron smith or bleacher or run a shop for doing business in it.[140]

According to al-Ṭaḥāwī, if a person leases-hires house for a certain period and does not move in it and take possession of it until the lease is expired, the rent is due on him regardless. In case, if he has not seen the house, he has right of option to hold the lease or reject it after seeing it. After taking the house into possession, if defect occurs causing damage to it, he has right of option to keep it leasing in that condition or if he pleases he can nullify the lease.

According to al-Ṭaḥāwī,[141] if a person leases-hires house, it is not valid for him to pay any rent, unless he has taken it into possession.

According to al-Qudūrī,[142] In case of dispute between an owner and the worker regarding the order he has received or regarding the wages, the assertion of owner is accepted.

According to al-Qudūrī[143] and al-Ṭaḥāwī,[144] lease-hire is of two kinds: (i) common lease-hire (*ajīr mushtarik*) and (ii) particular lease-hire (*ajīr khāṣṣ*). Al-Shaybānī describes such cases under the invalid leases-hires, but without making any distinction between them.

According to al-Shaybānī, if a person gives a piece of cotton cloth or fabric for weaving half of it for covering and other half of it as his recompense, and likewise, if he leases-hires a person to carry food and one *qafīz*[145] of it as a recompense for him, or if he leases-hires a donkey to carry manures and one *qafīz* of it as a recompense for it, it is invalid. Similarly, if a person leases-hires a person to bake bread of the tenth of the sixth part (*mukhānīm*) on this day for a *dirham,* it is invalid.[146]

A common lease-hire is when one with whom the contract of lease-hire is concluded for the work and there is no requisite mentioned such as dyeing and bleaching the piece of cloth. In such a common lease-hire, the article given to him for the work is considered deposit while it is in his possession. If it is destroyed, in this case and in all such cases, the worker is not responsible for it, but he is not entitled to any wages. This is the opinion of Abū Ḥanīfa. Abū Yūsuf and Muḥammad al-Shaybānī,[147] maintain that he is responsible for it such as when a dyer or a bleacher tears down the piece of cloth or the porter tumbles the load and it breaks down or the girth of a camel breaks or the boat sinks by the operation of the sailor. These differences of opinion between them are because of the different hermeneutical interpretations.

According to al-Ṭaḥāwī,[148] a person leases-hires (female) slave, who becomes protuberant in her appearance or an animal whose tusk begins to rise constantly effecting it to become defective, then the lessee-hirer is considered not responsible for it.

According to al-Qudūrī,[149] in the particular lease-hire one is entitled to the wages by submitting oneself for a term of the hire such as a person hired for a month or taking care of flocks.

According to al-Shaybānī, a bleacher can keep cloth (given as deposit) for the wages to be paid for his workmanship. If it becomes damaged in his possession he is not responsible for it, but there are no wages for him.[150] According to al-Ṭaḥāwī[151] and al-Qudūrī,[152] in case of particular lease-hire, the article given to the worker in his possession is considered deposit. If it becomes damaged not because of his action, he is not responsible for it, except in case of transgression on his part. Al-Ṭaḥāwī adds to this by stating that this is the opinion of all three eponyms. However, every worker whose work produces an effect on the article such as dyer and bleacher, he can retain the article unless he receives the wages. If the work produces no effect on the article such as porter carrying the load from one place to another, he is not at liberty to retain the article in his possession.

According to al-Shaybānī, a person hires a servant for his services in Egypt, and then he (asked to) travel (with him), it is valid.[153]

According to al-Qudūrī,[154] a person hires a slave for the services to render for him, he is not at liberty to take him on journey with him, unless it is specified as a condition in the contract.

According to al-Qudūrī,[155] a worker such as bleacher, tailor, baker, or cook is not at liberty to demand wages, until his work is complete.

According to al-Shaybānī, it is valid if a person gives to the tailor for sewing shirt and the tailor instead sews an outer garment (*qabā'*).[156] The same is expressed by al-Qudūrī with some variation[157] if a person asks a tailor to sew cloth in the Persian manner for a *dirham* or in Turkish (Romanian) manner for two *dirhams*. In both cases, he is entitled to wages.

According to al-Qudūrī,[158] if a person leases-hires house on the monthly basis in exchange for a *dirham*, then the contract is valid for a month and for remaining months is void, unless it is stipulated for all following all months.

According to al-Qudūrī,[159] keepers of bath and cuppers are entitled to wages, but no wages for caller of prayers, teaching of *Qur'ān* or *fiqh*, performance of pilgrimage and for the one who helps for covering of animals, that is, bringing a male to copulate with a female. Al-Marghīnānī, cites a prophetic *Ḥadīth* report that the Prophet has said "*la 'asab al-tīs*."[160]

According to al-Shaybānī, a person leases-hires land for cultivation and leases-hires someone else to cultivate it, it is not valid (*lā khayr*). Similarly, if the person lets half of his house on rent as a public place, it is not valid. Likewise, a person leases-hires land without mentioning what is to be cultivated in it, it is invalid. If he cultivates land and the lease is expired, it is valid for the future time, if it was specified in the contract. If a person leases-hires land for cultivation, it is valid for him to turn over the ground to plant seedling for cultivation and water it, even if it is not stipulated in the contract. The contract is dissolved, if the land becomes filled with water and becomes uprooted.[161]

According to al-Shaybānī, if a person leases-hires wet nurse for food and clothing as her recompense, it is valid according to the doctrine of *istiḥsān*. However, Abū Yūsuf and al-Shaybānī, only if the weight (quantity) of food and the quality of cloth is specified.

According to al-Shaybānī, if the tailor leases-hires servant to engage in sewing with him and becomes insolvent and relinquishes his work, it is excusable (valid), but if he wants to relinquish his work as the tailor and become the money changer, it is not valid.[162]

According to al-Ṭaḥāwī[163] and al-Qudūrī,[164] if a person leases-hires a shop and afterward becomes poor and gets involved into debt to the extent that he is unable to discharge his obligation to pay rent for the shop, then the *Qāḍī* must render a decree to dissolve the contract of lease-hire and sell his property for the payment of debt.

Al-Qudūrī states that if a person gives a piece of cloth to the tailor for sewing it with two conditions: If you sew it to-day, for you is two *dirhams* and if you sew it tomorrow, for you is one *dirham* and if he performs it according to that, his recompense is according to that, neither more nor less. According to Abū Yūsuf and al-Shaybānī, both conditions are valid.[165]

NOTES

1. Norman Calder, *Studies*, p. 105.

2. Christopher Melchert, "Traditionist-Jurisprudents and Framing of Islamic Law," *Islamic Law and Society*, 8.3, 2001, 386–387.

3. David R. Vishanoff, *Formation of Islamic Hermeneutics* (New Haven, CT: American Oriental Society, 2011), pp. 27–28.

4. Vishanoff, *Formation of Islamic Hermeneutics*, p. 28.

5. T. H. Juynboll, *First Encyclopaedia of Islam*, vol. I (Leiden: E. J. Brill, 1993), p. 90.

6. Melchert, "Traditionist-Jurisprudent" in Law and Society (Leiden: E. J. Brill, 2001), p. 186; Joseph Schacht "Aṣḥāb al-Ra'y," *Encyclopaedia of Islam*, vol. v (Leiden: E. J. Brill, 2001).

7. Al-Shāfi'ī, *K al-Umm*, vol. VII (Cairo: Bulaq, 1968), pp. 267–269.

8. Al-Shāfi'ī, *Risāla: Islamic Jurisprudence*, translated by Majid Khadduri (Baltimore: The John Hopkins Press, 1961), p. 71.
9. Sarakhsī, *Mabsūṭ*, vol. I (Beirut: Dār al-Ma'ārif, 1993), p. 5
10. Husain Kassim, *Sarakhsī, The Doctrine of Juristic Preference and the Concept of Treaties and Mutual Relations* (San Francisco-London: Austin & Winfield, 1994), pp. 14–44.
11. See, Weal B. al-Ḥallāq, "Was al-Shāfi'ī Master Architect of Islamic Jurisprudence," *International Journal of Middle East Studies*, 4, November 1993, pp. 587–605.
12. Abū al-Wafā al-Afghānī (edit), *Mukhtaṣar al-Ṭaḥāwī* (Cairo: Maṭba' Dār al-Kitāb al-'Arabī, 1370), p. 3.
13. F. Krenkow, "Al-Ṭaḥāwī" in *First Encyclopaedia of Islam*, vol. vii, 1987, pp. 608–610.
14. Yakov Meron, "The Development of Legal Thought in Ḥanafī Thought" in *Studia Islamica*, 1969.
15. Abū Ja'far al-Ṭaḥāwī, chapter *al-Buyū'*, *Mukhtaṣar* (Cairo: Maṭb'a Dār al-Kitāb al-'Arabī, 1992), p. 74.
16. Kamil Muḥammad Muḥammad 'Awīḍ, Introduction in the *Mukhtaṣar al*-Qudūrī (Beirut: Dar al-Kutub al-'Ilmīya, 1997), p. 5.
17. F. Krenkow, *First Encyclopaedia of Islam*, vol. vii, 1987, pp. 608–610.
18. Muḥammad Muhammad Tāmir and Ḥāfiz 'Asūr Ḥāfiz, *al-Hidāya*, vol. i, pp. 8–9.
19. Al-Ṭaḥāwī, Chapter *al-Buyū'*, *Mukhtaṣar*, pp. 74–75.
20. Abū Ja'far al-Ṭaḥāwī, chapter *al*-Buyū', *Mukhtaṣar*, pp. 74–75.
21. A measure containing about sixty-four pounds in weight.
22. A measure in varying meters in different Middle Eastern regions.
23. Al-Ṭaḥāwī, Section Sale of Trees, Palm Trees, and Fruits in chapter *al-Buyū'*, *Mukhtaṣar*, p. 78.
24. Al-Ṭaḥāwī, Sale of Tress, Palm Trees, and Fruits, chapter *al-Buyū'*, *Mukhtaṣar*, p. 79.
25. Al-Ṭaḥāwī, Sale of Tress, Palm Trees and Fruits, chapter *al-Buyū'*, *Mukhtaṣar*, p. 79.
26. Al-Ṭaḥāwī, Sale of Trees, Palm Trees, and Fruits, chapter *al-Buyū'*, *Mukhtaṣar*, p. 79.
27. Al-Ṭaḥāwī, Sale of Trees, Palm Trees, and Fruits, chapter *al-Buyū'*, *Mukhtaṣar*, p. 79.
28. Al-Ṭaḥāwī, Sale of Trees, Palm Trees, and Fruits, chapter *al-Buyū'*, *Mukhtaṣar*, p. 79.
29. Al-Ṭaḥāwī, Sale of Trees, Palm Trees, and Fruits, chapter *al-Buyū'*, *Mukhtaṣar*, p. 79.
30. Al-Shaybānī, chapter Right of Option of Inspection and Right of Option of Stipulation, *Jāmī' al-Ṣaghīr*, pp. 270–278.
31. Abū al-Ḥasan Aḥmad ibn Muḥammad bi Aḥmad ibn Ja'far Al-Qudūrī, chapter Right of Option of Stipulations and chapter Right of Option of Inspection, *Mukhtaṣar*, pp. 70 and 71.
32. A tribe of black Arabs who inhabited the fanny region between Wadis and Basra, Hamilton, The *Hidāya, Commentary*, vol. II, Footnote, p. 608.

33. Al-Ṭaḥāwī, chapter Sale of Trees, and Fruits, *Mukhtaṣar*, p. 73.
34. Al-Shaybānī, chapter Defects, *Jāmi' al-Ṣaghīr*, pp. 278–290.
35. Al-Qudūrī, chapter Defects, *Mukhtaṣar*, pp. 71–73.
36. Al-Ṭaḥāwī, chapter, *Bāb al-Muṣarra*, *Mukhtaṣar*, p. 79. *Muṣarra* denotes an animal that has been left without being milked for some days.
37. Hamilton, The *Hidāya, Commentary*, vol. II, p. 613.
38. Kassim, *Sarakhsī,* p. 33.
39. Al-Shaybānī, *Jāmi' al-Kabīr*, edited by Abū al-Wafā' (Lahore: Dār al-Ma'ārif, 1981).
40. Al-Ṭaḥāwī, *Mukhtaṣar*, p. 75.
41. Al-Qudūrī, *Mukhtaṣar*, p. 90.
42. Al-Ṭaḥāwī, *Mukhtaṣar*, p. 75.
43. Al-Sarkhsī, *Mabsūṭ*, vol. XIII, p. 14.
44. Al-Qudūrī, *Mukhtaṣar*, p. 90.
45. Al-Sarakhsī, *Mabsūṭ*, vol. XIV, p. 4.
46. Al-Qudūrī, *Mukhtaṣar*, p. 90.
47. Al-Sarakhsī, *Mabsūṭ*, vol. XIV, p. 4.
48. Al-Qudūrī, *Mukhtaṣar*, p. 90.
49. Al-Qudūrī, *Mukhtaṣar*, p. 88; Marghīnānī, *al-Hidāya al-Mubtadī*, vol. Iii, p. 1023; Hamilton, *Hidāya*, Commentary, vol. ii, p. 680.
50. Al-Marghīnānī, *al-Hidāya*, p. 1018; Hamilton, *Hidāya*, Commentary, vol. ii, p. 677.
51. Hamilton, *Hidāya*, Commentary, vol. ii, p. 677.
52. Al-Ṭaḥāwī, *Mukhtaṣar*, p. 88.
53. Al-Qudūrī, *Mukhtaṣar*, p. 89.
54. Al-Shaybānī, *Jāmi' al-Ṣaghīr*, p. 264.
55. Al-Ṭaḥāwī, *Mukhtaṣar*, p. 86.
56. Hamilton, *Hidāya*, Commentary, p. 679.
57. Al-Ṭaḥāwī, *Mukhtaṣar*, p. 86.
58. Al-Shaybānī, *Jāmi' al-Ṣaghīr*, p. 266.
59. Al-Qudūrī, *Mukhtaṣar*, p. 88.
60. Al-Ṭaḥāwī, *Mukhtaṣar*, p. 86.
61. Al-Shaybānī, *Jāmi' al-Ṣaghīr*, p. 266.
62. Al-Ṭaḥāwī, *Mukhtaṣar,* p. 86.
63. Al-Qudūrī, *Mukhtaṣar*, pp. 88–89.
64. Al-Ṭaḥāwī, *Mukhtaṣar,* p. 86.
65. Al-Ṭaḥāwī, *Mukhtaṣar*, p. 86.
66. Al-Ṭaḥāwī, *Mukhtaṣar*, p. 86.
67. Al-Qudūrī, *Mukhtaṣar*, p. 88.
68. Al-Ṭaḥāwī, *Mukhtaṣar*, p. 86.
69. Al-Ṭaḥāwī, *Mukhtaṣar*, pp. 86–87.
70. Al-Qudūrī, *Mukhtaṣar*, p. 88.
71. Hamilton, *Hidāya,* Commentary, vol. ii, p. 684.
72. Al-Ṭaḥāwī, *Mukhtaṣar*, pp. 86–87.
73. Al-Ṭaḥāwī, *Mukhtaṣar*, p. 84.

74. Al-Qudūrī, *Mukhtaṣar*, p. 89.
75. Al-Qudūrī, *Mukhtaṣar*, p. 89.
76. Al-Qudūrī, *Mukhtaṣar*, p. 89.
77. Al-Shaybānī, *Jāmi' al-Ṣaghīr*, p. 266.
78. Hamilton, *Hidāya*, Commentary, vol. ii, p. 692: Marghīnānī, *al-Hidāya*, p. 1030.
79. Marghīnānī, *al-Hidāya*, p. 1029; Hamilton, *Hidāya,* vol. ii, p. 697.
80. Al-Shaybānī, *Jāmi' al-Ṣaghīr*, p. 268; Hamilton, *Hidāya*, Commentary, p. 685.
81. Hamilton, *al-Hidāya*, Commentary, vol. ii, p. 685.
82. A certain measure of capacity.
83. Al-Shaybānī, *Jāmi' al-Ṣaghīr*, p. 267; Marghīnānī, *al-Hidāya*, p. 1027; Hamilton, *Hidāya*, Commentary, vol. ii, p. 687.
84. Al-Shaybānī, *Jāmi' al-Ṣaghīr*, p. 268; Marghīnānī, *al-Hidāya*, p. 1028; Hamilton, *Hidāya*, Commentary, vol. ii, p. 689.
85. Al-Shaybānī, *Jāmi' al-Ṣaghīr,* pp. 249–250.
86. Al-Marghīnānī, *al-Hidāya*, p. 1213; Hamilton, *Hidāya*, Commentary, p. 540.
87. Hamilton, *Hidāya*, Commentary, vol. ii, p. 542.
88. Al-Qudūrī, *Mukhtaṣar*, p. 110.
89. Al-Shaybānī, *Jāmi' al-Ṣaghīr*, pp. 349–350.
90. Al-Ṭaḥāwī, *Mukhtaṣar*, pp. 106–107.
91. Al-Qudūrī, M*ukhtaṣar*, p. 110.
92. Hamilton, *Hidāya*, Commentary, p. 542.
93. Al-Qudūrī, *Mukhtaṣar*, p. 110.
94. Al-Qudūrī, *Mukhtaṣar*, p. 110.
95. Al- Shaybānī, *Jāmi' al-Ṣaghīr*, p. 350.
96. Al-Ṭaḥāwī, M*ukhtaṣar*, p. 107.
97. Al-Qudūrī, *Mukhtaṣar*, p. 111.
98. Al-Qudūrī, *Mukhtaṣar*, p. 111.
99. Al-Qudūrī, *Mukhtaṣar*, p. 111.
100. Al-Ṭaḥāwī, *Mukhtaṣar*, p. 107.
101. Hamilton, Hidāya, Commentary, p. 550.
102. Al-Qudūrī, *Mukhtaṣar*, p. 111.
103. Al-Ṭaḥāwī, *Mukhtaṣar,* p. 107.
104. Al-Ṭaḥāwī, *Mukhtaṣar*, p. 107.
105. Al-Ṭaḥāwī, *Mukhtaṣar*, p. 107.
106. Al-Qudūrī, *Mukhtaṣar*, p. 111.
107. Al-Qudūrī, *Mukhtaṣar*, p. 111.
108. Al-Qudūrī, *Mukhtaṣar*, p. 111.
109. *Bayḍ'a* is a portion of profit made on a previous mercantile sold in partnership in traffic.
110. Al-Qudūrī, *Mukhtaṣar*, p. 111.
111. Al-Ṭaḥāwī, *Mukhtaṣar*, p. 107.
112. Al-Ṭaḥāwī, *Mukhtaṣar*, p. 107.
113. Al-Ṭaḥāwī, *Mukhtaṣar*, p. 107.

114. Al-Qudūrī, *Mukhtaṣar*, p. 111.
115. Hamilton, *Hidāya*, Commentary, p. 556.
116. Al-Qudūrī, *Mukhtaṣar*, p. 112.
117. Al-Qudūrī, *Mukhtaṣar*, p. 112.
118. Al-Qudūrī, *Mukhtaṣar*, p. 112.
119. Al-Ṭaḥāwī, *Mukhtaṣar*, p. 108.
120. Al-Qudūrī, *Mukhtaṣar*, p. 112.
121. Al-Ṭaḥāwī, *Mukhtaṣar*, p. 108.
122. Al-Qudūrī, *Mukhtaṣar*, p. 112.
123. Al-Qudūrī, *Mukhtaṣar*, p. 101.
124. Al-Marghīnānī, *al-Hidāya*, p. 1267; Hamilton, *Hidāya*, Commentary, p. 201.
125. Al-Qudūrī, *Mukhtaṣar*, p. 101.
126. Al-Qudūrī, *Mukhtaṣar*, p. 101.
127. Al-Qudūrī, *Mukhtaṣar*, p. 101.
128. Al-Marghīnānī, *Hidāya*, p. 1269.
129. Al-Ṭaḥāwī, *Mukhtaṣar*, p. 128.
130. Al-Ṭaḥāwī, *Mukhtaṣar*, p. 128.
131. Al-Qudūrī, *Mukhtaṣar*, p. 105.
132. Al-Shaybānī, *Jāmi' al-Ṣaghīr*, p. 105.
133. Al-Qudūrī, *Mukhtaṣar*, p. 101.
134. Al-Shaybānī, *Jāmi' al-Ṣaghīr*, p. 364.
135. Al-Ṭaḥāwī, *Mukhtaṣar*, p. 128.
136. Al-Qudūrī, *Mukhtaṣar*, p. 101.
137. Al-Shaybānī, *Jāmi'al-Ṣaghīr*, p. 364.
138. Al-Qudūrī, *Mukhtaṣar*, pp. 101–102.
139. Al-Ṭaḥāwī, *Mukhtaṣar*, pp. 128–130.
140. Al-Shaybānī, *Jāmī'al-Ṣaghīr*, p. 361.
141. Al-Ṭaḥāwī, *Mukhtaṣar*, p. 128.
142. Al-Qudūrī, *Mukhtaṣar*, p. 104.
143. Al-Qudūrī, *Mukhtaṣar*, p. 102.
144. Al-Ṭaḥāwī, *Mukhtaṣar*, p. 129.
145. A certain measure of capacity.
146. Al-Shaybānī, *Jāmi'al-Ṣaghīr*, p. 359.
147. Al-Shaybānī, *Jāmi'al-Ṣaghīr*, p. 365.
148. Al-Ṭaḥāwī, *Mukhtaṣar*, p. 129.
149. Al-Qudūrī, *Mukhtaṣar*, p. 102.
150. Al-Shaybānī, *Jāmi' al-Ṣaghīr*, p. 366.
151. Al-Ṭaḥāwī, *Mukhtaṣar*, p. 120.
152. Al-Qudūrī, *Mukhtaṣar*, p. 102.
153. Al-Shaybānī, *Jāmī'al-Ṣaghīr*, p. 358.
154. Al-Qudūrī, *Mukhtaṣar*, p. 102.
155. Al-Qudūrī, *Mukhtaṣar*, p. 102.
156. Al-Shaybānī, *Jāmi' al-Ṣaghīr*, p. 366.
157. Al-Qudūrī, *Mukhtaṣar*, p. 103.
158. Al-Qudūrī, *Mukhtaṣar*, p. 103.

159. Al-Qudūrī, *Mukhtaṣar*, p. 104.
160. Al-Marghīnānī, *al-Hidāya*, p. 1279; Hamilton, *Hidāya*, Commentary, p. 218.
161. Al-Shaybānī, *Jāmi' al-Ṣaghīr*, pp. 359–360.
162. Al-Shaybānī, *Jāmi' al-Ṣaghīr*, p. 358.
163. Al-Ṭaḥāwī, *Mukhtaṣar*, p. 120.
164. Al-Qudūrī, *Mukhtaṣar*, p. 105.
165. Al-Shaybānī, *Jāmi' al-Ṣaghīr*, p. 362.

Chapter 5

Ḥanbalī School of Law

Hermeneutical as Reflected in al-Khiraqī's Mukhtaṣar

A BRIEF BIOGRAPHICAL ACCOUNT OF AḤMAD IBN ḤANBAL

Aḥmad ibn Muḥammad ibn Ḥanbal Abū 'Abd Allah al-Shaybānī (241/855) is considered eponym of the Ḥanbalī school of law. He studied extensively in Baghdad. He started studying *fiqh* under Abū Yūsuf. After finishing his studies with Abū Yūsuf, he began traveling through Iraq, Syria, and Arabia to collect prophetic *Ḥadīth* reports and became a leading authority on the collections of prophetic *Ḥadīth* reports. After several years of travel, he returned to Baghdad to study *fiqh* under al-Shāfi'ī.

Aḥmad ibn Ḥanbal was called before the inquisition (*miḥna*) of the 'Abbasid Caliph Mā'mūn, who wanted to assert the religious authority of Caliph by pressuring the *'ulamā'* to adopt the Mu'tazila doctrine that the *Qur'ān* was created. Due to refusal to accept the Mu'tazila doctrine, Ibn Ḥanbal was imprisoned in Baghdad throughout the reign of Mā'mūn after whose death he was flogged to unconsciousness in the reign of Mu'atasim, after whose death his successor Wāthiq continued his predecessor's policies of the Mu'tazila doctrine, and Aḥmad ibn Ḥanbal was put to death.

AḤMAD IBN ḤANBAL, THE *MUSNAD* AND ISLAMIC LAW

Aḥmad ibn Ḥanbal was primarily a traditionist (*muḥaddīth*), and at the same time, "as a traditionist he was a *faqīh*."[1] Since ibn Ḥanbal bases the *dicta* (*qāla* Ḥanbal) strictly on the *Qur'ān* and the prophetic *Ḥadīth* reports and makes the legal rulings based on them, he can, to that extent, be hermeneutically considered *faqīh*. He strongly advocated relying on the prophetic *Ḥadīth* reports, especially those reaching back to the Prophet himself. He gave more weight to them than the prophetic *Ḥadīth* reports from others. For Aḥmad Ibn Ḥanbal, reliance on the prophetic *Ḥadīth* reports was essential for the law to know what the Prophet and other early Muslims had said and done.

AL-SHĀFI'Ī'S CONCEPT OF HERMENEUTICS AND AḤMAD IBN ḤANBAL AS A JURISPRUDENT IN RELATION TO AL-SHĀFI'Ī, MUḤAMMAD AL-SHAYBĀNĪ, AND MĀLIK IBN ANAS

The main contention of al-Shāfi'ī's hermeneutics was to hermeneutically relate the legal rulings to the legal canons in accordance with the revealed sources in the formation of Islamic law. But in doing so, he simultaneously made the traditionist position to prevail in Islamic legal theory which became science by setting out a methodology. In respect to the use and importance of the prophetic *Ḥadīth* reports in all four Sunni Islamic schools of law, we find only there are differences in the purpose they are pursued, degree, and the emphasis laid on the prophetic *Ḥadīth* reports. For al-Shāfi'ī, though the *Qur'ān* is ontologically primary, the prophetic *Ḥadīth* reports serve epistemologically more for relating legal rulings to the legal canons in the hermeneutical formation of Islamic legal system.

In Mālik's *Muwaṭṭa'*, we find the inclusion of the prophetic *Ḥadīth* reports. Mālik's *Muwaṭṭa'* is the first work in which the prophetic *Ḥadīth* reports themselves are used as the basis for the legal opinions. For example, the fruit of trees which have been sold belongs to the seller is based on what the prophetic *Ḥadīth* report exactly states: Yaḥyā related from Mālik from Nafī from 'Abd Allah ibn 'Umar that the Prophet said, "If palm trees are sold after they have been pollinated, *the fruit belong to the seller unless the purchaser makes a stipulation about its inclusion*."[2] This ruling neither needs hermeneutically further interpretation nor canonizing. The prophetic *Ḥadīth* report itself interprets what is intended in this transaction, although the final authority on any given legal opinion, according to Mālik, is *ijmā'*. Mālik, like al-Shāfi'ī, made use of the prophetic *Ḥadīth* reports, but like al-Shāfi'ī, made the traditionist position prevail. In terms of the position as *faqīh*, he is to be considered first a traditionist and then a jurisprudent, who makes the legal opinions based on the prophetic *Ḥadīth* reports. This limits his capacity to derive legal opinions involving hermeneutically interpretative process for further development in systemizing hermeneutically Islamic law. Aḥmad ibn Ḥanbal is considered foremost a traditionist. His *Masā'il Collections* manifest a traditionist "reaction" to the systematization of Islamic law of al-Shāfi'ī, Abū Ḥanīfa, Abū Yūsuf, Muḥammad al-Shaybānī, and Mālik. It is narrated by 'Abd Allah that his father Aḥmad ibn Ḥanbal saying that

> Abū Ḥanīfa wrote a book, then Muḥammad ibn Ḥasan (al-Shaybānī) came and wrote a book—there is no end to this. Whenever a man comes along, he writes a book. This Mālik wrote a book, al-Shāfi'ī came and wrote a book too. . . . These books that have been written are an innovation. Whenever a man comes along he writes a book and abandons the prophetic *Ḥadīth* reports of the Messenger of God.[3]

This is actually not the case as it is obvious from our discourse in the foregoing Chapters. This statement may not be quite accurate, but it indicates the extreme traditionist attitude of Aḥmad ibn Ḥanbal. When he was asked whether he preferred the books of al-Shāfi'ī and Mālik or Abū Ḥanīfa and Abū Yūsuf, his answer was that he preferred al-Shāfi'ī, who gives juridical opinions based on the prophetic *Ḥadīth* reports, whereas others give opinions based on *ra'y*. But, the fact is that al-Shāfi'ī uses it hermeneutically to systematize the Islamic law and does not limit himself to the prophetic *Ḥadīth* reports. For al-Shāfi'ī, the *Qur'ān* and the prophetic *Ḥadīth* reports are used as the hermeneutical method by which the jurist form rulings.

For Aḥmad ibn Ḥanbal, the revealed sources themselves determine the ruling and there is no need for further hermeneutical development and systematization of the Islamic legal system. It was later Ḥanbalī jurisprudents, who in interactions with the other Sunni schools of law, used a hermeneutical method to systematize the Islamic legal system. "The recording of Aḥmad ibn Ḥanbal's opinions by various disciples, the synthesis of most *Masā'il Collections* by Khallāl and the *Epitome* (*Mukhtaṣar*) by al-Khiraqī, and the work of the Abū Ya'la ibn al-Farra' made it acquire the character of a distinctive school of law."[4]

AḤMAD BIN ḤANBAL'S *MASĀ'IL COLLECTIONS* AND AL-SHĀFI'Ī'S CONCEPT OF HERMENEUTICS

Aḥmad ibn Ḥanbal's *Masā'il Collections* contains not only the prophetic *Ḥadīth* reports, but also his juristic *dicta* (*qāla* Ḥanbal) as a juristic authority. Aḥmad bin Ḥanbal is mostly humble in expressing the *dicta* assertions as his opinion, but later Ḥanbalī jurists took them as his *dicta* and his authority as a jurist raised his rank to the eponyms Abū Ḥanīfa, al-Shāfi'ī, and Mālik ibn Anas. To the extent Aḥmad bin Ḥanbal uses the revealed sources consisting of the *Qur'ān* and the prophetic *Ḥadīth* reports, he is considered in the party of al-Shāfi'ī, but that does not qualify him hermeneutically in his use of the revealed sources as a jurist for evolving, developing, and systematizing Islamic legal system in a hermeneutically. This hermeneutical task was undertaken later by the jurists of Ḥanbalī school of law as we find in Ḥanbalī jurist al-Khiraqī's composition of *Mukhtaṣar.*

A BRIEF BIOGRAPHICAL ACCOUNT OF 'UMAR IBN AL-ḤUSAYN AL-KHIRAQĪ

'Umar ibn al-Ḥusayn al-Baghdādī under the name of Abū Qāsim al-Khiraqī (324/946) was one of the most celebrated Ḥanbalī jurisprudent. He was first guided into the Ḥanbalī *madhhab* by his father Abū 'Alī Khirūfi. He was himself a student of Abū Bakr al-Mawardī.

When the Shi'ī Būyid arrived in Baghdad, al-Khiraqī left Iraqi capital seeking refuge in Damascus, where Ḥanbalī school of law was beginning to establish. It is said that al-Khiraqī had denounced publicly in Damascus a "reprehensible practice" *(munkar)*, whose nature is not specified for which he was condemned to be flogged, because of which he died.[5]

It is said that he wrote numerous works whose titles are not known and all of which are lost, except his *Mukhtaṣar* which has come down to us. The success of al-Khiraqī's *Mukhtaṣar* was so great that more than thirty *Sharḥ* were written on it by various jurists in the following generations as mentioned by Muḥammad bin Nāẓir al-'Ajamī.[6]

"Abū al- Qāsim Khiraqī was the most prominent jurist after Abū Bakr al-Khallāl. Al-Khiraqī seems not to have studied under Khallāl as Ghulam al-Khallāl."[7]

AḤMAD IBN ḤANBAL AND HIS *MASĀ'IL COLLECTIONS* IN CONTRAST TO THE WORKS OF EPONYMS OF OTHER SUNNI SCHOOLS OF LAW

Aḥmad ibn Ḥanbal's *Masā'il Collections* are the best source of his legal opinions. The *Masā'il Collections* differ greatly from al-Shāfi'ī's *K al-Umm*, Muḥammad al-Shaybānī's *Jāmi' al-Ṣaghīr*, and Mālik ibn Anas' *Muwaṭṭa'*. Al-Shāfi'ī is a jurist par excellence. He as a jurist who uses epistemologically prophetic *Ḥadīth* reports for making legal rulings besides the *Qur'ān* and other sources, as one of the vehicles for making rulings. Abū Yūsuf and Muḥammad al-Shaybānī were basically jurisprudents and besides using the revealed sources they used *ra'y,* though they do not seem to use al-Shāfi'ī's notion of hermeneutics and its techniques, but their procedure in practice is the same as we have discussed in chapter 3. Mālik ibn Anas'

Muwaṭṭa' manifests the same trends, only that his procedure is first to narrate the prophetic *Ḥadīth* reports and according to it, he asserts his juristic opinion relating to the various, situations, or issues (*masā'il*). However, Aḥmad ibn Ḥanbal's *Masā'il Collections* is visibly different. For him, the prophetic *Ḥadīth* reports and the *Qur'ān* are the primary authority and whatever rulings are provided in them, they are sufficient in the formation of Islamic law.

As far as *Masā'il Collections* concerning the civil and commercial law, Ibn Ḥanbal cites the *Qur'ān* occasionally, to be specific, only one time concerning *ribā* (2:279).[8] Thus, what the prophetic *Ḥadīth* report states itself sets the law rather than the jurist, who first states the problem for which he provides the prophetic *Ḥadīth* report as evidence in its support. For any ruling, Ibn Ḥanbal first states the prophetic *Ḥadīth* report and then in the second place as a jurist he gives his juristic opinion (*dicta*) regarding an issue. "The *Masā'il Collections* purport to record a series of short statements, either in response to the questions from his son 'Abdallah, the compiler of *Masā'il Collections* or from others, which the compiler has overheard. As a result, the *Masā'il Collections* "has a narrow range than that acquired in the century after his death."[9] It were later Ḥanbalī jurists, who adopting to al-Shāfi'ī's hermeneutic within the parameter and scope of the *Masā'il Collections*, systematized the Islamic law. The literary development of Ḥanbalī school of law was the synthesis in the last third of ninth century by all available *Masā'il Collections* by Abū Bakr al-Khallāl, followed by the composition of the first epitome of Ḥanbalī school of law by al-Khiraqī's *Mukhtaṣar*. As we shall see al-Khiraqī in the *Mukhtaṣar* accepts al-Shāfi'īs hermeneutics, though he also does not cite any prophetic *Ḥadīth* reports.

As far as the contribution of Aḥmad ibn Ḥanbal to the hermeneutical formation of Islamic law is concerned, the *Masā'il Collections* consists mostly of the prophetic *Ḥadīth* reports. The *qāla* assertions of Aḥmad ibn Ḥanbal are depended upon them amounting hermeneutically minimum interpretative use in formulating and articulating the legal rules in accordance with the legal canons. Thus, juristically speaking, Aḥmad ibn Ḥanbal's *Masā'il Collections* does not reflect hermeneutically a greater interpretative use. It was after his death that the Ḥanbalī *corpus* of legal doctrines evolved as the Islamic legal system by a group of scholars such as al-Khiraqī and others.

When one sees this from the point of hermeneutics, the Ḥanbalī legal *corpus* is the product refined over the generations. The real reason behind this phenomenon was that it was the acceptance and reception of al-Shāfi'ī' concept of hermeneutics by the later Ḥanbalī jurists, who developed it through respecting and recognizing Aḥmad ibn Ḥanbal as an authority, notwithstanding what was missing of al-Shāfi'ī' concept of hermeneutics in his legal doctrines.

HERMENEUTICAL GENERAL FEATURES AS REFLECTED CONCERNING THE NATURE OF CONTRACT AND CONTENTS IN AḤMAD IBN ḤANBAL'S *MASĀ'IL COLLECTIONS* AND AL-KHIRAQĪ'S *MUKHTAṢAR* CONCERNING THE NATURE OF CONTRACT IN CHAPTER *AL-BUYŪ'*

Aḥmad Ibn Ḥanbal in his *Masā'il Collections* as well as al-Khiraqī in his *Mukhtaṣar* do not discuss juristically the nature of contract.

HERMENEUTICAL GENERAL FEATURES OF RIGHT OF OPTION AS REFLECTED IN THE CONTENTS IN AḤMAD IBN ḤANBAL'S *MASĀ'IL COLLECTIONS* AND AL-KHIRAQĪ'S *MUKHTAṢAR*

Aḥmad ibn Ḥanbal states: It is narrated to us that the purchaser and the seller both have right of option, so long as they do not separate from each other.[10] Aḥmad ibn Ḥanbal's account of the right of option is short, whereas al-Khiraqī opens chapter *al-Buyū'* with right of option. It is extensive and describes all expanded additional elements involved in right of option stating with clarity that both parties to the contract have right of option. If the article of sale is destroyed or the purchaser emancipates a slave without taking him into his possession or if he dies, the right of option is void. If they separate from each other without canceling contract, neither the seller nor the purchaser can return the article of exchange, except if it is found with defect or if the right of option was stipulated in the contract.[11] Al-Khiraqī's account of right of option is concise and brings the expanded additional elements not included in Aḥmad ibn Ḥanbal's account of the right of option. This is simply because his account of it is limited to the extent of what the prophetic *Ḥadīth* states. Neither the interlocutor nor did his son ask any further questions. Aḥmad ibn Ḥanbal expressed his own opinion as jurisprudent what is stated in the prophetic *Ḥadīth* reports.

HERMENEUTICAL GENERAL FEATURES OF *RIBĀ* IN THE *ṢARF* SALE AS REFLECTED IN THE CONTENTS AḤMAD IBN ḤANBAL'S *MASĀ'IL COLLECTIONS* AND IN AL-KHIRAQĪ'S *MUKHTAṢAR*[12]

Al-Khiraqī in his Mukhtaṣar discusses *ribā* and *ṣarf* together under one heading.

Aḥmad ibn Ḥanbal's account of *ṣarf* sale is based on the prophetic *Ḥadīth* report that it is invalid to sell articles (in the same species) of weight at an unequal rate. It should not be different in weight in the balance of pans. How it can be pure (agreeable) when one article is more in weight than the other? It is like cheating.[13] In contrast to it, al-Khiraqī's account of *ṣarf* sale comprises expanded additional elements including articles of weight and measurement. It includes al-Shāfi'ī's classification of the things. If the articles are of the same species, one article should not exceed in weight to that of the other article, but if they are of two different species, then the weight of one article can exceed the weight of another article. The exchange of articles should be from hand to hand at the spot. The article (price) in exchange payable at a future specified time is invalid. Thus, Aḥmad ibn Ḥanbal's account is not only based on the prophetic *Ḥadīth* report but also is confined to that extent without further hermeneutically interpretative use in systematizing the legal rules by incorporating the expanded additional elements as we find in al-Khiraqī's account.

Al-Khiraqī being aware of al-Shāfi'ī's concept of hermeneutics and his classification of articles into species, and kinds, describes as the authors of the compositions of *Mukhtaṣar* in Shāfi'ī, Ḥanafī, and Mālikī schools of law do, that is, if the articles of the exchange are of the same species such as the exchange of grapes for raisin, it is valid only as the *'arāya.*

Wheat and barley are considered of two different species, but all kinds of meat are considered of the same species. It is not valid to sell one kind of meat in exchange for another kind of meat when they are moist. When they have become dried, the exchange of like for like by estimate is valid.

In the *ṣarf*, the sale of meat in exchange for an animal is not valid.

If one purchases gold in exchange for silver and one of them (either the purchaser or the seller) finds defect in the article of exchange, then he has the right of option either to accept it or to return it. If the defect has not occurred to it from mixing it with other things, then the purchaser takes the price in proportion to the loss. If the exchange was without any specification (*'aynayhi*), and he finds defect in the article of exchange, then the substitute for it is valid. If the defect has not occurred from (mixing) anything such as whitening it in gold and blackness in silver, then the substitute is void. When both parties have made exchange of articles and have not taken them into their possession, then there is no sale between them.

It is permitted on the authority of prophetic *Ḥadīth* report that the *'arāya* in the *ṣarf* sale is permitted, that is, when a person gives a gift of palm fruits to another person not of more than five *awsāq* in weight. The sale of the edible moist dates by estimate is invalid when they are left on the tree until they become ripe.

Al-Khiraqī's account of *ribā* and *ṣarf* sale differ in some minor respects from those of the other schools of law. Nonetheless, they are developed and to a certain extent al-Khiraqī incorporated them hermeneutically in the Ḥanbalī legal *corpus*.

HERMENEUTICAL GENERAL FEATURES AS REFLECTED IN THE CONTENTS OF SELLING FRUITS IN AḤMAD IBN ḤANBAL'S *MASĀ'IL COLLECTIONS* AND AL-KHIRAQĪ'S *MUKHTAṢAR*[14]

In Aḥmad ibn Ḥanbal's *Masā'il Collections* one does not find specific chapter under the heading "Principles of Selling Fruits." Al-Khiraqī's title "Principles of Selling Fruits" is as we find in al-Shāfi'ī's *K al-Umm.*

In Aḥmad ibn Ḥanbal's *Masā'il Collections*, there is only one narration based on the authority of Prophet. It is regarding the calamity which befalls the fruits while they are still growing (*raūs al-nakhl*) and the fruits become destroyed, then there is nothing for the seller, because there is no usufruct of it for the purchaser.

A person sells the dates still growing on a palm tree and when they appear to break up, namely when they become ripe, and if they are left for the seller to cut them down, they belong to the seller, except if it was stipulated that they belong to the purchaser.

It is not valid if a person sells fruits which are *dūna al-aṣl*, namely, they are not ripe until they are left to be plucked. However, if he sells it on the condition that they would be cut down, plucked and picked, then it is valid. If it is stipulated that until fruits are ripe, then its sell is void (since from the very beginning the condition was that it is invalid, if the fruits do not become ripe).

If one sells fruits on the condition that after they become ripe until after they are left to be plucked, it is valid.

If fruits on palm tree begin to become ripe, manifesting color yellow or red, then the sale is valid. If fruits become grapes and begin to be watery and sour while becoming ripe and do not look like the dates or grapes, then it is not valid.

It is valid to sell cucumbers, eggplants, and other similar things and, likewise, all moist articles when they are ripe, cut and plucked.

The harvesting is incumbent on the purchaser. If it is stipulated to be incumbent on the seller, then the sale is considered invalid.

If one sells orchard and makes a certain measurement of *ṣā'a* exempted from it, it is not valid. However, if he exempts certain palm trees or trees from it, it is valid.

One purchases fruits and the damage from nature befalls them before he takes them into his possession, it is considered damage from the property of seller.

If the damage happens on the articles of measurement, weight, or quantity, before they are taken into possession, it is considered from the property of seller, except when taking them into possession was not needed and they have been destroyed, then it is considered from the property of the purchaser.

If one purchases a thing which needs to be taken into possession, he is not allowed to sell it unless after he has taken it into his possession.

The partnership, friendly partnership and transfer of the property are considered species of the contract of sale and not cancellation, in contrast to it Aḥmad ibn Ḥanbal maintains that the cancellations are considered sale as they are related to it.

If one purchases food in lump, he is not allowed to sell it, unless it is transferred to him. If he knows approximately total amount of it and not its exact measurement, he is not allowed to sell it. If one purchases it in lump and knows its exact measurement, then it is valid.

HERMENEUTICAL GENERAL FEATURES OF *SALAM* SALE AS REFLECTED IN THE CONTENTS OF AḤMAD IBN ḤANBAL'S *MASĀ'IL COLLECTIONS* AND AL-KHIRAQĪ'S *MUKHTAṢAR*

Aḥmad ibn Ḥanbal's account of *salam* sale is based on three prophetic *Ḥadīth* reports with complete chain of narrations and the rest of others are *qāla* Ibn Aḥmad. In contrast to Aḥmad ibn Ḥanbal's account, al-Khiraqī's *salam* sale is precise and articulated covering the expanded additional elements related to the *salam* sale.

Qāla ibn Ḥanbal: the *salam* sale is *salaf* sale.[15]

Qāla ibn Ḥanbal: The *salam* sale is not objectionable regarding animals with description and specified time of delivery.[16] In contrast, al-Khiraqī's account is extensive and includes *salam* sale of all articles known with the description of their measurement, or weight, or quantity and specified time of their delivery. The articles should be in existence at the time of drawing the contract and the price is paid to the seller in advance before parties separate from each other.[17]

When any one of the descriptions is failing, then the *salam* sale before the article of exchange is taken into possession from the seller is void. Likewise, the *salam* sale is void failing any of the descriptions in the partnership, friendly partnership and transfer of food articles or any other articles.[18]

Qāla ibn Aḥmad that the price in *salaf* sale to be paid at a specified future time is not objectionable.[19]

According to al-Khiraqī, the *salam* sale of two articles in one price is not valid, unless the price of each single article is specified. If one of the articles is delivered at a different time from the other article, it is valid.[20]

According to al-Khiraqī, it is not valid to take security (*rahan*) or surety (*kafīl*) from a person to whom article is to be delivered. Al-Khiraqī is bringing this expanded additional element in his composition of *Mukhtaṣar*. The authors of other compositions of *Mukhtaṣar* have so far not included this point in their compositions of *Mukhtaṣar*.

Qāla Aḥmad ibn Ḥanbal on the authority of Prophet narrated by Ibn Mas'ūd: *salaf* sale is not objectionable of things other than animals.

The following *Qāla* Aḥmad ibn Ḥanbal are neither included in al-Khiraqī's account nor does he expound on their implications.

What is *salam* sale?

Qāla Aḥmad ibn Ḥanbal: when a person gives *dirhams* to another person in return for bringing a specified measure of food and says to him "I lent you (*dirhams*) to deliver it to the people of my land (*sawādī*), or to my town, or to my place of arrival (*mawṣūlī*)," and "I lent you *dirhams* not to purchase chicken or small country estate," because it is not known if from these chickens would come out something or not.'[21] In other words, *dirham* are given in advance to deliver the item as specified, otherwise *salam* sale is void.

Qāla Aḥmad ibn Ḥanbal: Likewise, regarding meat I said to him, "I lent you flesh of an elderly animal from its side or thigh as described as well as its head, and head load. Do not take what is superior but take lesser or inferior."[22] In other words, it is not valid to take more of something in weight or measurement in exchange for the other thing, but only equal in weight or measurement. Al-Khiraqī does not include it, since to take more in quantity of one thing in exchange for the other thing in quantity, weight, or measurement is considered *ribā* in all kinds of sales in general.

Qāla Aḥmad ibn Ḥanbal: A person sold wheat in the *salaf* sale and when the time arrived of its delivery, he did not have it into his possession and he said to the person take barley in exchange for *dirhams*, (or) take from me price, he said, "Do not take the barley except in exact measurement of barely or lesser, but not more than that. I said to my father: was it ten sacks of barely for which to take ten sacks of barely?"[23] He said: yes.

To conclude, al-Khiraqī's account of *salam* sale is in many aspects hermeneutically sound and in pace with hermeneutically evolvement of the Islamic legal system.

HERMENEUTICAL GENERAL FEATURES OF LEASE-HIRE IN AḤMAD IBN ḤANBAL'S *MASĀ'IL COLLECTIONS* AND AL-KHIRAQĪ'S *MUKHTAṢAR* REGARDING THE LEASE-HIRE[24]

In the *Masā'il Collections* of ibn Ḥanbal, we do not find any account of lease-hire. In contrast, al-Khiraqī's account is as extensive as we find in other compositions of *Mukhtaṣar* of Sunni schools of law. This shows that al-Khiraqī in his composition of *Mukhtaṣar* incorporates hermeneutically the expanded additional elements in the formation of Islamic legal system.

Al-Khiraqī, as other jurists of his time, does not cite any prophetic *Ḥadīth* reports. In his account of lease-hire, only one prophetic narration is referred.

When contract of lease-hire comes into effect for a specified time, then lease holder acquires right to usufruct the property. The full amount of lease-hire becomes due at the time of concluding the contract, except if it is stipulated to be paid later at a future specified time.

If the contract of lease-hire comes into effect for the whole one month by specification, neither party to the contract can cancel it, except until whole month is expired.

If immovable property is leased-hired for a specified period and if it begins before having taken it into possession, then payment for lease-hire becomes incumbent on leaseholder and owner of immovable property has no right to make usufruct of it, except at the expiration of the contract of lease-hire.

If owner of property changes before lease has expired, then there is no payment of rent for time during which the lease holder has lived in property, because usually the rent is paid at the time of lease agreement and it should have already been collected by the previous owner of property.

If lease holder is prevented from using it, then payment of rent is incumbent on him in proportion for the period he has lived in.

If lease holder becomes sick for any reason and stays in property longer, payment of rent is incumbent upon him for it. If the leaseholder or lessor dies, the contract of lease-hire remains the same without any change and does not become dissolved.

If a person leases-hires immovable property, he has right to let someone who is his representative to reside in it.

The expenses for food and clothing for the one who has been hired for any services is valid. Likewise, the expenses for food and clothing for wet nurse is valid. However, it is preferable to give wages to female slave, who weans the child as it is narrated in the prophetic *Ḥadīth* report "if she lets the child suckle."

A person leases-hires an animal to ride on it to a certain place and goes beyond it, then payment of rent is incumbent on him as specified in addition to payment of rent for what he has gone beyond. If animal dies during his travel, the price of the animal is incumbent upon him. Likewise, if the lease-hire an animal is to transport anything, and it is more than what is specified, then payment of rent is incumbent for that load.

It is not valid that one leases-hires going beyond the specified period. It is not valid to lease-hire, if the duration of lease is not specified. If the days for which the contract of lease-hire is specified, it is valid.

If one leases-hires an animal to travel to Mecca and the lessor has not seen that there are two travelers, their luggage, covering, and all other things, then it is not valid to rent it.

If there are two co-drivers and they are specified, and their load in the amount of in *raṭl* is known, it is valid.

Regarding wares, which is in the possession of worker, if it is destroyed while it is in his custody, he is not considered responsible for it, but there are no wages for the work he has performed. The cupper, circumciser, or medical doctor, who is known for his skills and there is no accusation against him, and has not transgressed, they are not held responsible.

HERMENEUTICAL GENERAL FEATURES OF PARTNERSHIP AS REFLECTED IN THE CONTENTS OF AḤMAD IBN ḤANBAL'S *MASĀ'IL COLLECTIONS*

Aḥmad Ibn Ḥanbal's remark regarding partnership is relatively very brief and much desired for its hermeneutical systematization. It does not describe all kinds of partnership. Like al-Shāfi'ī and Mālik ibn Anas, Ahmad bin Ḥanbal considers partnership in reciprocity invalid. Such a partnership when two persons say, "what we inherit or acquire profit or capital, it is between two of us," such a thing is for Aḥmad ibn Ḥanbal unthinkable.[25]

Aḥmad ibn Ḥanbal considers that two persons joining in partnership with the wares (*'ayn*) and if they are in debt, it is invalid.[26] The implications are that the partners should have capital consisting of *dīnārs* ad *dirhams*. It also suggests that the *shirka al*-wujūh, which is considered valid in the Ḥanafī school of law, is repugnant according to Aḥmad ibn Ḥanbal.

Aḥmad bin Ḥanbal narrates that the partnership of Muslim with *dhimmī* is not objectionable, if they join in partnership with *dirhams* and engage in trading, but a Jew or a Christian is not paid any wages, because he is himself the owner.[27] The last part of the statement is ambiguous, since a Jew or a Christian is presumably under *dhimma* and, secondly, if he is allowed to join in partnership with Muslim, then they should have an equal status with each other in the wages, profit or loss.

Regarding the provisions, a partner can be compensated, which is determined in proportion to the capital in partnership and not more than that.[28]

This account of Aḥmad Ibn Ḥanbal of partnership barely covers all kinds of partnerships and the details related to them. It is almost like al-Shāfi'ī's account of partnership narrated in a rudimentary form in the *K al-Umm*.

HERMENEUTICAL GENERAL FEATURES AS REFLECTED IN AL-KHIRAQĪ'S PARTNERSHIP[29]

Al-Khiraqī's account is extensive. It describes all kinds of partnerships systematically covering the essential elements of the partnerships comparable to the account of partnerships of al-Shāfi'ī', Ḥanafī, and Mālikī authors of the compositions of *Mukhtaṣar*. From this, it becomes evident that al-Khiraqī is one of the earliest jurists in the Ḥanbalī school of law, who is the pioneer in hermeneutically developing and comprehensively systematizing Islamic legal system.

The partnership in workmanship (*shirka abdān*) is valid. If two persons join in partnership having one partner or both partners capital or both with the manual labor without capital, or with manual labor and capital, or both with capital and one of them with manual labor, or both with capital and manual labor, whether in equal amount of capital or different, all of it is valid. The profit is divided between them as agreed upon between them.

It is not valid that the wages of one the partners exceed to the wages of another partner. If a silent partner (*muḍārib)* sells anything on credit without he has been commissioned by the other partner, then there are two legal opinions: according to Ibn Aḥmad Ḥanbal, he is held responsible for it. According to other narration, he is not responsible for it.

If he (silent partner) commissions a person to do any business transactions with the capital, then it is not valid that he commissions another person, because in that case there would occure loss to the first person who has been commissioned. If he does so and there is any profit, then it is returned to the first person who has been commissioned.

The profit is not valid for the silent partner (*muḍārib*) unless the full amount of capital in advance is received. If he sells two things in one transaction and there is a profit in one thing and a loss in other thing, then it is reciprocated from the profit. This is an expanded additional element incorporated by al-Khiraqī in his *Mukhtaṣar*.

If the partner thinks that the property in his hand is in excess, it is not valid that he takes anything from it except with the permission of the owner of capital.

If the owner and the silent partner (*muḍārib)* agree upon the profit between two of them to be divided according to the capital deposited as security money in the partnership, then the profit is divided accordingly.

It is not valid if it is said to a person, who is in a debt to tread with the property deposited as security money to him.

The deposit is determined in proportion to the capital each partner contributes in the partnership.

NOTES

1. Susan A. Spectorsky, "Ibn Ḥanbal's Fiqh," *Journal of the American Oriental Society*, vol. 102, no. 3, 1962, p. 461.
2. Mālik ibn Anas, *Al-Muwaṭṭa'*, translated by Aisha Abdurrahman Bewley (Scotland: Madinah Press Inverness, 2011), p. 251.
3. Melchert, *Aḥmad Ibn Ḥanbal*, p. 65.
4. Melchert, *Aḥmad Ibn Ḥanbal*, p. 79.
5. Muḥammad bin Nāẓir al-'Ajamī (edit), *al-Mukhtaṣar fī al-fiqh lī 'Umar bin Ḥusayn al-Khiraqī* (Kuwait: Dār al-Nawādir, 1429), p. 55.
6. 'Ajamī, *Mukhtaṣar fī al-Fiqh*, pp. 35–41.
7. Christopher Melchert, *The Formation of the Sunni Schools of Law, 9–10th Centuries C.E* (Leiden: Brill, 1997), pp. 148–49.
8. Aḥmad Ibn Ḥanbal, *Masā'il Collections*, riwāya ibnhu 'Abdallah ibn Aḥmad (Beirut: Kutab al-Islamīya, 1971), p. 292.
9. Melchert, *Aḥmad Ibn Ḥanbal*, p. viii.
10. Ibn Ḥanbal, *Masā'il* 1039, p. 1039.
11. 'Umar Ibn Husayn Al-Khiraqī, *Mukhtaṣar fī al-Fiqh*, p. 169.
12. Al-Khiraqī, *Mukhtaṣar*, pp. 170–171.
13. Aḥmad Ibn Ḥanbal, *Masā'il*, 1077, p. 279.
14. Al-Khiraqī, *Mukhtaṣar*, pp. 172–173.
15. Ibn Ḥanbal, *Masā'il*, 1067, p. 287.
16. Ibn Ḥanbal, *Masā'il*, 1069 and 1070, p. 287.
17. Al-Khiraqī, *Mukhtaṣar*, p. 178.
18. Al-Khiraqī, *Mukhtaṣar*, p. 178.
19. Ibn Ḥanbal, *Masā'il*, 1070 and 1071, p. 287.
20. Ibn Ḥanbal, *Masā'il*, p. 178.
21. Al-Khiraqī, *Mukhtaṣar*, pp. 278–279.
22. Ibn Ḥanbal, *Masā'il*, p. 288.
23. Al-Khiraqī, *Mukhtaṣar*, p. 179.
24. Al-Khiraqī, *Mukhtaṣar*, pp. 196–197.

25. Ibn Ḥanbal, *Masā'il,* 1099, p. 295.
26. Ibn Ḥanbal, *Masā'il,* 1099, p. 295.
27. Ibn Ḥanbal, *Masā'il,* 1100, pp. 295–296.
28. Ibn Ḥanbal, *Masā'il,* 1101, p. 296.
29. Al-Khiraqī, *Mukhtaṣar*, pp. 186–187.

Chapter 6

Mālikī School of Law

Hermeneutics as Reflected in al-Khalīl's Mukhtaṣar

A BRIEF BIOGRAPHICAL ACCOUNT OF MĀLIK BIN ANAS

The exact date of birth of Abū 'Abd Allah Mālik bin Anas ibn Mālik is not known. He died at the age of eighty-five in the year 179/795. He belonged to the Humayar who was included in the Banū ibn Murra. Legend is that he spent three years in his mother's womb. The Prophet himself is said to have foretold his coming as well as that of Abū Ḥanīfa, and al-Shāfi'ī. It is said that he wanted to become a singer but changed his career for the study of the *fiqh* on his mother's advice because of his physical appearance.

Mālik ibn Anas studied *fiqh* with Rabi'al-Farrūq, who cultivated *ra'y* in Medina. He transmitted prophetic *Ḥadīth* reports from al-Zuhrī, Nāfī, Mawla ibn 'Omar, and many others.

MĀLIK'S *MUWAṬṬA'*

The *Muwaṭṭa'* of Mālik is considered one of the oldest surviving books of the Islamic legal system. Mālik is the first jurist to use the name *Muwaṭṭa'*. Before whom those who authored books on law in his age used to call them the *Comprehensive* (*al-Jāmi'*) or the *Compilation* (*Muṣannaf*). "The word *muwaṭṭa'* means that which is made easy and is pruned and trimmed of superfluous matters."[1]

Mālik compiled the *Muwaṭṭa'* intending to include exclusively the strong prophetic *Ḥadīth* reports of the people of Ḥijāz combined with the sayings of Companions, and Followers. According to some, Mālik's *Muwaṭṭa'* is the first recorded collection of prophetic *Ḥadīth* reports. In that respect, it came to be seen as the transition from the simple *fiqh* to the pure science of prophetic *Ḥadīth* reports.[2]

"The transformation of Mālik into the mediator (through the *isnāds)* of ideally prophetic authority and into an exegete (through the appended juristic *dicta* (*qāla* Mālik) are one of the key elements in the creation of hermeneutics,"[3] though his *dicta* are entirely confined to the prophetic *Ḥadīth* reports. As a result, hermeneutical interpretations in it are limited to that extent. It was later that Mālikī jurists in the next succeeding generations, who developed it further with the acceptance of al-Shāfi'ī's concept of hermeneutics.

> The *Muwaṭṭa'* is composed of numerous discrete items, exhibiting two basic forms. First, there are prophetic *Ḥadīth* reports, characterized by a formal chain of narrations (*isnad,* pl. of *ṣanad*), introduced by *ḥaddatha-nī 'an Mālik.* This change of narrations may end at the Prophet, or at the Companion, or at the Follower, or an ancient Jurist. Secondly, there are juristic *dicta* characterized by the introductory formula *qāla Mālik.*[4]

DIFFERENT RECENSIONS OF THE *MUWAṬṬA'*[5]

There are about fifteen different recensions of Mālik's *Muwaṭṭa'*. Some of these include version of Yaḥyā ibn Yaḥyā (234/849), version of Abū Muḥammad 'Abdalla ibn Salama al-Fikhrī al-Miṣrī ibn Wahb (197/813), version of Abū 'Abd Allah 'Abd al-Raḥmān ibn al-Qāsim (191/807), version of Abū Yaḥyā Ma'īn 'Isā ibn Dīnār al-Madanī (198/814), version of Abū Muṣ'ab al-Zuhrī (242/857), and version of Muḥammad ibn al Ḥasan al-Shaybānī, the disciple of Abū Ḥanīfa.

A BRIEF ACCOUNT OF BIOGRAPHY OF KHALĪL BIN ISḤĀQ

Isḥāq bin Mūsa Shu'ayb Khalīl known also as al-Jundī died in the year 776/1374. He belonged to the Mālikī school of law. He was from a noble family of the army circle of Manṣūra. His father was Ḥanafī. It was through the influence of his teacher 'Abd Allāh al-Manūfī that he adopted Mālikī school of law. He was an ascetic completely cut off from the world devoting himself acquiring knowledge and doing pious deeds.[6]

He was an eminent scholar endowed with a brilliant mind, quick-witted, and perfect in combining nobility and honor, living a God-fearing life as an ascetic. He committed the *Qur'ān* to memory at the age of thirteen and attended the Jāmi' Azhar. He studied under al-Kawkab al-Munīr, 'Abd al-Jawād al-Shayāsī, 'Iwad Sunbāwī, and many others. He taught the *'Ilm al-'Aqalīya wa Naqlīya* at the Jāmi' Azhar.[7]

Khalīl composed the *Sharḥ al-Jalīl* which is in four volumes, the *Mawāhib al-Qādir* which is also in four volumes, *Hāshīya 'alā Hāmish*, and *Hāshiya 'alā Sharḥ al-Amīr*, which is originally *Mawāhib al-Qādir* known as the *Jāmi' al-Kabīr 'alā Majmū'a al-Amīr.*[8]

VARIOUS *SHARḤ* (COMMENTARIES) ON KHALĪL'S *MUKHTAṢAR*

More than one hundred *Sharḥ* have been written on Khalīl's *Mukhtaṣar*. The unique feature of Khalīl's *Mukhtaṣar* is that the entire treatise is composed by expressing the rulings denoted by a short phrase indicating *mashhūr* legal opinions of the jurists ranging from Mālik ibn Anas and 'Abd al-Salām bin Sa'd Saḥnūn and the jurists in next generations. More than one hundred *Sharḥ* have been written on Khalīl's *Mukhtaṣar*. Some of them are mentioned are as follows:[9]

(1) *Minḥa al-Jalīl Sharḥ 'alā Mukhtaṣar Khalīl* by Muḥammad bin Muḥammad Aḥmad bin 'Ulaysh.
(2) *Hāshīya 'alā Sharḥ al-Bāqī al-Zarqānī 'alā Mukhtaṣar Khalīl* known as *al-Fatḥa al-Rabbānī by* Muḥammad bin al-Ḥasan bin Mas'ūd ibn al-Fāsī al-Bannānī (1184/1770).
(3) *Al-Jalīl fī Sharḥ al-Khalīl* by Muḥammad bin Muḥammad bin 'Abd al-Raḥmān bin Ḥusayn known as al-Ḥaṭṭāb al-Ra'īnī (954/1547).
(4) *Jāmi' al-Umhāt lī Ibn Ḥājib,* whose *Sharḥ* is known as *al-Jawāhir.*
(5) *Mawāhib al-Jalīl fī Taḥrīr mā huwa Mukhtaṣar Khalīl* by Nūr al-Dīn Abū al-Irshād 'Alī bin Muḥammad Ibn 'Abd al-Raḥmān al-Ajhūrī.

Ibn Ḥaṭṭāb and 'Ulaysh both indicate the opinions of jurists whose legal opinions we encounter very frequently in the text. These are *mashhūr* legal opinions which have been developed over the course of time and are transmitted to the next generations. If no legal opinion had been transmitted concerning an issue or it had not been discussed by the jurists in next generations, Khalīl indicates it by the word *tarddud* (hesitation). Khalīl brings comprehensively all these legal *mashūr* opinions together which had been developed over the course of time until Khalīl compiled the *Mukhtaṣar*. This shows a constant and continued employment of the hermeneutics incorporating expanded additional elements by jurists.

'Ulaysh indicates in his text these legal opinions of jurists by mentioning their names and sometimes referring to their works without mentioning their names, and sometimes their last names, or the first names, or only the titles of their works.

AL-LAKHMĪ (478–1080)

Abū al-Ḥasan ʻAlī bin Muḥammad al-Rabīʻ known as al-Lakhmī died in 478/1080. He is the son of the daughter of Lakhmī al-Qayrwānī. He came to Tunisia with Ibn Muḥriz and others during the time when the formal legal opinions were evolving. He died in the year four hundred seventy-eight.[10] Al-Lakhmī discusses one higher form of later developments of hermeneutics regarding the sense or meaning indicated corresponding to the expression (*khiṭāb*).[11]

IBN YŪNUS (451/1059)

Abū Bakr Muḥammad bin 'Abd Allah bin Yūnus al-Tamīmī al-Ṣaqlī was a well-versed jurist in the *'Ilm al-faraḍīya*. He compiled *Jāmiʻ al-Masā'il* and annexed it with other matters from *al-Nawādir*. He died in the year 451.[12]

IBN RUSHD (520/1126)

Muḥammad bin Aḥmad bin Rushd, the grandfather of the philosopher Ibn Rushd. He was a jurist of Cordova in the region of Spain and the East. He was well known for the depth and knowledge in the *fiqh*. He is known for his composition called *al-Bidāya al-Mujtahīd*. He died in the year five hundred twenty.[13]

AL-MĀZARĪ (539/1145)

Abū ʻAbdallah Muḥammad bin ʻAlī bin ʻUmar al-Tamīmī al-Māzarī. He was from the place called Māzar in the Islands of Ṣaqlīya. He came to an African city in the Eastern part. To him belongs the *Sharḥ*. He died in the year 539.[14]

ṢAḤNŪN (240/855)

ʻAbd al-Salam bin Saʻīd al-Tanūkhī known as Ṣaḥnūn was born in the year 240/855 in Qayrawan where he died eighty years later. "In the *Mudawwana*, Ṣaḥnūn transmits as what was reported by Ibn al-Qāsim."[15] He studied under Mālik bin Anas, ʻAbd al-Raḥmān bin Qāsim, Ibn Qahb, Ashhab, and many others.[16]

KHALĪL'S *MUKHTAṢAR*

The most unique and striking feature of Khalīl's *Mukhtaṣar* is that Khalīl interprets by the word *mukhtaṣar* as a shorter statement in which all essential expanded additional elements are comprehensively brought together that are contained in a larger statement. Khalīl expresses these legal opinions denoted or so to say "coded" by a short phrase indicating *mashhūr* legal opinions including those of Mālik, Saḥnūn, and the jurists from earlier generations that have been developed hermeneutically over the course of time until the time when Khalīl compiled his *Mukhtaṣar*. Khalīl's *Mukhtaṣar* is considered the epitome of *sharī'a* law and is regarded as the most authoritative legal manual which gained him a great fame. It is the most concise and can be considered as the apex of codification of Mālikī school of law. It restricted to the *mashhūr* opinions while ignoring other opinions.

There are two major authorized texts of Mālik. The *Mudawwana* of Saḥnūn is one of the most widely used in North African and Andalusia. The other is the *Muwaṭṭa'* of Mālik in the recension of Yaḥyā' bin Yaḥyā'. The *Mudawwana* is associated with Qayrawan and the *Muwaṭṭa'* of Yaḥyā' bin Yaḥyā with Cordoba.[17]

KHALĪL'S *MUKHTAṢAR* IN CONTRAST TO THE COMPOSITION OF *MUKHTAṢAR* IN OTHER SUNNI SCHOOLS OF LAW[18]

Khalīl's *Mukhtaṣar* defies comparison with the ordering of material of Mālik's *Muwaṭṭa'*. Khalīl in the *Mukhtaṣar* follows in most part the arrangement of material from Saḥnūn's *Mudawanna* as we have separately expounded further in the Appendix.[19] Khalīl brings together larger statements from Saḥnūn's *Mudawwana* in shorter statements in the *Mukhtaṣar* with all the essential expanded additional elements which had developed over the course of time. Khalīl's main purpose is to provide the hermeneutical formation of Islamic legal system. Khalīl's *Mukhtaṣar* contains only *mashhūr* legal opinions entailing all the expanded essential elements, regardless of which jurists or schools of law. Since these *mashhūr* legal opinions are already hermeneutically related to the legal canons, Khalīl brings them together comprehensively based on which he asserts his legal opinions. It includes all the *mashhūr* legal opinions from Mālik, Saḥnūn, and the jurists in the earlier generations until Khalīl compiled the *Mukhtaṣar*.

The reference to indications of *mashhūr* opinions of the jurists would be expressed in our text in parenthesis based on which Khalīl's legal opinions are stated in an abridged form. In this sense, one can characterize Khalīl's

Mukhtaṣar as an abridgment in form, but its contents very rich, extensive, and hermeneutically the most comprehensive. Khalīl's opinions are explained "decoded" by 'Ulaysh in the *Mainḥ* as already mentioned in chapter 3. As we have already explored the idea of comprehensiveness was largely confined to hermeneutically relating legal rulings to the legal canons by the jurists in the Shāfi'ī, Ḥanafī, and Ḥanbalī schools of law as the continuous hermeneutical interpretative process. In contrast, Khalīl's *Mukhtaṣar* was designed to bring all *mashhūr* legal opinions together as they had subsequently developed in the formation of Islamic law. His *Mukhtaṣar* was written not to be read by the students in the *madrasa* or by ordinary persons, but it was meant to be taught by the man of knowledge well versed in the knowledge of *fiqh*.

HERMENEUTICAL GENERAL FEATURES AS REFLECTED IN NATURE OF CONTRACT OF SALE, ITS STIPULATIONS, AND VALIDITY AND INVALIDITY OF ARTICLES OF SALE AND ITS CONTENTS IN KHALĪLS' *MUKHTAṢAR*

Khalīl first describes in general the nature of the contract of sale and then separately the species of the contract of sale.

The contract (of sale) is concluded indicating an agreement between two parties and by reciprocal exchange of the articles using the words "sale" and "purchase" in the past sense, the seller stating, "I have sold it to you" and the purchaser stating, "I have bought it from you." If he says, "Sell me your commodity for such and such a price" and the seller says, "I have sold it to you" (Mālik, Ibn al-Qāsim, 'Isā bin Dīnār, and others).

If one of the parties has a conditional expression or expression in the future tense such as "I will sell this" or "I will purchase at so much" except to be obligated, his sworn statement shall be resorted to. If he refuses to take an oath, the contract remains obligatory. It is considered as a case of offer of sale and acceptance of purchase of the article as made in the transactions of market (Ibn Rushd).

If a person who drew the contract is intoxicated, the contract becomes incomplete. It is required that the parties should legally be competent.[20] The qualification that the person to the contract drawn should be sober and in the right frame of mind is implicit. Khalīl makes it explicit (Ibn Shās, Ibn Ḥājib, Ibn Rushd, and Khalīl).

It is not forced upon the purchaser as the force is unlawful. If it was executed by force, it is returned to the seller without any price (Ibn al-Qāsim, Saḥnūn, the *Tawḍīḥ*).

It is forbidden that Muslim sells the copy of *Qur'ān* and slave of minor age to an unbeliever, who is forced to emancipate him or preferably to donate him to his mother.[21] He is given as a slave with the contract of emancipation (*bi kitābati*) and as a pledge (*rahan*), or surety only to the reliable person. The delay is granted for the execution of emancipation and in case of an unbeliever he is asked to expedite it as in the contract of sale, if he has become Muslim. It is valid that the slave with defect is returned as in the right of option in the contract of sale. If the owner is absent and far away for a long time, then it is permitted to sell him by the one, who has accepted Islam voluntarily. For Khalīl, the contract is indecisive "(*taraddud*) as no definite verdict has reached to us from the jurists in earlier generations"[22] (Abū al-Ḥasan, Ibn Yūnus, Abū Bakr bin 'Abd al-Raḥmān, Būlū).

If the purchaser is prevented from buying a slave of minor age because he is not of the same religion or because the father of the child is not with him under the circumstances, then there are two interpretations: if a Muslim purchases a slave who is Zoroastrian, or from among the people of book, or from non-Muslim territory, he is forced by intimidation and beating (to accept Islam) or sold to the person of his religion as his representative (guardian) and no one else is preferred.[23] (Saḥnūn, al-Basāṭī)

The object of the contract of sale should be pure (lawful), not such as manure, contaminated oil, or something of no good use or advantage.

It is valid to sell a cat, predatory animal for its skin, and animal which is about to give birth to offspring. Regarding the sale of predatory animal for tanning is considered valid by Abū Ya'lā as we have discussed in chapter 2 (Ibn Rushd, Ibn Ḥājib, Ibn Salmūn, Ibn 'Urfa).

The subject of contract should not be uncontrollable (usurped) such as the runaway slave and unattended camel. It should be controllable, otherwise it is invalid to sell the unattended camel without having the permission of its owner or under whose control (*ghāsib*) the camel is (Ibn al-Qāsim, Ashhab, Ibn Mājshūn, Ibn 'Urfa, Abū al-Ḥasan, Ibn Ḥājib).

However, according to Khalīl, it is indecisive (*tarddud*), if the runaway slave or unattended camel returned after a long time.

The contract of sale by the owner is canceled, if runaway slave is inherited but in case he was purchased, then it is not canceled. If it is placed as a pledge with the consent of mortgagee or for the property of someone else with his consent and if the purchaser knew that slave is a criminal and there is a claim against him and the purchaser claims that the seller sold the slave knowingly that the slave was criminal on whom there is a penalty for crime, then the purchaser has right of option to take the price and returned the slave which was purchased, or take it with the price if it is less. If he intends to reject sale mixed with some other transaction (such as defect), it is not valid to return the slave.

The sale of a column with structure is valid. If it is destroyed because of the negligence on the part of the owner and the safety is infringed, then the sale is void. If the natural calamity befalls it beyond any control or explanation, the sale is void. The structure must be surely secure against its breaking or demolition. The lease-hire is void if the structure along with the palm tree (*gharẓa*)[24] in the orchard has become dry and is destroyed (by natural calamity), except if it was described originally (*aṣl*) in the contract for a specific period such as ten years. It is not valid to sell property such as hawk, free person, or container made of gold or silver. This is requisite by the stipulation of the subject matter of the contract (*ma'qūd).* If some unlawful things are mixed with the lawful things in the contract, the sale is void. (Then, detailed comments are followed. ('Urfa, Ibn Yūnus, Abu al-Ḥasan, 'Ayāḍ).

It is not valid to sell if the price or value is not known of something which was sold and its other description such as the price of slave purchased by two persons for such and such. It is not valid to sell *riṭl* of the sheep meat before it has been skinned.

It is not valid to sell jewelry molded with soil, because of not knowing details as to the quantity or measure of gold or silver in it. It is prohibited to sell gold or silver in mine without knowing its description because of the uncertainty of it.

However, it is valid to sell meat of a sheep before it has been skinned by estimate and not by weight, but it is prohibited if it is measured in scale (Ibn Rushd).

It is not valid that the purchaser takes exempted amount of four *riṭls* of animal meat from some other animal, because it is like the sale of food in exchange for meat of four *riṭls* of meat before it has been taken into possession.

If animal dies, there is nothing incumbent on the purchaser. However, if the animal is slaughtered and the buyer has enjoyed four *riṭls* of meat, the price for it is incumbent on him.

It is valid to sell by estimate wheat growing in the ears and the wheat after it has been trodden by feet of known quantity in the measure of one-third of it and not more, but it is not valid when it is inflated as a standing up crop. It is valid to sell by estimate wheat growing in the ears and straw if they are measured, and fodder when it is not inflated. It is valid to sell olive oil in the known quantity of weight before it is extracted, and its description is known by custom. If description is different, then sale is not valid, except that the purchaser has right of option when he comes to know the description after olive oil has been extracted.

It is valid to sell wheat flour by the measurement of *ṣā'* or *irdabb* if it is known before it is grinded. If it is different from what has been described, then it is not valid, except with the stipulation by the purchaser as recorded in the *Mudawwana*.

It is valid to sell one or more *ṣā'* from a heap, whether it is known of what is in it or not, and the purchaser knows the number of them or in every *ṣā'* of heap. But it is not valid to sell measured by *ṣā'* or by *ḍhīrā'* or by numbers of *riṭl* from the heap.

The sale of meat of a sheep whether alive or slaughtered before it has been skinned is in the amount of four *riṭl*. The *sharī'a* limit is four *riṭls* as recorded in the prophetic *Ḥadīth* report. The exception is four *riṭls* and the purchaser does not take meat of any other animal in its place. The sale of meat which does not exist (*mughīb*) is nothing over the meat which is existing as the meat of sheep. Thus, if it dies, the purchaser owes nothing. If he has enjoyed meat of slaughtered sheep, then he owes equivalent in the amount of *riṭls* of meat which he has consumed. It is like if I intend to purchase some meat of sheep and not meat of the whole sheep, the difference between intending to purchase whole of it and intending to purchase only some of it is that if I intend whole of it I can estimate it by inspection but estimating some of it is ambiguous (uncertain).

It is valid to sell (things) in lump and fruits by estimate excepting one-third in measurement, weight, or specified by numbers, but not like in case of fruits which are not yet existing.

It is valid to sell the animal's *jild* (skin), but not *sāqiṭ* (meaning, head, feet, liver, and stomach attached to it) in accordance with the ruling of *jild wa sāqit*.

As to the exception concerning *sāqiṭ*, Mālik considers it valid only if one is on the journey and there is no price attached to it. It is valid to sell anything that is commonly accepted as one-fourth, one-third, or one-half absolutely during the journey (Mālik, 'Ayāḍ).

If one has sold an animal in the form (*ṣawra*) of exempting the *sāqiṭ*, regardless if the animal was sold to slaughter or not, the purchaser becomes representative of the *jild wa sāqit,* because he is not forced to slaughter it and give its substitute or pay the price to the seller as it becomes his responsibility. The seller has no right in the sold animal. This is incumbent on the purchaser from their mode of expression (*kalām*), even if it is not declared.

There are contrary (*khilāf*) legal opinions concerning the issue (*mas'ala*) of exception, if the purchaser is forced to slaughter animal which he has bought exempting it in the amount of four *riṭls* in this way, the seller does not receive his share of meat from what has been exempted. If there is a disagreement between them regarding slaughtering of animal in the portion of exemption four *riṭls*, then the seller gives all expenses and wages for slaughtering and skinning animal as specified according to what has been specified for its portion (*juzhu*) between the two and the purchaser must pay for *sāqiṭ*. The choice is either to pay price or value, whichever is fair. What is the choice for the seller and the purchaser? if the person for whom exception was specified, he would be held responsible for *jild wa sāqiṭ* and not for meat. The sale is valid by estimate if seen and should not exceed too much, when it is measured, weighed, or counted.

If the seller knows weight, measurement, and quantity of the commodity that was sold, and the purchaser did not know it, then he is given the choice either to accept it or return it. If he is informed later, the contract becomes void such as in case of a singing girl for whose service charges to be paid are informed later.

If both parties to the contract know or think at the time of sale that the land which was sold was leveled, it is valid. If they come to know of it later or think that it was not the case or they are in doubt about it, the sale is void, because of the uncertainty (*gharar*) involved in the transaction. If they thought that it was leveled at the time of sale, but later it was found not to be the case, then there is right of option for the seller either to reduce the price or increase the land in measurement.

It is not valid to sell by estimate those things, which one can count individually by number such as eggs and watermelons. It is narrated by Saḥnūn from Ibn Wahb from Mālik: "Do not sell walnut by estimate, if it can be known by number," but the sale of cucumber by estimate is valid, if they are different in size, some bigger and others smaller or average. The sale is valid of something filled second time after the first fill has been emptied out. It is considered as the article of known measurement (Mālik, Ibn Wahb, and Saḥnūn).

It is not valid to sell by estimate living sparrows confined to the cage, because they do not enter the category of estimate. It is not valid like selling pigeons confined to a pigeon-turret, because there is no possibility of selling them by estimate.

It is not valid to sell cloth, slave, and animal by estimate in parts separate from the whole. Nor is it valid to sell by estimate gold and silver used in business transactions. It is sold separately counting one by one by number or by weight as authorized by the Sulṭān, because there is a gamble and risk involved from both sides, lightness of *dirhams* from one side and gold from the other side of what is received. Likewise, it is not valid to sell by estimate *falūs* made of copper used in transactions, because there is no possibility of selling them by estimate, except if gold or silver is molded as coins, whether used in traffic by weight or counted by numbers as single units one by one or as molded coins. If it is not used in traffic by counting one by one in number, but by weight, then its sale by estimate is valid. Ibn Nājī said it is *mashhūr* (Ibn Nājī).

If there is an exchange of articles by estimate between two contracting parties and one of them knows and the other comes to know of its quantity after the sale, it is good. However, it is void such as in case of a female slave of whose services one is informed later that she would be his singer for an increase in price.

It is not valid to sell wheat by estimate. It is sold by measurement only.

It is valid to sell things having the same description, regardless whether by estimate, or by measurement, or one thing by measurement and the other by estimate.

It is not valid to sell an *irdibb* of wheat for a *dirham* from a lump without specifying the price of whole lump bought by measurement, because the price of whole lump was not specified. This is absolutely restricted to the things (*sil'a*), which are not sold by estimate.

It is valid when the description of the articles is known by seeing similar (*mithlī*) of its kind such as wheat which is measured, cotton which is weighed, or eggs which are counted, and shelled pomegranate, watermelons, walnuts, almonds, and hazelnuts.

It is valid to sell wares or food corresponding to the knowledge of description gained by hearing or seeing with confidence (certainty).

The sale of non-estimable articles by a blind person is valid, if his mind was able to comprehend the transactions of sale and purchase when he was able to see as a child and then became blind. The ruling remains the same, if a person was blind as child for whom everything was hidden or opaque. However, Abharī prohibits the sale by a person who was born blind or he could have distinguished different colors that rest upon seeing (Abharī).

The sale or purchase which has been relied upon the knowledge of the description of sold item by seeing before the time of conclusion of contract is not allowed to be changed after it has been concluded in the meeting (*majlis*) as a custom. Absolute sale or purchase is not allowed except with right of option.

If the purchaser takes sold article into his possession relying upon the testimony of seller that it is corresponding to the entry in the official register and afterward withdraws from it and comes with a cause to return it, claiming that he found it different from what is recorded in the register on which he had relied. If the register is destroyed or it is no longer existing, and the seller claims that it was corresponding to as it was recorded in the register, then the word rests with him with an oath confirming that it was corresponding to what was recorded in the register (Al-Lakhmī, Abū al-Ḥasan).

If a person gives *dīnārs* or *dirhams* for *ṣarf* sale or for the price of wares, or paying debt, or as a loan to other person and that person takes it into his possession testifying that he would return every unit, and then he withdraws from it and returns all of it or some of it, claiming that he found them counterfeit, or less in weight or quantity and the person who gave them refuses it and takes an oath opposing against the claimer that what he gave was without any counterfeit or less and says that in his knowledge they were all good and takes an oath to that effect. If he refuses to take an oath, then the word rests with the claimer who had taken them into his possession.

If one purchases an article which he had seen before and thinks and claims that a change was made in the description afterward, then it is decided in the favor of the seller with an oath to the effect that there was no change made between what he had seen before contracting sale and after it has been taken into possession by him. If the seller refuses to take an oath, it is decided in the favor of purchaser with an oath confirming that the change has occurred between what he had seen before the contract was concluded and after he had taken it into his possession.

The sale of a specified thing with known description is valid if the seller is not present at the place where the contract was concluded, but it is void if it is without descriptions such as kind, or species, or with right of option either to execute sale or reject it after seeing sold article, because of not knowing of it as required or keeping silence (*'alā luzūm wa sukūt*), that is, not accepted.

If the seller is not too far away and it is not possible to see article without encountering difficulty, then contract of sale is not valid. The meaning is that if it is possible to be present at the place of concluding agreement without encountering difficulty, the sale is not valid with only description of the article.

It is valid to expedite voluntarily the payment of sale of an immovable property by the seller without any stipulation, whether the sale is in the absence of seller or not, it becomes the responsibility of purchaser.

It is valid to sell immovable property by estimate in the absence of the seller without any absolute stipulation of cash or not, whether it is immovable property or other property like it.

After the sale of immovable property with the description in the absence of seller, no change is allowed. It is valid to stipulate sale of a vacant land and other immovable property in exchange for *dīnārs* and *dirhams* without its description in the absence of seller. The sale of vacant land by estimate is absolute.

Affecting the immovable property, it is valid to sell it in exchange for *dīnārs* and *dirhams* with stipulation in the absence of seller making it requisite that the purchaser expedite payment within near future such as two days.

If movable property is sold in the absence of seller with the stipulation of payment in cash or not, the seller is not considered responsible, but the purchaser who is responsible to expedite payment. However, if there is a dispute from the side of purchaser affecting the sale of movable property, whether it is in existence, destroyed, or unimpaired, or regarding its description, then it is the responsibility of seller.

It is unlawful to sell *dīnārs* and *dirhams* in exchange for gold and silver. Likewise, it is unlawful to sell food in exchange food, because of the possibility of *ribā* or credit involved in it. It is also not valid to sell things of the same nature in different weight such as *dīnārs* and *dirhams*, because one of them can be either more than the other or lesser than the other, or one them to be paid at a future specified time.

ṢARF SALE

Hermeneutical General Features as Reflected in *Ṣarf* Sale and its Contents

In an absolute *ṣarf* sale, it is unlawful that one of the parties to the contract makes payment at a future specified time in exchange for the other party paying it immediately before separating from each other. Even when payment is deferred from either party without breaking meeting, it is repugnant according to Mālik. If the payment from one of them is prolonged or he appoints a representative to take the article of exchange into his possession, then the *ṣarf* sale is void, or if the deferment occurs with an agreement (*muwā'ada*) on the part of one party to exchange gold for *dirhams* or with debt and is deferred, then other party has right of option for the payment of debt at a future appointed time (Mālik).

If one hundred *dirhams* are deposited and they become damaged for which one hundred different kind of *dirhams* are given as substitute, it is not valid. It is valid to take the same kind of specified one hundred *dirhams* which were given as deposit. With respect to the *'ārya* and *rahan* the ruling is the same.

If the gold or silver jewelry is usurped and at the time of its exchange it was presumably believed to be safe from any defect, then the price is incumbent on the usurper as in case of debt. It is *mashhūr* ruling (*Al-Tawḍḥī*).

The credibility in *ṣarf* sale is unlawful, when one party to the contract claims against the other party in respect to the number, or weight, or description of gold and silver that was given to him which he found less in quantity, or it was damaged thus, causing impediment in executing *ṣarf* sale. However according to al-Lakhmī, it is valid with the testimony of a reliable person. Ibn 'Urfa considers it repugnant (Al-Lakhmī, Ibn 'Urfa).

It is void, if *ribā* or *nisā'* is involved in the *ṣarf* sale between two persons such as *dīnār* in exchange for its kind in excess, or *dirham* in exchange for its kind in excess, or food of its kind in excess or different in kind. However according ibn Rushd, if the *ṣarf* has occurred or exchange of two articles in excess with testimony, it is not void because of the difference. According to Ibn Yūnus, the testimony is not valid in the *ṣarf* sale and the substitute of one thing in exchange for the other thing in excess, debt or price for the sold article payable at a future specified time as in *salam* sale (Ibn Rushd, Ibn Yūnus).

It is unlawful to combine the sale and the *ṣarf* sale in one contract, except if *dīnārs* are combined separately for the sale and the *ṣarf* sale and there is no stipulation that one follows after the other. Thereafter, it is valid that the sale excluding the *ṣarf* sale for half a *dīnār* and the other half excluding the sale for the *ṣarf* sale combined for one *dīnār*.

It is unlawful to sell wares in exchange for *dīnārs* and *dirhams* with them and it is prohibited to expedite sale, nor is it allowed to combine *dīnārs* from the purchaser and *dirhams* and wares from the seller in contrast to (*bi khilāf*) only *dīnārs* and *dirhams* and wares payable at a future specified time. Ashhab narrates from Mālik that it is valid, if *dīnārs* and *dirhams* are in cash and wares to be delivered at a future specified time. According to Ibn al-Qāsim, it is valid that *dīnārs* and *dirhams* to be payable at a future specified time to expedite the sale of wares (Mālik, Ashhab, Ibn al-Qāsim).

The *ṣarf* sale with *dīnārs* excepting one-third, one-fourth, or more is valid, if it is all in cash. It is not appropriate that any of it with a deferred payment, such as if one sells fifteen of animal skins of which every piece for a *dīnār*, except one *dirham* with a differed payment, it is not valid, except if the exchange of one *dirham* is severed before the sale is concluded and nothing more.

It is valid that a person in the *ṣarf* sale exchanges wares for *dīnārs* after exempting one or two *dirhams* payable at a future specified time so that he can expedite the sale of wares.

In the *ṣarf* sale if two *dirhams* are exempted and if they are more than two, then it is valid only as the sale for cash but not valid as the *ṣarf* sale, if payment of more than two *dirhams* is differed to be payable at a future specified time.

If one gives silver to a goldsmith to make jewelry or *dīnārs* to make gold nuggets or metal or *dirhams* for engraving silver to jewelry and gives him wages which can be realized in two ways: either he purchases molded gold from goldsmith and leaves with him to make jewelry and in addition to it wages. In this the *ribā* and *nisā'* is involved, or if he purchases jewelry already molded in weight of gold, or silver, or wages in addition to it, there is only the possibility of *ribā* involved in it. In the second case, it is valid because he does not need to travel to mint house to get gold or silver, and in the first case it is preferably not allowed.

It is valid, in case if one gives olive, sesame, seed, sunflower, radish, or sugar cane to a presser for extracting juice from them and gives wages, contrary to (*bi khilāf*) to the previous case of molded gold, a traveler gives wages for the performance of work, it is valid because the traveler does not need to travel to mint house to pick up gold.

If a person has exchanged *dīnārs* in the *ṣarf* sale with other person for *dirhams* and after a few days he meets him and says to him "I permit to increase it for more *dirhams* or for a differed payment", it is valid, and it becomes contract of sale and contract of *ṣarf* sale becomes invalid. It is recorded in the *Mudawwana.* Thereafter, Mālik said that if defect appears in original (*aṣlīya*) exchange of *dīnārs*, it is returned. If defect appears afterward, it is not returned, since it is with increase (*ziyāda*) of *dirham* because of differed payment (*Mudawwana*, Mālik).

Ibn al-Qāsim says in the *Mudawwana* that if you make a transaction in the *ṣarf* sale with a person and you say to him "I permit you *dīnārs* and you increase *dirhams* to pay in cash or at a future specified time, it is valid and the *ṣarf* sale is not invalidated and he takes from you what was your increase with *dirhams*, because it is the *ṣarf* sale in which increase is also returned with permitted *dīnārs* given to him. It is absolutely (*muṭlaq*) not valid to return increase of *dirhams*, if he finds them with defect, except if it was made requisite, and if he finds it with defect, then it is incumbent on the person, who permitted *dīnārs* for increase in *dirhams* to substitute it" (Ibn al-Qāsim).

It is valid, if a person exchanges *dīnārs* in the *ṣarf* sale to another person for *dirhams* and if in either one of them appears any defect in what has been taken into his possession as agreed, then the loss of price and weight in *dīnārs* or *dirhams*, which one has taken into his possession is incumbent on the other person, because from the very beginning some of it which is canceled due to the loss of weight or quantity such as *raṣāṣ* (copper, iron, lead etc.) in which due to the appearance of defect, its quality depreciates. Or it is valid if one agrees to remove that defect replacing the *raṣāṣ* in the *ṣarf* sale.

In an absolute *ṣarf* sale, if it is valid to return defective gold or silver (*naqd*) caused by the corruption lowering its value such as *dīnārs* mixed with silver and *dirhams* mixed with copper.

If there is a dispute regarding the corruption, the contract of sale is restored by substituting corrupt *raṣāṣ*. If there is a lapse of long time between the appearance of defect and the time of conclusion of contract and according to the contract it was specified that the separation between the two parties to the contract without a lapse of long time, the contract is void in all what has preceded concerning the appearance of defect. After the separation of parties to the contract or a lapse of long time, the defect appears in respect to the loss of quantity or corruption in *raṣāṣ* and the one who finds it, demands to complete the contract by replacing the loss of quantity or corruption in the *raṣāṣ*, does in such a case the *ṣarf* sale become void? There is a hesitation (*taraddud*) on the part of Khalīl, since no definite ruling has been transmitted. However, according to al-Lakhmī, substitute for it is valid (Al-Lakhmī).

The sale is invalidated for a smaller amount of *dīnārs* in the *ṣarf* sale when they are not combined with a larger amount of it such as five *dīnārs* and other ten *dirhams* and still other twenty *dirhams* and if defect is found in five *dīnārs*, then the *ṣarf* sale of five *dīnārs* is invalidated as in this case the defect is found in smaller amount of *dirhams*, it does not invalidate the *ṣarf* sale of all larger and smaller amount of *dīnārs*. It is a *mashhūr* ruling, because every *dīnār* is considered by itself a single unit, regardless whether it is one *dīnār* or it is with other *dīnārs*. However, Ibn al-Qāsim considers that the *ṣarf* sale of all *dīnārs* is invalidated. What if numbers of all units of *dīnārs* are not known, does the *ṣarf* sale become invalid? In this case also Khalīl expresses his hesitation (*tarddūd)* as there is no definite ruling transmitted from jurists from earlier generations (Ibn al-Qāsim).

However, it is described in the *Tawḍīḥ* in two ways: one of them is by Māzarī and other is by Ibn 'Abd al-Salām (Sanḥūn). According to them, if *dīnārs* are different, the *ṣarf* sale of all of them is invalidated or the *ṣarf* sale of smaller amount of *dīnārs* is invalidated. This is *mashhūr* ruling, regardless if number of *dīnārs* are known or not. The other is described by Bājī. According to him, both are invalidated (*Tawḍīḥ*, Māzrī, Saḥnūn, al-Bājī).

If *dīnārs* traded in the *ṣarf* sale are of different descriptions such as higher and lower in quality and defect appears in any one of them, the *ṣarf* sale of all coins becomes invalidated because of defect, whether it was known or hidden, or it was counterfeit, the value of it becomes less as coins differ in their purpose from one other (Saḥnūn, Ibn Yūnus, Ibn Rushd, al-Bājī).

If in the *ṣarf* sale substitute is stipulated for defect of counterfeit coins or any kind of *raṣāṣ* when it is not perfect, or it is not of the same description or it is less in weight or quantity and they are not of the same species, then substitute is not valid, except if they are combined in the sale and the *ṣarf* sale.

The stipulation for substitute is to expedite from preventing the *ribā* or credit (Ashhab).

If the adulteration is caused in jewelry or it has occurred due to the setting (molding) by work, contract of sale of it is unlawful. Ibn 'Urfa says it is permitted if one knows that the excellent quality of gold has not been affected by molding, relying upon the information given by the people in that profession. If the adulteration has occurred with or without sale and one believes or has doubt that it is clearly an adulteration, then sale is not valid (Ibn 'Urfa).

If any unusual thing is found in jewelry after the separation or a lapse of long time, then based on the entitlement it is not permitted to return it, even if it was with right of option.

What? If both parties had agreed for the substitute and one of them denies, then he is not forced to rectify for anything unusual based on the entitlement. This is contrary to the case of defect in which it is incumbent to rectify it.

Khalīl expresses the hesitation (*tarddūd*) and holds back any opinion. The jurists from earlier generations held different opinions in this respect.

It is valid to sell gold or silver attached to anything such as to the copy of *Qur'ān*, sword, and cloth after heating each of them gold or silver is taken out, then each of them is not considered part of jewelry. Thus, it is valid to sell it for gold or silver or with differed payment. If there is a dispute regarding its quantity, it is appropriate to take gold or silver out of them. This is exception to the sale of *naqdayn* (*dīnārs* or *dirhams*) mixed with other things.

It is permitted to take out gold attached to the copy of *Qur'ān*, sword used for the holy war, and women's clothing in the combination of sale and *ṣarf* sale, but it is forbidden when it is attached to inkwell, weapons used in war excepting sword, saddle, riding animals, men's clothing to sell for gold or silver and not in exchange for wares except that it is all *dīnārs* or *dīnārs* less embellishment. But, if the embellishment is made of silver in saddle, or arrow, or knife, or bridle, or rider's silver clade, sewing needle, or sharp sword, or silver clade and the like, it is not valid to sell it in exchange for silver, even if one says that it is embellishment, because taking these things out not knowing that which is taken out. It is contrary to what is permissible such as in case of taking gold or silver out from the sword, copy of *Qur'ān,* and finger ring. According to Mālik, it is not objectionable. However, it is repugnant regarding things which are casted in silver such as jug glittered with silver, flask fumigated with silver and gold, jugs, bridle, knives molded in silver, because they follow the nature of weapon (Mālik).

If an ornament is nailed in with silver in a bag or bowl and is not decomposed in its structure, then it has no effect on its permissibility to sell (Al-Bājī).

What? It is not valid to sell the ornament weighing more than one-third in exchange for an article of the same species, but it is valid to sell it with an article of different species which is not ornamented when it is stipulated that it is an exchange of articles from hand to hand (*ṣarf* sale). It is said in the *Mudawwana* that it is invalid to sell a sword that it has the same nature as that of silver or gold at a differed payment (*Mudawwana*).

What? Is it valid to sell the ornament which is one-third in price and not one-third in weight? There are two contrary *mashhūr* opinions: one *mashhūr* opinion is by Ibn Yūnus that it is *ẓāhir* based on the *Muwaṭṭa'*. The other *mashhūr* opinion is by al-Bājī, who said that it is considered *ẓāhir* in the Mālikī school of law (*madhhab*) and, that is, if one sells sword ornamented with gold in exchange for seventeen *dīnārs* and ornament weighs equivalent to twenty *dīnārs* and its price is three *dīnārs* for its molding and price for sword is forty *dīnārs*, it is valid considering the weight and more of price (Mālik, Ibn Yūnus, al-Bājī).

If an ornament is molded with gold and silver, it is not valid to sell it in exchange for gold or silver by weight, regardless if it is equivalent to it or not, except if gold and silver ornamented are one-third combined in exchange for lesser than that according to opinion of that profession. Regarding sale of more than half of it, there are two opinions: according to Ibn Ḥājib, it is valid, if one of them follows other (in its description), and excess is considered as the deferred payment. Other opinion is that the excess of it as what has preceded in the sale in exchange for one-half. The meaning is that excess of it in one of them in sale such as sale of wares, gold, and silver in exchange for gold and silver, there is a meaning of *ribā* in it (Ibn Ḥabīb).

The sale of jewelry molded with gold and silver with any other wares (e.g., metal) in exchange for gold and silver is not allowed. Ibn al-Qāsim prefers this legal opinion, referring to Mālik (Ibn al-Qāsim).

The exchange of the lesser amount of molded *dīnārs* and *dirhams* of the same kind for each other such as *dīnārs or dirhams* in the same number with the stipulation to benefit lesser amount of them is valid, but not for more amount of them. Similarly, it is valid if it is stipulated in exchange of six *dīnārs* or *dirhams* for six *dīnārs* and *dirhams* of the same kind when they are weighed, they become approximately equal compared to what was given.

The exchange (substitute) of lower quality of gold or silver for good quality of gold or silver lesser in weight is not permitted. Mālik said that the excess from one side is not good, except if good quality of gold or silver with ornament is less in weight, it is valid (Mālik).

The substitute of gold or silver for the like in gold or silver counterposing *naqd* (*dīnārs* and *dirhams*), regardless if they are in the form of coin or not or are different, or if they are used in the transactions as coins counted by numbers or they are weighed if they are bigger from both sides or only from one side in the known weight by placing them in one palm of scale and measurement of weight in other palm, when palms of scale are in balance, then the exchange is valid. This is the opinion of Ibn Yūnus which is preferred by Khalīl (Ibn Yūnus, Khalīl).

If either all gold or all silver is of superior quality in comparison to all *dīnārs* such Western *dīnārs* counterposing Miṣrīyya or Iskindirīyya *dīnārs* measured in *riṭl* or the *naqd* (*dīnārs* or *dirhams*) are of superior quality and the other is equivalent to the superior quality of Western *dīnārs* and two Egyptian *dīnārs,* then it is not valid if one of *naqdayn* is of lower quality compared to some of other superior quality. According to the interpretation of most jurists, it is not valid to sell lower quality of one of *nqdayn* counterposing good quality of which value is more than that of lower quality of coin in circulation (Ibn ʻAbd al-Salām).

It is valid to sell *dīnārs* adulterated with silver or copper or *dirhams* adulterated with copper counterposing of its like or in exchange of one with other, if adulterated thing is not more according to Ibn Rushd and the *dīnārs* have not been damaged (Ibn Rushd).

The sale of adulterated *dīnārs* is void, if one has doubt about it. It is also invalid if one knows there was an adulteration existing in it, thus it is incumbent to invalidate it.

It is valid to sell adulterated *dīnārs* in exchange for *dirhams* free from adulteration, meaning counterposing it with the pure *dīnār*, but its opposite is prohibited (Ibn 'Urfa, *Tawḍīḥ*).

If one knows that *dīnār* or *dirham* is adulterated, and the adulteration is still existing in it, then contract of sale to the extent of adulteration is void. As to the price of invalidated sold adulterated *dīnār* or *dirham* falls into the property of the purchaser and was not made requisite for its replacement, then it is not replaced, because the sale was not contracted making it requisite to return the price to the purchaser, except if the authorization was made requisite for it. If the unadulterated *dīnār* or *dirham* is sold, then only the price for the remaining adulterated of it is authorized to return. This is consistent with the contract of lease-hire in which it is authorized more than one-third. There are several opinions regarding more than one-third.

It is valid to execute payment of loan regardless whether it was a specific thing, food, and wares and regardless if it is to be paid now or to be paid at a future specified time for its equivalent in quantity or description for which he was responsible. It is better if one pays more in quantity or better in quality even if it was not stipulated in the contract, except in case of loan drawing profit as the custom, because the custom is considered as the stipulation. It is valid to loan wheat in measurement and the wheat flour is paid in the same measurement, but it is not valid to pay less in measurement. According to Abū al-Ḥasan, it is valid so long as the wheat flour is better in quality and enjoyable to eat. Al-Ashhab maintains that if wheat flour paid for wheat is less in measurement, it is not objectionable, if the quality of wheat flour is better (Abū al-Ḥasan, al-Ashhab, Khalīl cites here a prophetic *Ḥadīth* report in support).

If the debt of loan is resolved of differed payment or paid in the beginning, it is valid to execute it by lesser of it in quantity or quality such as half *dīnār* or *irdabb* damaged coin in place of good *dīnār*, because it is better to execute payment of loan preferably with either lesser in quantity or lower in quality. The meaning is that the stipulation was preventing to resolve differed payment, because of the loss and deferment of some right, and the execution of payment of loan would generate profit. The execution of payment of more than loan is invalid. The payment in the like manner is incumbent on him in the same amount counted in number. Generally, if it is less than the loan incumbent, it is valid to pay it more in weight (Mālik).

If you loan to a person one hundred *dirhams* half of it counted in number and the other half of it by weight and he pays you back one hundred *dirhams* by weight without any stipulation, it is valid. But, if he pays you ninety *dirhams* by weight, it is not good. Then, he said if you loan one hundred *dirhams* by weight and counted in number and it is paid back fifty in halves and the other fifty in halves, it is valid. However, if one hundred *dirhams* fifty in halves and the other half of one hundred *dirhams*, it is not valid if they are less in weight. The *aṣl* is that if you loan one hundred *dirhams* counted in number, it is valid that the payment of loan is executed in the like manner counted in number, regardless if *dirhams* weigh approximately equal. It is valid to execute payment of loan which is lesser counted in number of the same weight, if the commodities are destroyed. But it is not valid to execute payment of loan if it is less in number and more in weight or more in number and less in weight. There are also different views held by jurists in earlier generations on this issue.

As to the numbers, he said that it is not valid to execute loan payment more in weight or quantity in the transaction for allowing differed payment, except when it is more in weight or in the form of good quality such as in preponderance (*rujḥān*) of one of the *naqdayn* (*dīnār or dirham*) over the other and they are equal in weight, it is valid if the transaction is carried out by weight. If the transaction is carried out by number only, it is valid to execute payment with excess in weight equivalent to weight of it in number. If it is a loan payment from both sides, namely the lender and the borrower, it is void.

If the price of the sold article in *dīnārs* or *dirhams* is arranged as the responsibility of the purchaser to execute it, it is considered as the execution of debt with permissibility of a superior description absolutely or of inferior quality to resolve the deferment.

It is valid to execute the payment for sold article with the same kind of article more in number or weight to resolve deferment.

If loan payment of coin is received from one side and from the other side it is remaining to be received, it is not valid if payment is of inferior quality of coin and other was of superior quality and vice versa, nor is it valid if loan payment of inferior quality of jewelry and the other was of superior quality and vice versa. If the payment of the molded coin is different from the jewelry, it is valid, according to Ibn al-Qāsim (Ibn al-Qāsim).

It is void, if *falūs* used in transactions fall in disuse after it was arranged as the responsibility of person indebted or sale or if *dīnārs or dirhams* fall in disuse in transactions, If one purchases in exchange for *naqd* or lends or borrows it and then it falls in disuse, there is nothing incumbent on him If it becomes renewed, except the price (Ibn Rushd and other shaykhs).

The *falūs* which were used in the transactions become void by their disuse after it was arranged as the responsibility of the borrower or its price changes with its continuity in the business transactions, then what he has owed is considered *rahan* and there is nothing incumbent on him.

Al-Ḥaṭṭāb describes that if one borrows *dīnārs, dirhams,* or *falūs* and they are authorized currency by the ruler and, thereafter, they become deauthorized by the ruler without their replacement, then it is incumbent on the one to pay the like of what he had taken into possession on the day it was executed as the authorized currency. It is said in the *Mudawwana* that if a person owes *falūs* from borrowing and if they fall into disuse, then it is considered as if there was no borrowing (Al-Ḥaṭṭāb, *Mudawwana*).

If the adulteration is caused in gold or silver or it has occurred due to setting, the contract of sale is unlawful. The depreciation is not incumbent, and the sale of the adulterated commodity is void by consensus. Ibn 'Urfa says that it is permitted, if the good quality has not been affected by molding it, relying upon the information provided by the people in profession of molding. If one believes or has doubt that the adulteration has clearly occurred in it before or after the sale, it is not valid (Ibn 'Urfa).

If one sells to someone the unadulterated gold or silver with adulterated gold or silver without any clear indication (explanation), then the purchaser can keep the unadulterated gold or silver, if he knows its quantity and sale of adulterated gold or silver is void.

It is valid to accept the adulterated gold or silver, if the adulteration is not in an exceeding quantity. If it is in exceeding quantity, Mālik alludes it to the urine. According to the verdict of Ibn al-Qāsim it is not permitted (Mālik, Ibn al-Qāsim).

The exception to the adulteration is not permissible, except it is valid when the one who purchases the adulterated gold or silver has its knowledge or if the purchaser knows that the adulteration with water is for the fermentation of wine, it is valid. But, it is not permitted to adulterate an esculent article or keeping it in store. It is also not permitted casting gold or silver with lower quality of metal and mixing meat of female animal with that of male animal, the meat of lean animal with that of flashy animal, the meat of the goat with that of the sheep, the barley with the wheat, and inflating the animal after skinning to raise it for showing that it is fat.

RIGHT OF OPTION[25]

Hermeneutical General Features as Reflected in Right of Option and its Contents

The right of option in contract of sale is established with the execution of the contract of sale, each party to the contract has right of option to reject it or accept it. It comprehends right of option of seeing and reflection.

The duration of right of option is one month in the sale of house as narrated in the *Mudawwana*. In the elucidation and explanation, it is narrated two months. Ibn Yūnus and Ibn Rushd make it as a rule, Ibn Ḥājib maintains opinion contrary to their ruling. 'Abd al-Salām says that this ruling is for the sale of land and not house, because in the sale of land more time is needed than in the sale of house. In the sale of house one month is generally accepted (*mashhūr*) and some say two months. In the commentary, it is said three and four months for the land. It is narrated from Mālik one year in the case of a landed estate (Saḥnūn in the *Mudawwana*, Ibn Yūnus, Ibn Rushd, 'Abd al-Salām, Mālik).

It is valid if the purchaser buys house for his family and for (keeping) his possessions, he has right of option to enter the house by himself (without his family and possessions) to examine it. Ibn 'Urfa says that he has right of option to stay in house overnight for getting acquainted neighborhood without occupying it as a residence. Ibn Muḥriẓ and others say that he may not bring his family and his possessions with him and he can move alone in house to explore and get to know it. The rent for that duration is incumbent on the seller (and not on the purchaser), because of right of option before the purchaser moves in the house. If the purchaser makes a condition to reside in it with his family and to bring his possessions during that time of right of option, he is wrong (at fault) and the contract of sale is void. According to al-Lakhmī, if the purchaser resides in the house during the time of right of option, the rent becomes void for him, if he owns or rents it. However, if he resides in it while on lease, and then he vacates it or subleases it, it is not valid that he resided in it without paying rent (Ibn 'Urfa, Ibn Muḥriz, al-Lakhmī).

It is valid that right of option is executed in the sale of a slave, and his services, wages, and usufruct all together (Ibn 'Urfa al-Lakhmī).

It is valid in the contract of sale of an animal to ride for a day during three days of duration with the stipulation of right of option, if it is not a place of residence to ride and return, or when it is not certain of the services rendered by the servant, in such a case it is determined according to the need by stipulation. Ibn Yūnus explains the ruling regarding riding of an animal for a day from the *Mudawwana*. Ibn Ḥabīb allows right of option to ride an animal for a day or two or three days and return it and such like this. There follows some more commentaries and explanations from the various jurists (*Mudawwana*, Ibn Yūnus, Ibn Ḥabīb).

It is not objectionable to stipulate riding animal to bring messages from one place to another place and return. This is the ruling of Ashhab with Ibn a-Al-Qāsim, if he carries message as indicated in his discourse (*kalām*) of going from one place to another place and return. Likewise, it is said bringing message from one place to the other place, stopping and bringing message to the first location and going to the second location and returning. Khalīl shows hesitation (*taraddud*) as in case of right of option in case of piece of cloth. 'Imran and some other jurists differ in their opinions regarding right of option of three days in sale regarding the piece of cloth and other things of similar nature (Ashhab, Ibn al-Qāsim).

It is valid to stipulate in the contract of sale after one is settled from the beginning when contract is concluded, and the purchaser gives price to the seller and more if it is incumbent on him. This is according to most of our shaykhs. Ibn Bashīr limits it only to the price which is incumbent on him. If the contract of sale is not in gold or silver, it is not valid that the seller takes price that was the responsibility of purchaser, if it was in exchange for the wares with right of option. This is not valid because of the invalidation of what was the responsibility of purchaser or validity and permissibility, regardless if the contract of sale was in exchange for gold or silver, or not. This is *ẓāhir* according to *al*-Lakhmī, because it is not the contract of sale in reality (*ḥaqīqa*). However, if the intention was pure in making right of option, there are two interpretations as an answer: one interpretation is that it is restricted to if there was no clarification by the seller to take price which was the responsibility of purchaser and other interpretation is that it is prohibited according to the consensus, because of the invalidation of responsibility of purchaser. In the *kalām* of *al-Ṭawḍīḥ* first interpretation is preferred (Al-Lakhmī, *al-Tawḍīḥ*).

The right of option takes place after the purchaser has settled, the contract of sale is considered to become the sale with right of option. If it is the purchaser who has made right of option with the seller, then it is the responsibility of purchaser according to the consensus. If the seller has made right of option with the purchaser, then there are two juristic opinions: one juristic opinion is from the *Mudawwana* that it is considered the responsibility of purchaser, the other juristic opinion is narrated by al-Makhzūmī that it is the responsibility of seller (*Mudawwana*, al-Makhzūmī).

Regarding the interpretation of sale with the stipulation of consultation when the seller is absent and far away from the place where it was contracted, and it is not known how to consult him except after the end of duration of right of option, then it is interpreted according to the right of option and agreement. According to al-Lakhmī, if it is right of option of stipulation or agreement, or consultation in case a person who is absent and far away, the contract of sale is invalid, even if it is included in the contract that he would be absent and far away. If the right of consultation is relinquished to permit the sale, it is not valid. The meaning of being far away is that the right of consultation is permitted when a person to the contract is in the nearby vicinity. The stipulation of right of option is to give more time for enabling article to be sold in good faith. The time of exceeding is a month or so for the house, seven days or so for the slave, and three days or so for the animal and wares. According to Ibn 'Urfa if the duration of being far away is stipulated, then its void by the *naṣṣ*. Thereafter, follow many interpretations and comments, which contributes little to the main contention (Ibn 'Urfa).

The stipulation of right of option is void either from the seller or the purchaser when it is not certain if it is a loan or sell.

Concerning the stipulation of right of option of piece of cloth without measuring it, if the purchaser after wearing it brings it defiled to the seller and wishes to return it after the expiration of right of option, because of the responsibility of seller to measure it, then one of the parties to the contract with right of option in whose possession sold piece of cloth is responsible for its price because of the expiration of time. If he wishes right of option at a future specified time, then after the sunset of the last day of time of right of option or tomorrow or near future and like that. Abū al-Ḥasan means by near future one, two, or two days after three days of the duration of right of option (Abū al-Ḥasan).

It is invalid to defer the payment of price in the contract of sale at the end of time of right of option and, likewise, to stipulate (cash) payment after or at a near future appointed time (Ibn Ḥājib, *al-Tawḍīḥ*).

The lease-hire of land for cultivation not protected from calamity cancels contract, because of the requirement of replacing and bringing it back to the safety. Khalīl shows hesitation *(tarddud)* ('Abd Abū Isḥāq al-Gharnāṭī, al-Shu'bī, Ibn Hindī).

The lease-hire stipulated to begin after a month or more than half a month is prohibited with the stipulation of (cash) payment, but it is obligatory if a female slave is sold in exchange for something.

If a person purchases one of the two pieces of cloth without specifying which one and takes both pieces of cloth into his possession to choose one of them to keep and the other to return, then by the stipulation of right of option, he determines which one to keep and which one to return. If the purchaser claims without providing any evidence that one of them is destroyed which was bought with the other the cloth, then legal ruling is that the purchaser is responsible for the price of only one, if evidence establishes it. This is *ẓāhir* according to al-Rajrājī and *Mudawwana* (*Mudawwana*, al-Rājrājī).

The purchaser is responsible for the price of one piece of cloth, if the seller has not asked to take both pieces of cloth in his possession, but if the purchase has asked the seller to take both pieces of cloth in his possession, then according to Ibn al-Qāsim, it is considered for only one piece of cloth. Būlū indicates that the other ruling is for both pieces of cloths, unless the seller voluntarily taking the price of one when the purchaser asked him to accept that the purchaser takes both pieces of cloth into his possession (Ibn al-Qāsim, Būlū).

Or if the purchaser claims that one piece of cloth from the two pieces of cloth is destroyed, then he is responsible for the half of price of what has been destroyed without knowing which one. Thus, he is responsible for the half of price with all likelihood in practice.

Regarding the absoluteness of responsibility such as a person demands from another person loan or payment of debt, he has a choice of one-third for himself and pays two-thirds assuming as if two-thirds is destroyed. That is so (described) in the *Mudawwana*. Saḥnūn adds and describes that it is two-thirds (*dīnārs*) is not known except by his statement. Abū Muḥammad bin Abī Ẓayd holds back his opinion and raises the objection against Saḥnūn. Ibn Yūnus says that this is right. There is no difference between knowing and not knowing it, except by his statement or by evidence (*Mudawwana*, Saḥnūn, Abū Zayd).

The one in whose possession are *dīnārs* is considered partner in the remaining undamaged *dīnārs* and damaged *dīnārs*, one-third of them is returned and two-thirds of all damaged becomes incumbent on him. If he has returned two-thirds which are damaged, he must take an oath to that effect. If he takes an oath, he is not responsible for two-thirds after seeing or weighing. If he finds them safe, otherwise he returns all of it and as to the claim regarding that which are damaged or some of them are damaged, nothing is incumbent on him, because *dīnārs* which were in his possession were security (deposit) and its possession into his hand is considered *rahan*. If they do not agree regarding the condition of possession, the word rests with an oath with the one who has taken it into his possession.

If a person purchases two pieces of cloth together and takes them into his possession on the condition that he has right of option to buy both pieces of cloth or reject them. The two pieces of cloths or more which are sold to the purchaser and they are either in the possession of purchaser or if they are in the possession of seller and the time of right of option has expired, there is nothing incumbent on him.

If two cloths were in the possession of purchaser and he claims that they became damaged, he is responsible for the price of both pieces of cloths at which he has bought them. If he claims that one of them became damaged, he is responsible for its price in proportion. The contemporary jurists and those who have narrated it from the *Mudawwana* have said that if their descriptions have changed, then he is responsible for each of them.

If the purchaser has bought with right of option to choose one of two pieces of clothes or two slaves and takes both in his possession and after that the purchaser and the seller have separated from each other, then there is no longer right of option to choose one of them after the expiration of duration of right of option, regardless both pieces of cloth or slaves are either in the possession of purchaser or seller. The price in half becomes obligatory upon the purchaser for one piece of cloth or one slave, not knowing for which one. Consequently, the purchaser becomes partner with the seller in both articles. Likewise, in case one or both articles are damaged. According to Ibn Yūnus and some other jurists, if he has purchased one of them and both are damaged or one of them is damaged which was in his possession, regardless evidence is established or not that they were damaged. And there is no longer any right of option of the purchaser in taking remaining all of it. If the duration of the right of option has expired and they have separated from each other and both articles are in the hand of the seller or the purchaser, the half of price of cloth is incumbent on the purchaser and he does not have right of option, because he did not know the price of which one piece of cloth from two pieces cloth, consequently, it becomes obligatory on him to become partner in both of them. Similarly, it is described in the *Jawāhir.* Abū al-Ḥasan says if he bought both pieces of cloth with the option of three days, whether one or both pieces of cloth, he becomes partner in both pieces of cloth with the seller (Abū al-Ḥasan, *al-Jawāhir*).

If one purchases one piece of cloth from two pieces of cloth with right of option and the duration of right of option expires and both cloths are in his possession, then he is not allowed to choose one of them, since the right of option has expired and it has not taken place as it was required in the contract to choose one of them, if it is in the possession of seller, then the purchaser becomes partner in it as previously stated.

If the description of article of sale is not known, it is valid that the purchaser returns it to the seller, because of the description of stipulation is not given or found by the purchaser, regardless it was in excess of price as in case of a female cook whose description is not given or found and, likewise, in case of a deflowered woman from the seller that she had no intercourse as a virgin, it is valid to return her to the seller testifying with an oath. If it is not testified with evidence or reason (cause) such as it is established that a Christian female is married to a Christian male slave and she is found to be a Muslim or deflowered woman is widow and not virgin, she is returned because of the defect, the contract of sale is void.

The article of purchase is returned, if it is not for the purpose for which it was bought. This is according to the stipulation which is clear and plain.

If it is claimed that a slave was Muslim who was bought by the purchaser from the seller who claimed that he is a cook, failing that description it is valid for the purchaser to return him.

The article of sale is not returned if it was not stipulated, because the purpose and the price of it is not stipulated. It is void such as in case of the stipulation regarding a female slave that she is scribe, and a female slave that she is widow, but one finds her that she is virgin, because purpose for which they were bought is not different (Ibn al-Lakhmī).

The article of sale is returned in which the defect is found due to which its price is reduced such as a runaway slave, or a thief, or a slave with difficult personality, or hermaphrodite, or having fearful appearance such as leprosy by birth, and a fortiori the blind person not able to see when the object is visible or some vision in one eye is lost, he is returned though according to the custom it may be considered good and sound (Ibn 'Urfa).

It is narrated by Ashhab from Mālik that if a runaway slave or a thief urinated while he was minor and then he is sold when he became of legal age, it is valid for the purchaser to return him. According to Ibn 'Urfa al-Bājī, it is not valid to return the thing with defect such as whiteness in eyes, or blindness in one eye, or dumbness, or deafness that does not decrease price. It is not valid to return a slave of minor age with defect of dumbness, or deafness, except if it is known that such is found from his birth (Ashhab, Mālik, Ibn 'Urfa).

Ibn 'Urfa says if some part of body such as cut in a finger and it shows that it is light (i.e., finger has not been diminished), then likewise it is not valid to return him because it would go away and be cured in time. It is *ẓāhir* established by textual evidence according to *al-Tawḍīḥ* (Ibn 'Urfa, *al-Tawḍīḥ*).

It is valid to return a female slave who has been castrated and her genitals are cut off and after they have been repaired, her vagina and rectum have become one. If it is included in her price, it is invalid by the *sharī'a* as in case of a female slave who charges more in price for entertaining. A stallion, sheep, or goat intended for work is not returned because of castration as the custom. It is said that the meat of stallion is purer than the meat of castrated animal, thus right of option for its return is valid according to the custom (Ibn 'Urfa).

The female who has continuous flow of blood after her days of menstruation while she is in the possession of the purchaser, she is not returned if she is cured (purified) while she is in his possession. This is *ẓāhir*. Ibn 'Urfa narrates from al-Lakhmī that if he takes her into his possession and there was a continuous flow of blood from the very beginning, it is valid to return her. Ibn 'Urfa al-Bājī narrates from Muḥammad al-Shaybānī that the duration of two months of menstruation is considered defect (Shaybānī, al-Lakhmī, Ibn 'Urfa).

According to Ibn Ḥabīb, anyone whether male, or female, or castrate person who works with hands and has a difficulty with his right hand and has any defect in the eyes or in one eye the inclination of turning its pupil to the pupil of the other eye, causing difficulty in fixing gaze and looking in other direction, as well as neck of which one side is cracked are considered defects (Ibn Ḥabīb).

According to Ibn 'Urfa, concerning adultery if a slave is of ignoble character, it is considered defect, According Ibn Muḥriz, if he had intercourse with a female by force, it is considered defect. Ibn 'Urfa says that if the female or male slave takes on drinking wine even if it does not smell on his breath, it is considered defect and stinking mouth is also defect. According to bn Ḥabīb, if a slave is of mean character or foul mouth, it is considered defect, if it is imposing (frightening). Thinning or losing of hair in a female or male slave that includes also losing hair on eyebrows such as in case of leprosy, if it is publicly not showing, it is considered not defect (Ibn 'Urfa, Ibn Muḥriz, Ibn Ḥabīb).

If there is a growth in male or female slave behind teeth or length of teeth becomes longer and penetrates in front of the mouth due to any cause or growth in the place of palate harming teeth, it is considered defect. According to Ibn 'Urfa, ibn Ḥabīb, Zufar, growth of meat and growth of hair on eye, and 'Isā narrated from what he heard from Ibn al-Qāsim, that the hair on eyes and growth of skin on whiteness of eye projecting in the direction of nose to the blackness of eye are not considered defects. According to al-Bannānī, the slave is not returned if the protuberance on outer part of his body emerging as swelling on naval caused by the movement of bulkiness, it is considered defect. It is said of a big bellied person as having natural disposition or preferably natural disposition as well as emergence of swelling and if there is a suspicion that one of them exists, the slave is not returned (Ibn 'Urfa, Ibn Ḥabīb, Zufar, al-Bannānī).

If the husband of a female is free person or slave, or the wife of a slave is free person, the slave is not returned with the existing growth, whose father or mother had it before or if he has step brothers or mother and the cause is sperm which produces it and spreads after forty years, like leprosy. It is strong and powerful, and it cuts off other usual blood circulation to the subsidiary veins, or the slave whether male or female, becomes overwhelmed by gloomy temper or madness, then he is not returned because of such defect (Ibn Ḥabīb).

The slave whether male or female is not returned if he or she has been subdued by black bile or devil who is residing on this earth with human beings, so long as God has created him with human beings and thus, fit and insinuation caused by the blood circulation of subsidiary veins are natural disposition. A slave touched by the devil is not returned.

The slave is returned who has dull teeth imposing vile appearance of front part of mouth and the female imposing upon her beauty because one of her front teeth is falling. The meaning is that if it is not imposing, it is not returned. Ibn Ḥabīb describes that the loss of teeth in a slave in the back part of his mouth has no legal value. The loss of teeth and excessive growth of one of teeth is considered absolutely defect in both female and male slave. The greyness in hair of a female slave is not like menstruation, that is, it is not vile, except if it decreases her price because abundance of it is imposing, then she is returned. Ibn Muwāz says, if all greyness in hair of a female slave is causing vile appearance, she is returned. And the curliness of hair appearing long and fleeing in the open air that makes her look beautiful and increases her price, she is returned because it is not stipulated for that purpose (Ibn Ḥabīb, Ibn Muwāz).

If the hair of the female slave turns into red which the purchaser did not see at the time of buying her and then found out that her hair was not natural, but it was black or curly, it is considered defect and she is returned. According to al-Lakhmī, a female slave with curliness of hair for an increase in price is returned. According to Abū al-Ḥusayn, if her hair is slander and thin and if it is turned to curliness to make it better looking, it is considered cheating and fraud, then she is taken for less in price, or if a slave is adulterer repugnant to the soul and vile, it is considered as in previous two cases of curly hair and coloring of hair from black turning into red (Al-Lakhmī, Abū al-Ḥusayn).

The slave who urinates in bed while sleeping and it has developed seriously, then he is returned with evidence that he has begun urinating when he attained puberty while he was in the possession of seller. If the seller takes an oath that slave did not urinate while he was in his possession, then the slave is not returned (Ibn 'Abd al-Salām).

If the slave is put as deposit with trusty and he urinates in his sleep while in the possession of trusty and there is a dispute whether such was the case or not, then the word rests with testimony by a trustworthy witness. The information given by the trustworthy wife or the trustworthy husband is accepted confirming that slave urinated. Ibn Ḥabīb and Ibn Rushd consider that information provided as a testimony is valid (Ibn Ḥabīb, Ibn Rushd).

If the quality of bisexuality in male slave and in female slave is displayed, they are returned. The bisexuality is displayed by mutual sexual act of one male with another male and bisexuality in female is displayed by mutual sexual act of one female with another female. They are not returned because of doubtful resemblance from their speech or movement. Khalīl maintains that it is restricted to display of baseness in character as a defect (Khalīl).

The male slave lacking hardness in sexual organ in the male and the female slave having depressed sexual organ are returned regardless, if they are high or law ranking Muslim visitors, they are not returned. Regarding this, there are three *aqwāl*: (i) they are born and raised as Muslims, but they are not of Arab origin (ii) both male slave and female slave are from a Muslim land, and (iii) they have stayed long time among Muslims and are from their land and one of them at the time of death developed sickness of vile character and surgical procedure (circumcision) was done for it. Thus, there are three conditions: the slave is Muslim, born in the Muslim country, or have stayed a long time with her in the Muslim land and dies at the time of surgical procedure.

Similarly, the return of slave for any old defect is the responsibility of the seller as in the contract of sale. If the seller has a slave for a long time in his possession and did not know that he was having defect, he is retuned, because according to the stipulation slave should have been free from any defect. This is explicit and established by ruling, as in case of an endowed or inherited property, if there is no evidence that the sale of property was an endowment or inheritance, it is returned.

Similarly, regarding defects occurring in an animal, such as wound inside its hoof preventing smooth walk and making it stumble. If is established that the defect had occurred while it was in the possession of the seller or those who have seen both legs (paws) of animal and other marks indicating that the defect did not occur after the animal was sold. Except, if the seller takes an oath that he did not have knowledge that the defect has occurred while it was in his possession. If he refuses to take an oath, the animal is returned.

According to al-Bājī, stubbornness of an animal, excessive aversion in an animal, eating less food and such persisting marks in an animal are considered defects (Al-Bājī).

If one purchases an animal or a she camel and rides on it as usual and it does not run fast, nor can one sit on her because of her is slenderness, it is valid to return her.

The female slave is not returned, if she exposes herself to the minors because it is not obscenity.

The female slave is not returned because of adultery confined to her kissing, because it is one of the good qualities. In some manuscripts, it is considered minor thing and is considered preferable (to return her), because it is considered defect. Ashhab narrates from Mālik that kissing the minor is not a defect, except if it leads to adultery and then it is considered defect (Ashhab, Mālik).

According to Ibn Ḥājib, a female slave becoming thin in her heaps which makes her unattractive is considered not defect, if it is insignificant and less, it becomes defect.

The slave is not returned, who is accused of stealing while he was in the possession of seller, because of accusation and a fortiori if he was not confined to prison with evidence that it was someone else who had stolen. Ibn Yūnus said that the stolen property was found with someone else is evidence for it (Ibn Yūnus).

The sold article is not returned with appearance that does not emerge, except with change of personality as in an animal or something else such as an adulteration in the body of animal having disease termed as *sawās* (Ibn Ḥabīb, Māzrī).

If decay appears in walnuts, hazelnuts, figs, bitter cucumbers, spices of cucumbers, whiteness in watermelons and greenry, if it is less than one-third of it and not more than that, it is not returned except if in all or more of them decay appears, then it is it returned. If the defect is less or a little, it is not returned with more of those not decayed, unless it was less of them with more of them according to the custom. The custom is considered stipulation. It is *ẓāhir*. The price is not incumbent on the purchaser for any appearance of defect, if it emerged without breaking walnut, the bitter cucumber, and change of personality due to the disease in an animal as mentioned before.

Eggs are returned in which defect appears without purchaser breaking it, because it is known that they were defective before breaking them, the purchaser returns the broken ones and whole price is given to him, as the seller has deceived him in the matter. Otherwise, if after he has broken them, and defect appears, then the whole price is incumbent on the purchaser on the day when they were sold.

The price of house is not returned because of small defect in it. There are three kinds of defects in which the price of house is neither reduced nor is it returned such as in the collapse of balcony, sinking of the pavement, and fear of its collapse. The mediation between two of them is that it is not returned and the repair cost for it is deducted from the price of house. According to the author, it is *ẓāhir* intending the middle ground considering the indication that the value of house has been diminished (Khalīl).

If a female slave says to the purchaser "I am the mother of the seller's child and a fortiori a free person" and if it is established with evidence before or after the contract of sale, then the seller is liable for one-third of the price or compensation. If she in her claim is accused of lying, then she is returned to the seller, but it is valid for the purchaser to return her because of her claim that she is the mother of child of seller.

It is invalid to sell a goat, sheep, camel, or horse, or donkey keeping milk in the udder creating an impression that her udder is big to hold more milk or creating an impression of a female slave's breast that it is larger. It is valid for the purchaser to return her. Ibn Shās said, because it is a great deception to make the purchaser think that it was perfect without any defect. Ibn 'Urfa said that it is repugnant, if it is established that such has been done by the seller or he ordered his slave to do not in his presence (Ibn Shās, Ibn 'Urfa).

According to Mālik, coloring an old piece of cloth to make it look good is a gross repugnancy and one should safeguard from such a temptation. Ibn Abū Zamīn said that if it happened, then the purchaser has a choice (either to accept or reject it). This is also said by 'Abd al-Mālik. Similarly, if the seller says that he makes inkwell and pen by his own hands or his servant does it by his order, then the purchaser can return it (Mālik, Ibn Abū Zamīn, 'Abd al-Mālik).

If the purchaser buys milk of an animal measured in *ṣā'* with vessel of measurement and when he measured it again, it was not according to his contentment. It is clearly (*ẓāhir*) a transgression according to Ibn Muḥriz (Muḥriz).

If stipulation is by *ṣā'* regarding an article of nutrition with the inhabitants of certain place such as milk (*laban*) in exchange for coagulated sour milk (*ḥalab)* in an approximately equal quantity with an insignificant difference, if they differ in price of nutrition as in wheat, dates, rice, it is valid. This is according to the *Mudawwana* (*Mudawwana*).

It is forbidden to sell milk left in the udder of animal, because it is the sale of food (article of nutrition) before it is taken into possession.

It is not allowed for the purchaser to return milk that was left in udder, if he knew it. Al-Lakhmī says that if he purchases knowingly that the milk was left in udder, he does not return it, except if he finds milk less in quantity. Thereafter, follow different comments (Al-Lakhmī).

It is not obligatory to return *sā'*, if the milk was left in udder after animal has been milked. It is narrated that Ashhab returned it with *sā'* to prove that it was the milk left in udder which is returned after animal has been milked (Ashhab).

If the milk left in udder has been left three times, then purchaser has a choice for second time with agreement, that is, for the milk from the udder in quantity of three times, then it is not valid to return it.

SALAM SALE[26]

Hermeneutical General Features as Reflected in *Salam* Sale and its Contents

Khalīl describes that there are following seven conditions for a valid contract of *salam* as described also by al-Qudūrī in the *Mukhtaṣar* and al-Marghīnānī in the *Hidāya*: (i) the possession of the price by the seller for the sold article, (ii) the genus of article of sale is specified such as wheat or barley, (iii) the species of article of sale is specified such as wheat grown in soil watered by rain or by means of a canal, (iv) the quality of the article of sale is specified such as good, bad, small, or large, (v) the quantity of the sold article must be specified such as the measurement, weight or numbers, (vi) the period of delivery of the sold article is specified, and (vii) the place of delivery must be specified.

According to al-Lakhmī, the possession of an advance payment by the seller ensures that there would not be any loss due to the delay in the delivery of article of sale. If the delivery of the article is delayed, for example, for two days or the price is delayed for a long time, there are different legal opinions. According to Mālik and Ibn al-Qāsim, the delay is permitted in its entirety for three days. It is narrated that al-Saḥnūn and other Baghdādī jurists consider that it is void. Al-Māzarī narrated from 'Abd al-Wahāb that it is permitted only for two days and no more. Al-Ṣaqlī and others ascribe three days according to the right of option and two days more. Regarding the price to be delivered in three days is vague, whether stipulation of delay of three days and other such days is requisite or not. Complying to attach it with the taking possession of price in advance is implied in the sense that it is the stipulation in *salam* sale, whether it is explicitly stated or not (Mālik, Ibn al-Qāsim, al-Saḥnūn, al-Māzarī, 'Abd al-Wahāb, al-Ṣaqlī).

Regarding the dispute because of the delay of the price of three days without any stipulation and if the delivery of the article of *salam* sale is delayed not too long, there is no definite ruling transmitted by the earlier jurists (*tarddud*). Al-Ḥaṭṭāb narrated two legal rulings of Mālik. Saḥnūn indicates hesitation (*tarddud*), which he copied from it (Al-Ḥaṭṭāb, Saḥnūn).

It is permitted in the *salam* sale to have right of option, either of the price or usufruct of the article of sale or only for one of them or not anyone of them, for the delay in the payment of price is three days and not more than that for the slave and house. It is applied as in the article of sale if the price is not in cash payment. If it is not in cash payment (voluntarily), it is void, for it is wavering between the loan and the price and the sale and the loan. The reason is that it is an invalidated stipulation.

In the contract of *salam* sale, the usufruct is permitted of specified object such as an immovable property or an animal in which delay is enacted of taking into possession of the article of sale first or later. The debt is prohibited because debt cancels debt as in this case to begin with there is a debt against debt in all transactions of *salam* sale. This is *ẓāhir*. It is not appropriate to usufruct the article of sale before the completion of three days, except in case of an animal, the delay of taking an article into possession without any stipulation for a longer time is valid by analogy (*qiyās*) (Al-Bannānī).

The *salam* sale of an article by estimate is permitted and it is stipulated as in the contract of sale. According to Ibn Ḥājib, the *salam* sale by estimate not specified is valid as in the contract of sale, including to make specified usufruct of the sale of article. This ruling is *ma'rūf* (well-known) legal ruling. It is valid to stipulate to delay the payment of price exceeding three days after the appointed time has expired. The meaning or the idea is that without stipulation, the delay of the payment in price exceeding three days is forbidden (Ibn Ḥabīb).

The price to be paid for food and the wares in the *salam* sale, the delay of three days without stipulation is permitted, but not more than three days. More than three days is prohibited, if the food is measured and it is green and ripe at the time of contracting sale, then the purchaser is responsible to transfer it and its possession is relinquished by the seller after both the purchaser and the seller have taken the article of exchange into possession. It is not valid if at the time of concluding contract, the food was not green and ripe to be enjoyed by the purchaser as it does not enter the responsibility of the one to whom it is to be delivered. It is *ẓāhir* from the discussion (*kalām*) of the author. If the permissibility of equality is not found from both sides, then according to Ibn Bashīr, if the price is delayed in the *salam* sale, it is not void, whether it was stipulated or not and the time is extended for the delay, whether the price is known such as for the thing or animal, or the price is not known specifically that the payment is in cash (Ibn Bashīr).

It is valid to return *dīnārs* or *dirhams* in three days, if the defect such as the counterfeit is found in all or some of them recently or later, as it is requisite by the ruling of three days delay. It is *mashhūr* legal ruling. If one demands to substitute it before the expiration of two or three days, the delay is permitted, if he wishes. If it is not stipulated in fact or by ruling, and the delay is more than three days, then the *salam* sale in some of the articles is void, namely in the portion of counterfeit *dīnārs* or *dirhams* of them. This is according to the verdict of Ibn Muḥriz and that is also the verdict of Abū 'Imran and Ibn Sh'abān. However, Abū Bakr bin 'Abd al-Raḥmān considers it void for all of it (Ibn Muḥriz, Abū 'Imrān, Ibn Sh'abān, 'Abd al-Raḥmān).

The testimony of the seller is permitted regarding the measurement, weight, or counting of sold article, if it is returned after the expiration of period of delay, but it is not accepted in the payment in advance after the appointed time, because of the prohibition. According to Ibn al-Kātib, one who takes food on loan, his testimony has no bearing before the expiration of appointed time, because when the appointed time comes, it becomes a loan generating profit resulting into a loss from the delay of payment. Similarly, the permissibility of testimony regarding the measurement of weight in sale of food, it is valid. If it is testified regarding the measurement or weight of food in the contract of sale or the *salam* sale and if one finds it less or more. If it is more, it is returned (to you). If it is less, then according to the custom among the people. It is *ma'āruf* legal ruling (Ibn al-Kātib).

If the sale of article was taken into possession or the seller measured or weighed it (as in the sale of food) and it was found less and the one to whom the article was sent (delivered) does not establish it with evidence that he himself measured or weighed it or he was present when it was measured or weighed it, then it is considered as prescribed by the contract. If either the seller or the purchaser was not present, then without an oath the claim is not accepted.

If you deliver an article in the *salam* sale in which its price is in your possession and it becomes destroyed, whether it was due to the negligence on the part of purchaser not to take it into his possession or it was placed as *rahan* with you for trading with it or as a loan to you and if it was destroyed without establishing it with evidence, then the *salam* sale is void. If it was established with evidence that it was in your possession or by someone else, the *salam* sale with an oath is not void. If you (the seller) do not take an oath, then the purchaser has right of option to nullify the contract and take its price back.

If a person sells an animal or immovable property and it becomes destroyed by the seller or a sranger due to the transgression, then contract of *salam* sale is not void and the seller is considered responsible for the price of the sale of animal or immobile property. Ibn Bashīr' says in the *Kalām al-Mufaṣṣīl*, if the purchaser destroys the article afterward, he is responsible for the article of sale. There is no doubt in the validity of it in the *salam* sale (Ibn Bashīr).

See, if God destroyed it or the one to whom it is delivered destroyed it, the price is not returned in either case. If it is destroyed by the seller, the price is returned to the purchaser or its like for what was destroyed. Likewise, it is returned if a stranger destroyed it and it was in the responsibility of seller, the contract of *salam* sale is void, except if it was destroyed not intentionally by taking it into possession to a place of delivery and it was destroyed, then the contract of *salam* sale is valid. If it is not known who has destroyed it, in that case there are two legal opinions: one legal opinion is that the contract of *salam* sale is void, and that is *mashhūr* legal opinion and the other legal opinion is, if the cause of its destruction is not known, the price is returned to the one whom it was to be delivered. It is not conceivable to consider that the contract of *salam* sale is void (Ibn Bashīr).

According to one of the conditions of valid *salam* sale, if the price (capital) and the articles of *salam* sale are such as food in exchange for food, it is not valid, if they are of different species because there is a possibility of the *ribā* and the *nisā'* in it, and if it is *dīnārs* and *dirhams* (*naqdayn*) in exchange for *dīnārs* and *dirhams* in the *salam* sale, if one of them is more than the other or one is better than the other of the same species, then it is not valid because of the *ribā* in it. In the same manner, the *salam* sale of lesser quantity or lower quality of a thing in exchange for more in quantity or better in quality of the same species is forbidden, and one is responsible to pay the price even if it is not stipulated, except if the usufruct of entities of the same species is different, regardless the entities of one species are more, or less, or lower, or better than that of another species, because of the different usufruct of the entities of the same species, they are considered of two different species.

It is not valid to deliver perished things or good things with perished things. However, it is valid if he delivers more good things with some perished ones. It is not valid to return them one by one, regardless if they were good or perished beforehand, because of the loan that generates profit. If they differ in number and the perished ones are included more in number in the transaction, then they are replaced with the good ones. If they both are equal in number, then the more good ones in number are for the owner and bad ones are not admitted in the transaction, and if the half of good things are delivered without perished ones, they are permitted to be admitted in the transaction.

In the *salam* sale, there is no difference between the horses which are faster in racing and some slower in racing, if they are of the same species ('Imrān, 'Ayāḍ).

However, it is not valid in the *salam* sale to sell good horses in exchange for bad horses, nor bad horses in exchange for good horses. However, it is valid in the *salam* sale to sell tamed (good) horses for more wild horses and more wild horses for less good (tamed) horses.

As narrated by 'Abd al-Salām regarding the horses which are not racing horses, there is no difference between smaller and larger horses. Ibn Dīnār said, there is no difference between a smaller horse and a larger horse, if they are from the same species. Al-Lakhmī considers invalid to sell in the *salam* sale racing camels for ambler horses which are good and swift having an easy gate, except if they have not wider gates to carry rider and is helpless. There is no objection to sell in the *salam* sale an ambler horse for more horses of other species which are devoid of the qualities of racing ('Abd al-Salām, Ibn Dīnār, Al-Lakhmī).

The *salam* sale of male camel is valid for multiple carriages intending not to unite him with female camel. The different usufructs of riding for multiple carriages without racing is valid. According to Ibn 'Abd al-Salām, Arabs considered this only for the camel and not for the racing horse. For example, when Arabs were wedging war riding on it and some of them intended to ride it without carrying any load and that has continued that way even today ('Abd al-Salām).

The different kinds of cattle for different kinds of work such as plowing, thrashing grain, watering (irrigation), regardless if cattle are female or male they are considered of the same species (Ibn al-Qāsim).

In a *salam* sale, delaying goat from milking for the abundance of milk in exchange for the milk of sheep in double the amount is not allowed. Al-Māzarī agrees with it (Al-Māzarī).

As narrated in the *Mudawwana,* the *salam* sale of the milk of sheep in exchange for the milk of goat is not valid and vice versa, except if abundance of milk of goat is described (*mawṣūf*). It is not objectionable to accept the milk of wild (small) cattle. The inclusion of abundance of goat's milk is exception to what is ruled in the permissibility of the milk of wild (small) cattle in the *salam* sale. Ibn Yūnus says it is considered *ẓāhir* in the *Mudawwana* that the sheep and the goat are equal as they are both known for the abundance and magnanimity of milk. The exchange of milk of each other is permitted in the *salam* sale. Regarding the usufruct, the abundance of milk in the sheep is like the abundance of milk in goat, despite the prominence of wool in the sheep. Ibn Ḥabīb narrates from Mālik and his companions that it is valid. Ibn 'Abd al-Salām traces it to Ibn al-Qāsim and said "God knows that the milk of the sheep follows the usufruct of wool, because its milk is prominently less than that of the goat." He said the *salam* sale of two small animals for one large animal of the same species is valid when their usufruct is different such as mixing water with wine for the fermentation and vice versa. Or the *salam* sale of one large animal in exchange for two small animals in the same species is forbidden, if their usufruct is not different as in exchanging large animal for small and young animal, until it grows and becomes big and large. It is as explained in the *Tawḍīḥ* that it is like the *muzābana* (selling of fruits on the tree in exchange for fruits ripe and measured) which is forbidden, because of the gamble and risk involved in it (Mālik, Ibn Yūnus, 'Abd al-Salām, Ibn al-Qāsim, *al-Tawḍīḥ*).

If a large animal which is giving birth to younglings, the *salam* sale of it for a young (smaller) animal is prohibited and vice versa, but the *salam* sale of two young (small) animals for one larger animal is not prohibited. It is invalid in the *salam* sale to sell an animal, relying on that it would become larger when it would be delivered. It is considered *muzābana*. Similarly, its usufruct and its offspring are also prohibited such as in case of human (slave) and sheep. In is not valid in the *salam* sale to sell the offspring of a larger animal in exchange for a smaller animal whose usufructs are nearly the same (Ibn al-Qāsim).

Likewise, the *salam* sale of an animal of one year (or few months) is inviolable, relying upon that it would become bigger or larger in one year, or two or three years. The *salam* sale of a tall and vigorous animal for smaller animal in the same species is not allowed, unless it is established that they are of different species. Then several comments follow.

If the jewelry is taken out of sword and is separated from it, then the jewelry and the sword without it are considered of two different species and the *salam* sale of it is valid. If they are both equal, it is forbidden according to the consensus, because of the increase in payment at a future specified time (*salaf bi ziyāda*) and their usufruct. Likewise, the *salam* sale is valid of one thing for another of two different species, if their usufructs are different.

Likewise, it is valid to sell one thing in the *salam* sale for two things of different species, if their usufruct is the same, if their usufructs are approximately the same such as the linen cloth and cotton cloth, it is valid to sell one for the other in the *salam* sale, because they are of different species. However, it is not valid to sell in the *salam* sale one camel for two camels for a differed payment at a future specified time. This is *mashhūr* legal ruling, because the differed payment at a future specified time as if it is loan with excess.

The information sent (by the bird) from one place to another place for the *salam* sale of one thing known in exchange for one thing or more things unknown, relying upon the knowledge sent by information is valid. However, it is not valid to sell in the *salam* sale a chicken with eggs for two chickens without them. Ibn 'Urfa and 'Abd al-Salām do not describe the knowledge sent by the bird. The *salam* sale is not valid of one rooster for two chickens and vice versa. According to Ibn 'Urfa and ibn Rushd, there is no difference, if the acquisition is of a bird in exchange for a poultry and eggs such as of rooster, goose, and dove in their species, whether they are bigger or smaller, and male or female. If the eggs and poultry are having disparity in quantity and they are of different species, it is valid to sell one for two for the differed payment at a future specified time in future. (Ibn 'Urfa, Ibn Rushd)

The difference between the male and the female animals and humans is of no consideration. This is valid and is considered *mashhūr* legal ruling. This is according to Mālik, but majority of the succeeding jurists in earlier generations disagree in case of humans, because the males differ from the females. They render different services. The male renders services outside the house, travels, and such things, but the female renders services inside the house such as cooking, baking bread and similar things and the difference is the usufruct of services rendered (Mālik, Later Jurists).

There is no difference in the usufruct of a female rendering service in spinning and cooking, even if she has not attained high degree of perfection in them and in other services like them.

There is no difference of the usufruct in knowledge of arithmetic and skill of writing of a slave, if they are both combined according to Ibn al-Qāsim. And Yaḥyā bin Sa'īd said that there is a difference in the usufruct of both. Ibn 'Urfa following Ibn Sa'īd says there is no difference in the sale of a slave with the knowledge of arithmetic and skill of writing as they are of the same description. Ibn Ḥabīb said the same. However according to Abū 'Imran, the opinion of both is contrary to that of the *Mudawwana Kubra*. According to the *Mudawwana Kubra,* a slave with the knowledge of writing includes reading, trading, dress making, and such other things (Ibn al-Qāsim, Yaḥyā bin Sa'īd. Ibn 'Urfa, Ibn Ḥabīb, Abū 'Imrān).

Any food or *dīnārs* or *dirhams* (*naqdayn*), or wares, or animal, or slave given as loan or in sale or *salam* sale is paid back with its like, regardless whether it is stated in wordings or not, or it is not specified of the thing or animal. However, it is valid in case of food and cash when it is specified as loan. If it is specified as the sale or *salam* sale or not specified anything, it is prohibited because it is sale of food in exchange for food at a differed payment. In case of *dīnār* or *dirhams* (*naqd)* the substitute at differed payment for a thing is allowed generally as well as in particular cases.

It is valid to delay the execution of *salam* sale when the appointed time is known such as harvesting of seed, thrashing of grain, and returning of pilgrim to his land after performing pilgrimage. The postponement is valid if it one knows by calculation the severity of snow in the winter or the severity of heat in the summer. It is necessary relying on calculating the deferment of fifteen days from the day of conclusion of contract and the time when crop is to be produced and not more delay than what is described and as the custom. If the crop is prevented from being produced, it is not objectionable to sell it when it is produced as described in the *Mudawwana.* If it is New Year day, or Celebration of (Christian) Easter, or (Judiac) Passover, or Lebanese Christian Festival *(maharjān),* or Lent, or Christmas, if the time of their occurrence is known, it is valid.

Except if it is stipulated that the article of sale for bringing it to a place is more than half a month. However, the distance of that place to bring it in two days is stipulated, then it is delivered on the third day. Al-Māzarī says one day is enough, which Ibn Ḥājib enters in his register. Al-Ṭafī's opinion is that it is not less than three days, but if it is more than that, it is contrary to what is described in the *Mudawwana.* Khalīl's desires bringing the article of sale in three days (Al-Māzarī, Ibn Ḥabīb, al-Ṭafī, *Mudawwana*).

If the distance is of two days to travel by land or sea gliding with the flow of waters or an oar with which ship is propelled or pulling it manually by the person going along with it on foot securing it by regulating from the wind in less than a day, then the *salam* sale becomes sale at that day.

Postponing the *salam* sale of an article of sale for one month or two months is counted by the appearance of new moon, regardless if it is after three days or nineteen days of month, the contract of *salam* begins from the first day of month. If the contract begins not from the first of month, but other than that and the contract is for three months, then the second and third months are counted to begin at the appearance of new moon and if the new moon appears after twenty-nine days, the fourth month begins on first night of it. If the appointed time of article of *salam* is first or second month, the first day of month begins on the night when the new moon appears and breaks up by down.

If the article in the *salam* sale is to be taken into possession at a place where the inhabitants are accustomed to measure, for example, wheat, meat, fat, fresh dates, raisin, and rice which are measured in some places and weighed in other places, then in the first case, it is to be taken into possession by the measurement and in the second case by the weight. In case of pomegranate, quince, eggs, watermelon, and such kinds of things which are either counted by number or weighed, they are measured by the known length of span of hand or measured by length of arms for different things, or they are measured by two equal cords, one measured by the seller and another by the purchaser.

It is doubtful, if the eggs to be taken into possession counted by number and other things are measured by the strings of the pan to be consistent with making up the difference. Khalīl omits in some of the explanations the measuring of eggs by the strings of the pan indicates that in the first case it is the *salam* of the eggs and it is not valid to give eggs as a loan, except if it is counted by number and the *salam* sale of the walnuts counted by number or measurement is valid as the custom. It is not objectionable to loan (*salaf* sale) pomegranate counted by number and, likewise, apple and quince known counted by number.

Or taking possession of an article packed in a bundle in the *salam* sale, the seller says that "I sell ten loads of clover or wood to you in the *salam* sale all packed in a bundle by this rope or one hundred each of it packed in a bundle to be taken into possession is not valid, because of the deception (uncertainty) due to the difference of lightness and heaviness in their weights." Ashhab approves it (Ashhab).

If the seller gives choice (to select) in the *salam* sale, for example, bread or meat in such and such a quantity of *qinṭār or irdabb,* it is according to Ibn Abū Zamnīn when the seller gives in the *salam* sale meat of sheep or bread in the quantity of ten *riṭls* and such other things, does it mean choosing to take meat or meat by weight or to take bread or meat? According to Ibn Zarib Abū al-Ḥasan 'Ayāḍ Ḍahab Ibn Zamnīn it means to take quantity of ten *riṭls* of meat or ten *riṭls* of bread (Ibn Abū Zarib Abū al-Ḥasan 'Ayāḍ, Ibn Abū Zamnīn).

It is void, if the article of *salam* sale is taken into possession in exchange for the thing of an unknown measurement or weight or number in a container filled with wheat or oil weighed by this stone or quantity of eggs in the palm of the scale measured by stone as the amount of thing filled in a container is unknown.

It is valid to take an article of the *salam* sale into possession which is measured by forearm (*ḍara'a*) of a specified person, resting elbow to its middle. According to Ibn Rushd, if the ruler does not authorize an article measured by forearm, it is forbidden. Aṣbagh heard from Ibn al-Qāsim that it is valid if the average of the measurement taken two times, however, Aṣbagh himself considers it invalid according to the doctrine of juristic preference and the doctrine of analogy (*qiyās*). Khalīl narrates that it is like its permissibility such as in the *wabyata* and *ḥafnata* wheat when they are measured by the handful of the different sizes, smaller or larger making them consistent to make it equal in the *salam* sale. It is valid to sell one-third of cloth with the description of measurement taken by forearm by a specified person at a deferred payment, if the measurement is seen. They are taken into possession measured by forearm as in the purchase of wheat measured by handful in exchange for *dirham*, if handful is seen, because they can be different. 'Ayāḍ said that the wheat measured ten *madds* is five *ṣā'* and the *ḥafnata* wheat filled with one handful. Al-Jawharī said it to be filled with two handful. The different articles do not obligate different prices, because the validity of it is not related to the description of the articles in the transactions (Al-Aṣbagh, Ibn al-Qāsim, 'Ayāḍ, al-Jawharī).

The example of the descriptions in establishing the prices of articles differ shows in the humans, horse, Roman citizen or black man, and their descriptions, whether they are good or bad which is taken into consideration overall. According to al-Mutīṭī, it is established by the textual evidence (*naṣṣ*). Some of the jurists claim that there is no doubt that these descriptions are acknowledged in all articles of *salam* sale. If it is not a slave, more description is required such as color of an animal, cloth, honey, oil, and palm dates. Similarly, Ibn Ḥājib corroborates with it in the *Tawḍīḥ* with the discussion (*kalām*) of al-Jawharī. Thereafter, he says that if it is not a slave we do not acknowledge the description of color. In this case he relies on al-Māzarī's *kalām*, who does not describe color in other things, but it is not *ẓāhir*. If the price is different in other things and some of them are described (such as) in horse and other animals and the description of color such as in cloth and honey without seeing honeybee, then there are no differences in their prices (Al-Mutīṭī, *al-Tawḍīḥ*, al-Jawharī, al-Māzarī).

More description is required in case of the palm dates and fish imported from different places such as the palm dates grown in Medina, or Swīyā, or al-Wāḥiyā and fish from Alexandria, or Sawīyā or Fayyūmiya, or Suez and other more descriptions such as if it is large, or small, or average. Al-Māzarī says that in case of the palm dates it is required to describe its kind and whether it is of the superior or inferior quality. According to some jurists, more description is needed such as place in which was grown, color, big or small, and if it is newly grown or it is old, and in case of fish, its length, width, or weight. In the *Mudawwana* it is said that the one who sells palm dates in the *salam* sale and does not provide their descriptions, if they are Barnīyā dates backed in a clay bowl and their species, or if he provides descriptions of their species, but not of their quality such as of the superior or inferior quality, then it is void until their species and descriptions are provided. Regarding the moist fish if its species is described, it is valid if it is stipulated with the known quality, length, and the orchard in which it was grown, if the *salam* sale is by the number or weight (Al-Māzarī, *Mudawwana*).

In case of wheat, additional descriptions are needed such as if it is grown newly, or it is old, if their prices are different. According to Ibn Futūḥ, it is preferable if it is described that it is one year old or two years old with some authentication. It is necessary to describe that it was not buried or covered by soil or was left to be dried for a year or watered manually. The price is different for wheat intended for cultivation and not for eating and vice versa. If the price is not different, their description is not requisite. The additional description is needed of wheat, if it is from greater Syria or Egypt or it is cultivated in both places or if they are transported from somewhere else. Būlū indicates the opinion (*qawl*) of Ibn Ḥabīb that it is not obligatory to describe them, if they are in a place where they are bought and to be transported. Al-Bājī holds the opinion against the requisite of these narrations. According to Ibn Bashīr, this is described as an abridgment in the *Ṭawḍīḥ*. If the wheat is cultivated in both places, it is necessary by the textual evidence (*naṣṣ*) to describe the species of each, otherwise the *salam* sale is void. And if both are imported, then Ibn Ḥabīb does not see its invalidation, if they are left there. If the prices and the articles are different, the description of each is necessary, otherwise there is no sense (meaning) of describing them. Ibn al-Qāsim said, "I do not know that there is any repugnancy in it." According to Ibn Muwāz, the reason for it is mixing of the good (superior) articles of food with the bad (inferior) articles of food. According to 'Abd al-Ḥaq, if it is sale of an article of food as a substitute before it is taken into possession, its description is required. In addition, according to the *Muqaddmāt* Mālik, if two articles are combined in the *salam* sale without measurement, then measuring of both articles is not obligatory. This verdict is permitted in case of two articles of food. According to Abū al-Ḥasan, if articles of food are different, then by requirement sale is absolutely void (Ibn Futūḥ, al-Bājī, *al*-Tawḍīḥ, Ibn Bashīr, Ibn al-Qāsim, Ibn Muwāz, 'Abd al-Ḥaq, Abū al-Ḥasan).

HERMENEUTICAL GENERAL FEATURES AND CONTENTS AS REFLECTED IN PARTNERSHIP

Khalīl first describes the very broad features of partnership expounding on the various aspects applicable to all partnerships, and then he describes different kinds of partnership.

The partnership between two or more persons is valid when each partner allows the other partner the usufruct, profit, or loss in the share of his property in partnership, including the manual labor and the responsibilities. Each partner has right in partnership to appoint an agent as his representative. It is also valid for his appointed representative to appoint another agent to commission property of partnership. Both agents must be of legal age and rightly guided Muslims and not the inhabitants of non-Muslim territory. According to the *Mudawwana*, it is valid to appoint a *ḍhimmī* as an agent on the condition that he makes transactions in the presence of owner. In this case, the legal opinions of the *Mudawwana*, Ibn 'Urfa, and al-Lakhmī vary from not allowing *ḍhimmī* as an agent in partnership to its being repugnant, or on certain conditions. Khalīl indicates various legal opinions which are accepted as the *mashhūr* legal rulings. If no legal rulings have reached from the jurists in succeeding generations, Khalīl shows hesitation (*tarddud)* (*Mudawwana*).

If the *ribā* is involved in the profit of partnership, it is preferable to make it charity.

The execution of partnership by the female with the female or the male is valid. If the female is virgin traveling a lot for business purpose and meets or encounters any males, it is preferable that she has an intermediary with her.

The partnership by an owner with his slave with limited rights is valid for business purpose.

If both partners bring gold or silver in equal proportion in weight with negligible difference, it is valid. However, if one of them brings in partnership Ḥāshmīya *dīnārs* and other partner Damashqīya *dīnārs* in equal weight but their usufruct is different, it is not valid. However, the difference is insignificant when they bring gold or silver in greater amount. If they make profit and work together between themselves as agreed, it is valid. If the profit is more of one partner to the profit of another partner, it is invalid.

It is valid to exchange in partnership gold or silver or both for wares not intending it for the articles of food.

If the wares from both sides are in partnership, or capital from one side and wares from another side, then the value of wares is determined on the day when they were rendered in partnership. If the wares are destroyed, their value is determined on the day they were destroyed. If the partnership is canceled, the capital is taken from the price of wares by which they were bought for the business transactions in the partnership.

According to the author of the *Mudawwana,* if the partnership has taken place concerning the articles of food, then each partner is responsible for the capital for which articles of food were bought.

If two persons join in partnership and all or some of the property is destroyed, then the partnership is not invalided, but it continues without mixing the property of one partner with the property of the other partner and is determined as stipulated. It is *ẓāhir*, if the mixing of each other's property has not occurred, the loss is considered in the property of its owner.

If the wares which were bought by the property of one partner for the transactions in partnership and if they become destroyed, they are considered in the partnership with the property of other partner whose property is safe.

Regarding the wares which were bought, if they are considered safe in every circumstance, there are two opinions: (i) if it was in the knowledge at the time of its purchase, then they are considered not in partnership and the profit or loss is as specified for the owner of safe property. This is according to Ibn Rushd. Or (ii) If the owner of safe property claims that he intended to purchase it for himself.

According to Mālik and Ibn al-Qāsim, partnership is valid, if the cash of one partner is not at hand (*ghāba*). However, some jurists restrict it that if the cash is not contributed in partnership, the trading is not allowed in the partnership.

The partnership with the articles of food different in genus, description, and quantity is not valid, but if they are they are of the same kinds, species, and description, it is valid. This is *mashhūr* legal ruling, referring to Mālik. However, if the articles are of the same species having different value, it is forbidden.

DIFFERENT KINDS OF PARTNERSHIP

According to Khalīl, there are seven kinds of partnerships: the partnership in reciprocity (*shirka al-mufāwada),* the partnership in traffic (*shirka al-'aynān),* the partnership in restoration (*shirka jabr),* the partnership in workmanship (*shirka al-'amal*), the partnership in responsibility or credit (*shirka dhiman*), the silent partnership (*shirka muḍāraba*), and the partnership in loan or borrowing (*shirka qurūḍ*). We are specifically going to deal with the partnership in reciprocity, partnership in traffic, partnership in workmanship, and partnership in responsibility or on credit.

PARTNERSHIP IN RECIPROCITY

The partnership in reciprocity is when both partners trade with all or some their capital in the presence or absence of each other for the sale, the purchase, usufruct, and lease-hire. It is valid, if one partner donates gratuitously something from the capital of partnership. If it was not gratuitously donated, it is charged as debt against him. If it is in an insignificant amount, it is permitted. It is not valid that a partner lends money to anyone from the partnership, but it is valid if he lends or makes a gift from the share of his own property.

It is not permitted that a partner deposits the property in partnership in reciprocity without any good reason. If he deposits property with a good reason at the lodging or boarding house and it becomes stolen, he is not responsible for it. However, if he deposits without any good reason, he is responsible for it.

If the partnership in reciprocity is not defined as partnership in reciprocity, it is valid. However, Basāṭī says restriction is necessary in the partnership when it is partnership in reciprocity. Ṭafī says if there is an uncertainty in the ruling, it is not valid for each partner to trade with the property, except with the permission of other partner.

The partnership in traffic is valid without the partnership in reciprocity, because it is simply another kind of partnership.

According to al-Lakhmī, it is valid if one partner takes one-third of his property from the partnership in reciprocity and keeps his remaining property in the partnership in reciprocity for the business transactions.

It is valid for a partner to trade or lend profit made in the partnership in reciprocity without the permission of his partner, if it is for some other specified wares.

It is valid to return the article of purchase for the price, if one fears that it would not be saleable, or there would be loss.

If an old defect appears in the article after it has been purchased, it is valid to return it by one or both partners. If one partner agrees to accept it and another rejects it, it is returned. In the *Mudawwana*, the author says that if one partner accepts it, it is incumbent on the other partner to accept it.

It is valid to sell wares for the price on credit in the partnership in reciprocity. This is *mashhūr* legal ruling. But, it is not valid to purchase wares on credit.

It is not valid in the partnership in reciprocity for each partner to purchase a slave with the contract of emancipation without the permission of another partner, because the price of emancipation of the slave would be prepaid and if that price is more than the price for which he is purchased.

It is not valid in the partnership in reciprocity to take property exclusively for himself for trade for a specified amount of property, except with the permission of another partner. However, it is valid in the partnership in workmanship, because it is excluded from the partnership in reciprocity.

If a partner leases-hires an animal to load goods of partnership on it without the permission of the other partner, then the wages and loss for it are connected to the partnership in reciprocity, but he is responsible for girdle and bridle. According to Abū al-Ḥasan, this is ẓāhir (Abū al-Ḥasan).

Each partner is representative of the other partner in the sale, purchase, execution and termination of contract, claims, and responsibilities for defective articles. If his partner has sold an article and is absent and far away and defect appears in it after purchaser has bought it, it is valid for the purchaser to return it to the other partner. However, if he reappears, the purchaser returns it to him only.

If a partner entrusted to commission sale and purchase and is absent and far away for two days of distance between two safe places to travel and ten days by sea, then his absence is considered not long.

It is obligatory that the profit or the loss is divided equally in the partnership in reciprocity of each partner. If the distribution of profit or loss is stipulated differently and not in proportion to the property of each, it is invalid. The wages for workmanship of each is applied literally (in fact) and the profit or the loss figuratively according to the amount of property.

If one of the partners lies claiming that some of the property which was in his possession is destroyed or lost, then the word rests with him with an oath confirming that the property was destroyed, because he is considered only a custodian.

In the following few paragraphs Khalīl discusses the partnership in reciprocity in which circumstances and conditions the word of a partner is accepted with testimony.

If one of the partners says that the partnership between two of them was fifty and fifty for each partner and the other partner says two-thirds for me and one-third for the other partner, then the word rests with the one who says it was fifty and fifty for each partner (confirming with testimony).

If one of the partners in partnership in reciprocity acquires something and claims that it was only for himself and the other partner says it was in the partnership, then the word rests with the claimer with testimony.

If one of the partners in partnership in reciprocity takes one hundred *dīnārs* from the partnership and claims that he has returned them in the remaining property in partnership, the word of the other partner against him is accepted with testimony. However, if a long time has elapsed between the time when it was contracted and whether dispute between them took place or not, then the word of the one, who claims that he has returned it is accepted with an oath. Ibn Muwāz said that if a short time has elapsed, then the word rests with one, who claims he has returned it without testimony.

If a partner residing at the place of partnership in reciprocity relinquishes expenses for food and clothing and does not charge it, then the expenses are determined according to the custom of place. Likewise, if prices are different at the place of residence and at the place of partnership, then according to Ibn Yūnus, expenses are charged to partnership for the sake of convenience.

Similarly, the expenses for food and clothing for the family members of partners are eliminated, if the ages and numbers of family members of partners are residing at two different places where the prices are different.

If a partner buys a female slave to render services for himself or he has intercourse with her and has paid the price for her from the property of partnership, then the female slave is abandoned from the partnership and he is responsible for the price of her. But if he had purchased her with the permission of his partner, then she is considered the property in partnership and the profit and the loss is for both partners, because his partner has given half of the loan (property) in the partnership.

If one of the partners has bought a female slave with the permission of the other partner and has a speedy intercourse with her, it is disapproved. If she becomes pregnant from the intercourse without having permission of his partner to have intercourse with her, the rectification of price for it is to be established. This is *mashhūr* legal ruling.

PARTNERSHIP IN TRAFFIC

The partnership known as the partnership in traffic is valid when both partners stipulate the usufruct of the property in the presence or absence of each other. If it is stipulated that a partner can have usufruct of the property only in the presence and with the permission of another partner, it is invalid.

It is valid, if one partner brings male birds and the other partner brings female birds with an agreement to hatch the eggs by bringing them together.

If a person says to his representative to buy a thing for him exclusively for the purchase, then the representative does not transgress without his permission, because it is specified for only the purchase.

It is not valid to prevent a person who has been commissioned to usufruct thing in what is paid from his portion of property, except if he says "sell it for me and for you and give me the cash to me until my portion of it is paid." Then, it becomes *rahan* with the one who has been commissioned.

It is valid if a person commissions to purchase and says, "Take these *dīnārs* and buy for me and give me by selling it until the commission is paid to you."

The food articles purchased with the stipulation to trade with them in one place are not to be purchased to trade with them at another place.

PARTNERSHIP IN WORKMANSHIP

Partnership in workmanship is valid with the agreement between two persons to join with each other in workmanship. If both partners work together, the earnings of each are determined according to the work each has performed. Otherwise it is void, because in that case one partner would be taking earnings of workmanship of the other partner.

If the revenues are needed for workmanship, they are taken from partnership in proportion to the workmanship of each partner.

It is not valid for a partner to accuse or blame the other partner. If one of the partners claims that the earnings made in the workmanship were only for him and not for the other partner, it is void. The cooperation between two partners in the workmanship is necessary. It is required to be corrected if partnership to work is at one place. If it is at two different places, it is void.

The tools in the partnership for the workmanship remain in partnership after deducting expenses and profit of each partner.

It is permitted to lease-hire tools owned by one of the partners. This is *ẓāhir*. If tools are taken care of by owning them in partnership or on lease-hire from someone, it is valid.

If two persons join in the workmanship in the same kind of compatible workmanship, it is valid. If their workmanship is different, it is void.

If two persons join in partnership in hidden treasures not knowing whether it is gold or silver or well springs or graveyard and if the Imam permits a person to perform digging to take what is extracted from it for himself. If he dies before finishing the digging, the inheritors are not entitled to the treasures. It is returned to the Imam and he gives it first to the inheritors or anyone else. If the legator dies after all the treasures taken out, no inheritor is entitled to it. The Sulṭān distributes it among Muslims whomever he wishes.

If one partner works in the absence of other partner, then according to the contract of lease-hire it is incumbent on the other partner to pay wages in proportion to the work his partner has performed in his absence. If two partners join in the contract of partnership in workmanship and if one of them falls sick, it is incumbent on the other partner to complete the work.

If the duration of sickness is short, it is not counted, and the wages are divided between them. However, if the sickness is of more than two days, then wages for the partner for the work he has done are determined in excess for those days.

PARTNERSHIP IN LIABILITY OR ON CREDIT

Partnership in liability (*shirka al-ḍamam*) also called partnership on credit (*shirka al-wujūḥ*) is when two persons agree to engage in partnership to purchase for trading without having capital. The responsibility or liability without capital for which each partner purchases on the condition that in what they purchase is not valid, whether both partners are in the same place or at different places. Likewise, the partnertship in liability with little amount of capital by borrowing from each other is not permitted.

Khalīl states several reasons as narrated by different jurists of the earlier generations as to why the partnership in liability is invalid, which one does not find with Shāfi'ī, Mālikī, or Ḥanbalī jurists. We will describe only Ibn Rushd's objection.

According to Ibn Rushd the profit follows the responsibility, because the borrowing from each other is like when the workmanship brings capital from only one partner. It is said in the *Mudawwana* that if a worker sits in a shop for transporting goods and trading with them, and profit made from it is divided between the two is not valid. According to Ibn Ḥājib and Shās that in such a partnership the transactions of purchase and sale are not allowed.

Hermeneutical General Features as Reflected in the Contents of Partnership[27]

As we have already seen in chapter 3, al-Shāfi'ī's account of the partnership was hermeneutically not developed sufficiently. It was later that al-Muzanī and al-Shīrāzī undertook to hermeneutically develop it further. Same could be said of Abū Ḥanīfa, Muḥammad, Abū Yūsuf, and al-Shaybānī as we have seen in chapter 4. It was later that al-Ṭaḥāwī, al-Qudūrī hermeneutically developed it further. Aḥmad bin Ḥanbal's account of partnership is very short, which al-Khiraqī tried to expound hermeneutically further. The case of Mālik's and Saḥnūn is not very much different. Al-Shāfi'ī's concept of hermeneutics was adopted subsequently by Khalīl. His account of partnership is based on the opinions of Mālik, Saḥnūn, and the opinions that were developed hermeneutically over the course of time the jurists in earlier generations.

According to Khalīl, there are seven kinds of partnership: partnership in reciprocity (*shirka mufāwada*), partnership in traffic (*shirka 'aynān*), partnership in restoration (*shirka jabr*), partnership in workmanship (*shirka 'amal*), partnership in responsibility or credit (*shirka ḍhimam* or *wujūh*), and silent partnership (*shirka muḍaraba*). We are going to deal specifically with the partnership in reciprocity, partnership in traffic, partnership in workmanship, and partnership in responsibility or credit as we have done in other compositions of *Mukhtaṣar*.

Khalīl in his account of partnership first describes very broad features of partnership and then he expounds on the different kinds of partnerships.

Partnership between two (or more) persons is valid when each partner allows other partner usufruct of his property, profit or loss, and responsibility, including manual labor. Ibn 'Urfa calls it common or general partnership (*al-shirka al-'amīya*), which is a fortiori valid in contrast to the exclusive partnership (*al-shirka al-shakhṣīya*) when an owner of the property allows partnership only in some of the property, which is invalid (Ibn 'Urfa).

The property acquired in inheritance and booty is not allowed in partnership.

It is valid for a partner to appoint an agent to represent him for the usufruct in his property. Each partner makes usufruct with the permission of other partner. Ibn Ḥājib agrees with Khalīl it and before him Ibn 'Abd al-Salām, and others. It is valid for an agent to commission other person to commission in the property. In the usufruct of property, both agents should be of legal age, of sound mind, free persons, and rightly guided Muslims, and not inhabitants of the enemy territory. Ibn 'Urfa follows (agrees with) all of it. Al-Ghazālī allows it, but he rejects exceeding obligations (Ibn 'Urfa, al-Ghazālī).

The blind person who owns property does not need any agent to sell it, because the sale by a blind person himself is valid. This is *mashhūr* legal ruling.

It is not valid to appoint *ḍimmī* or an inhabitant of enemy territory as an agent. His representation is not valid as indicated by Ibn Shās and Ibn Ḥājib. Probably Khalīl also intends to exclude them from the partnership. It is considered *ẓāhir* from the discourse (*kalām*) in the *Mudawwana* the validity of partnership with *ḍimmī*, though in the beginning he (Saḥnūn) considered it invalid. He said in the chapter partnership that it is not valid for Muslim that he joins *ḍhimmī* in partnership except in his presence and not far away to sell, purchase, settle, and execute contract (Ibn Shās, Ibn Ḥabīb, Saḥnūn).

Ibn 'Urfa al-Lakhmī says if there is any doubt that there was *ribā* involved in the profit made in partnership, then it is preferable to make charity of all the capital in which profit was made such as in trading wine. It is transmitted by al-Qarāfī. It is *ẓāhir* that the ruling of partnership of Muslim should be safe and profit is not indebted to charity and such other things. He said that partnership with *ḍimmī* is valid in his presence when he is executing sell. Then, he said that it is repugnant to join in partnership with *ḍhimmī* who is in debt, if he is commissioned to purchase and sell, otherwise it is permitted (Ibn 'Urfa, al-Qarāfī).

The execution of partnership by a female is valid as described by the author in his discourse (*kalām*). It is said in the *Mudawwana* that the execution of partnership between females and females and between females and males is valid. Al-Lakhmī desires that when female is traveling around, or she is virgin, she should not come in direct contact with a man who is single, because her frequent conversation with a young man in business, it is feared that it can cause temptation. If there is an intermediary between the two, then there is no objection. Ibn 'Urfa desires that the intermediary should be a trustworthy female. Ibn Hindī considers it valid if female and male both are well known to be pious, charitable, believer, and respectful, otherwise not. Abū al-Ḥasan allows it with a person in a degree of consanguinity precluding marriage (*Mudawwana*, al-Lakhmī, Ibn Hindī, Abū al-Ḥasan).

Partnership of an owner of property with his slave with limited rights is valid for business purpose. Al-Lakhmī says that if the slave having no limited rights and is commissioned to purchase or sell, he is not responsible for the loss and destruction of property. Likewise, if he (the slave) is authorized to represent purchase, sale, and weight of an article and if misfortune befall it, it is forfeited. If he is separated from authorization to represent, he becomes responsible for the capital which is destroyed or lost. If there are two slaves who are authorized and if the destroyed property was that generates profit, they are not responsible for it.

According to Abū Isḥāq bin 'Abd al-Rafī', it is required that the ruling is specified in the contract of partnership. It is *mashhūr* legal ruling narrated from Mālik and his companions. Ibn 'Abd al-Salām says that according to the Mālikī *madhhab* it is required that the ruling is specified in the contract of partnership (Abū Isḥāq bin 'Abd al-Salām).

As narrated by Ibn Ḥājib, if in the partnership both partners bring gold or silver approximately in equal proportion, and after weighing them, if there is a negligible difference of weight between them, it is valid. In the *Mudawwana*, it is narrated that if one of them brings *Hāshmīya dīnārs* and the other brings *Damasqīya dīnārs* equal in weight, or one of them brings *Yazidīya dīnārs* and the other brings *Muḥammadīya dīnārs* and their usufruct is different, it is not valid, except if the difference is insignificant when both partners bring gold or silver more in quantity. If both partners make profit and work with it between themselves as agreed, it is valid. If the profit for one partner is in excess of another partner, it is invalid. This is not valid as in the rulings of the contracts of sale, and partnership, and weight (Ibn Ḥājib).

Partnership is valid with gold and silver in which one partner brings gold and silver and in the same way other partner brings gold and silver as stipulated in equal amount of weight and their usufruct. It is valid to exchange gold or silver, or both gold and silver in exchange for wares not intending with it to include articles of food. It is valid to exchange it without food articles in exchange for other articles, indicating absolutely that they are of the same species such as cotton and silk, consisting of wares for one of them and the food article for the other. In the *Mudawwana*, partnership with food articles and *dirhams*, and with things and wares, is valid and the profit and workmanship are determined in their proportion (*Mudawwana*).

If there are wares in partnership from both sides or capital from one side and wares from the other side, then the value of wares is determined on the day it was rendered in partnership. If the value of wares is equal in comparison to capital, then the partnership is half and half for each, otherwise in proportion to the values of wares and capital mixed. If the wares are destroyed, their price is determined on the day they were destroyed. If the partnership is invalidated, the capital is taken from the (price of) wares by which the wares were bought for business purpose, because it was his property and it was in his responsibility.

As narrated in the *Mudawwana*, if partnership has occurred in an invalid food, then each partner is responsible for his capital by which the food was sold (*Mudawwana*).

If two persons or more join in valid partnership and then all or some of property of the one partner is destroyed, which was in his responsibility, then he is not removed from partnership. Partnership remains intact and is continued without mixing the property of one partner with the property of other partner as indicated in the ruling, otherwise the destruction is considered loss in owner's property. It is *ẓāhir* as the acquisition of partnership is with respect to profit and loss, and not with respect to responsibility. Al-Rajrājī aids that according to Ibn al-Qāsim loss was due to the destruction of property and not in profit (increase) of it, because it was from his property before mixing their properties in partnership. Ibn 'Urfa said that the stipulation establishes responsibility of partnership between them with mixing of gold or silver by ruling. Al-Bannānī says that according to the author, it is *ẓāhir* that the mixing of property as stipulated was required of it. It is also the opinion of Saḥnūn (Rajrājī, Ibn al-Qāsim, al-Bannānī, Saḥnūn).

If the mixing of property of both partners is not occurred, neither in fact nor by ruling, and if the property of both or one them is destroyed, then it is the responsibility of its owner only. If the wares were bought for trading with the property of one which is destroyed, then it is considered in partnership with the one whose property is safe as narrated in the *Mudawwana.* In case of profit or loss, it belongs to both partners, then partnership between two of them is half and half for each of them, otherwise it is calculated in proportion to one's property (*Mudawwana*).

Whether wares which were bought are in partnership considered safe of its owner in every circumstance? (i) if it was in the of knowledge of owner of safe property at the time of purchase, then wares are considered not in partnership between the two of them and the profit or loss is as specified for the owner of safe property for the article purchased with it. This is the opinion of Ibn Rushd. (ii) Ibn Yūnus, contrary to what has preceded restricts, if the owner of safe property claims that he intended to purchase it only for himself. If that is what he claims that wares were bought for him by the agreement between them, then the answer is *tarddud* as the jurists in the earlier generations did not discuss the meaning of the legal opinion in the *Mudawwana.* If the remaining money is in the possession of owner until one of them has bought a female slave with the property in partnership and the property of other partner is destroyed, then the property destroyed is considered to belong to its owner and the female slave bought is considered to belonging to both partners. Ibn Rushd and others understand the first meaning of ruling of the *Mudawwana* and Ibn Yūnus the second meaning. Then several comments follow about the secondary issues (*Mudawwana*, Ibn Rushd, Ibn Yūnus).

According to Mālik and Ibn al-Qāsim, partnership is valid if the cash of one of the partners is not at hand (*ghāba*). This is *mashhūr* legal ruling. According to al-Lakhmī, it is preferable. Some of the shaykhs restrict it. If the cash to be contributed in partnership is not at hand for a long time, it is valid. However, the trading is not done if one of the partners has contributed cash in partnership but not the other partner (Mālik, Ibn al-Qāsim, al-Lakhmī).

The partnership is not valid when gold of one partner is combined with silver of other partner in the partnership and *ṣarf* sale. Ibn 'Abd al-Salām takes an objection against regarding that partnership and *ṣarf* sale are not separated ('Abd al-Salām).

The partnership with articles of food of different species or description or quantity is not valid, but if they are of the same kinds (species) and descriptions, then it is valid and *mashhūr* legal ruling which refers back to Mālik, because it is obligatory to sell food for substitute before it is taken into possession, since each partner sells to his partner some food in exchange for food of other partner and each partner sells the remaining some of food available to anyone (stranger). Mālik discusses it in partnership with the articles of food, things or wares and permits it. According to Ibn 'Urfa, it is forbidden, if there are two articles of food of the same species having different value of one exceeding to the value of other. Al-Ṣaqlī agrees with it (Mālik, Ibn 'Urfa, *Mudawwana*, al-Ṣaqlī).

And Ibn al-Qāsim says, "I do not know if there is apparently any repugnancy." Ibn Muwāz's reasoning is that there is mixing of good and bad articles of food in it. 'Abd al-Ḥaq's considers it sale of article of food as substitute before it is taken into possession. For Ismā'īl, the requirement of partnership is the equality in value of articles and the sale requires their equality of measurement, both are not found in this case. Furthermore, others have said that combing of two things with or without measurement is permitted. According to Mālik, it is permitted in case of food. According to Abū al-Ḥasan, if articles of food are different, then by requirement it is absolutely void (Ibn al-Qāsim, 'Abd al-Ḥaq, Ismā'īl, Mālik, Abū al-Ḥasan).

PARTNERSHIP IN RECIPROCITY

The partnership in reciprocity between two persons is when each partner trades with all the capital of partnership in the presence or absence of other partner, without the permission or knowledge of other partner regarding purchase, sale, lease-hire, and such kinds to which it is applicable. However, if it is in one kind of article in which it is traded such as linen cloth or perfume and it is known that it is a property with which he is trading for himself. If the workmanship enters the property of partnership, then it is determined in proportion to the capital of each in partnership. If one of the partners in partnership in reciprocity has things or wares and not the other partner, it does not invalidate the partnership in reciprocity. In the *Tawḍīḥ*, it is not invalidated according to the Mālikī school of law (*madhhab*). As mentioned earlier in chapter 4, according to Abū Ḥanīfa, Abū Yūsuf, and al-Shaybānī, partnership in reciprocity was valid contrary to which al-Shāfi'ī and Mālik considered it invalid. In fact, Mālik does not acknowledge partnership in reciprocity. Khalīl and after him Ibn Ḥājīb, contrary to the opinion of Mālik, hold a different view. This should be attributed to the acceptance of al-Shāfi'ī's concept of hermeneutics and its further develpements. Furthermore, this shows that Khalīl is concerned only with the *mashhūr* legal opinions, regardless from which individual jurists or school of law.

It is valid, if a partner in partnership in reciprocity donates something gratuitously from the capital of partnership without the permission of the other partner as narrated in the *Mudawwana*. If it is not given gratuitously, it is forbidden and is charged as debt against the partner who donated it, or if it is not given gratuitously and is of very insignificant amount such as lending bucket, axe, hand mill, giving a slice of bread, or drinking water to poor, and lending servant to bring animal to drink water, it is valid. The idea is that if is in less or in very insignificant amount, it is allowed. If it is in a large amount and due to which the other partner may become victim of debt or similar calamity befalls him and he suffers loss in the trading in future, then it is prohibited. Similarly, if a partner authorizes an agent to work without authorization of his partner, then the partner who authorized agent is responsible in his portion of capital and pays him for his work performed from it, except if what agent has performed is destroyed. It is also not valid for partner in partnership in reciprocity to lend property (capital) of partnership, except if he is permitted, or it is in very insignificant amount such as lending servant an animal to drink water. I (the author) hope, it is not objectionable to lend it. This is well known (*ma'ārūf*) that no partner is permitted to do it except with the permission of other partner, except if it is intended for the trade as the custom.

If a partner makes a gift or lends from the known portion of his partnership for which he is responsible, it is valid except if he does it with the payment received in advance. It is valid for him to invest the known profit from the partnership to purchase goods from such and such a place and sends it to his partner and pays for it from the property of partnership to the one who trades for the known portion of his profit without the permission of other partner. According to al-Lakhmī, this is only if the property is large that it would need excessively large amount like its price. However, if it is not excessively large, then with the permission of his partner, or if the thing is unsaleable and it is expensive to bring it to the other place and there is no (safe) road to travel with the goods to bring it at that place in good condition (Al-Lakhmī).

It is not permitted that a partner deposits anything from the property of partnership, except if there is some good reason or excuse. If the person to whom it is deposited dies and the deposited property is not found for which he was responsible, whether it was the property in partnership in reciprocity or not, he is not responsible. However, if the property was deposited with a good reason and he has deposited it at his arrival to a place of lodging and boarding not safe from theft, he is not responsible, but if he has deposited property without any reason, he is responsible for it. Abū al-Ḥasan says that if there was any suspicion, he is responsible to pay for it (Abū al-Ḥasan).

If the partnership is not specified as the partnership in reciprocity, it is valid according to the *Mudawwana*. Regarding this, al-Bisāṭī says that the restriction is necessary to specify that it is the partnership in reciprocity. Ṭafī says that if the partnership in reciprocity is specified and there is an uncertainty (*gharar)* in its ruling (*qawl*), then it is not valid for each partner to trade with it, except with the permission of the other partner (*Mudawwana*, al-Bisāṭī, Ṭafī).

However, if partnership is specified as the partnership in traffic (*sharka al-'aynān*) without the partnership in reciprocity, it is valid, because it is simply one kind of trade among other trades.

According to al-Lakhmī, it is valid if one-third is taken out from the partnership in reciprocity in any specified thing such as wares or slave or *dīnārs* and keeping remaining other two-thirds in partnership for trading with it (Al-Lakhmī).

Abū al-Ḥasan accordingly says that a partner in the partnership in reciprocity can trade with the profit made in it and lend it without the permission of the other partner. Ibn Yūnus says giving profit and to lend it to others is valid, if partnership is for the specified of wares or wares for trading. However, if it is the partnership in reciprocity and property of one partner is for the usufruct in partnership, then it is not valid for the other partner to usufruct it (Abū al-Ḥasan, Ibn Yūnus).

It is valid for him to return wares in partnership in exchange for the same price with which he has bought it, if he fears that it would not be saleable or there would be loss. This is according to the opinion (*qawl*) from the *Mudawwana* (*Mudawwana*).

It is valid to return the article, if any old defect appears after it had been purchased by one partner or both partners. If one partner rejects it and the other partner accepts it, it is returned to the seller. In the *Mudawwana*, it is said that if a partner buys a slave and finds him defective and agrees to accept it, then it is incumbent on the other partner to accept it (*Mudawwana*).

If the article is purchased in the partnership in reciprocity in exchange for something such as food or something else, then the partner who has bought it is responsible for it. Ibn al-Qāsim specifies that it should be consistent (agreeable) with the thing purchased. Ashhab further specifies that the article of food is purchased for business transaction in the place where it is bought, but not at a different place where one needs to travel for trading it or it was purchased for acquisition or ransoming a prisoner of war (Ibn al-Qāsim, Ashhab).

If one of the partners is accused of lying concerning partnership in reciprocity, it is incumbent on the other partner to accept what is established by the testimony of a stranger, who is not in near relation to the one who has been accused of lying without favoring him. If one who testifies is his father, or offspring, or friend, his testimony is not accepted.

It is valid to sell wares from the property of partnership in reciprocity for the deferred payment at a future specified time. This is according to the *mashhūr* legal ruling, but it is not valid to buy wares for partnership in reciprocity on credit. According to Ṭafī and Ibn Shās except Ibn Ḥājib, the article of purchase (on credit) for the trading is valid. Ibn 'Abd al-Salām says that the sale on credit is valid. This is *mashhūr* legal ruling in the Mālikī *madhhab* of the *Mudawwana*. However, Mālik says that it is repugnant to take any property for trading on credit in the partnership in reciprocity. If they do it, then it is considered as if what each of them has bought is from his own property. He said that it is valid, if the price of article of purchase is delayed for two or three days. This is what the people must do it. Then some miinor points are discussed by earlier jurists in the succeeding generations (Ṭafī, Ibn 'Abd al-Salām, Ibn Ḥājib, Ibn Shās, Mālik).

Similarly, it is not valid for each partner without the permission of the other partner, except with the permission of the other partner such as to purchase a slave with the contract of emancipation in partnership in reciprocity, if the price is more than of his emancipation, because it is possible that the slave withdraws from it without emancipation and similarly for the slave with the limited rights in the partnership in reciprocity, it is not valid except with the permission of the other partner. It is not permitted for one partner to take property exclusively for himself to trade with it for a specified amount of profit, except with the permission of his partner. However, it is valid in the partnership in reciprocity to trade with a specified amount of property exclusively for himself with the permission of his partner, because the workmanship is excluded from the partnership in reciprocity and there is nothing for his partner in it. This Saḥnūn said in the *Mudawwana* (*Mudawwana*).

If a partner hires independently an animal to load goods for partnership without the permission of other partner, then for the wages of carriage, profit, or loss he is responsible, including girdle and bridle. If one of the partners borrows an animal to ride on it for himself or carry property in partnership and it becomes destroyed, he is responsible for it and there is nothing incumbent on his partner, because he says, "I am engaged in the workmanship and not responsible for any loss" and other partner says, 'There is no responsibility for borrowed animal, except in case of transgression." Abū al-Ḥasan says it is *ẓāhir* from the discourse (*kalām*) of Ibn al-Qāsim concerning the animals. (Abū al-Ḥasan, Ibn al-Qāsim)

Each partner is representative of the other partner in sale, purchase, leasing-renting, execution, and termination of the contract, and discharging claims and responsibility for defect. If one partner has sold an article and he is absent and far away and, then the old defect appears in the article after the purchaser has bought it, it is valid that the purchaser can return it to the other partner who is present, as he is representative of his partner to commission it. However, if his partner reappears, the purchaser does not return article to any other person except him.

If the partner, who is entrusted to commission sale, is absent and far away for ten days of distance between two places with the safe streets and two days (more) with the fear, then the absence is considered not long. It is not conceived in the conscience as the absence. This is according to the divine statute (*ḥadd*).

If one of the partners lies claiming that some property in his possession is destroyed or incurred loss, then the word rests with the claimer in whose possession was property as in case of robbery, because he is only a custodian. In the *Tawḍīḥ*, it is restricted to the absence of appearance of any lie. If his partner accuses him and takes an oath to that effect, then it is considered that he lied and the partner who claimed that it was destroyed is responsible for its loss (*Al-Tawḍīḥ*).

It is obligatory that the profit and loss in the property of partnership is divided in proportion to the property of each, otherwise there is no partnership (it is void). If the distribution of profit and loss is stipulated at different rate and not in proportion to the amount of the property of each, it is invalid. For each partner, the wages for the workmanship is applied literally (in fact) and the profit is applied figuratively according to the amount of the property.

If one partner says that partnership in the property between us is fifty and fifty for each and the other partner says it was two-thirds for himself and one-third for the other partner, the word with an oath is accepted of the one, who claims it was half and half.

If one of the partners in the partnership in reciprocity acquires something and claims that it was only for himself and his partner says it was from the property of partnership, then the word rests with the claimer in every case with the testimony as in case of the inheritance. But if he says we did not know beforehand, the word rests with him except the testimony of evidence is not inserted in it.

If one of the partners in partnership in reciprocity takes one hundred *dīnārs* from the property of partnership and claims by lying to his partner that he has returned them with the remaining property which was in his possession, then the word of other partner is accepted with the testimony against him confirming that he has taken one hundred *dīnārs* from the property of partnership and he (the other partner) takes them from the property in partnership, except if long time has elapsed between what had taken place and the dispute between them arises or not, he is not freed from it, except with the testimony that he has returned it. Ibn Muwāz said that if only short duration of time has elapsed between what he has taken place and dispute regarding that he has returned. If the long time has elapsed and he does not testify, then the word rests with the one who claimed that he has returned that property he had taken (Ibn Muwāz).

Similarly, regarding the verdict concerning the claim of responsibility in partnership in reciprocity, he said that one of the partners claims that he has made tax payment of the other partner from the property of partnership without furnishing any evidence, then if his partner or his inheritor after his death claims that it was paid from the property of partnership, then the word rests with the one who claims that tax was paid from the property of partnership in reciprocity. Except, if the long time has elapsed between when the tax was paid and the dispute such as one year, then the word with the testimony is accepted of the one, who claims that he has paid tax from the property of partnership in reciprocity and it is free and clear in every way (circumstance).

If each partner relinquishes what he spends on himself to buy food and clothing from the property of partnership in reciprocity and does not charge it to the partnership, whether they are residing in the same place or two different places, where the prices for food and clothing are the same or different in those places, then the expenses for food and clothing are determined according to the custom and, likewise, for the provision for each of them. In case, the prices are different, then it is considered for the business transaction for making it convenient. This is the opinion of Ibn Yūnus (Ibn Yūnus).

Similarly, expenses of food and clothing for the family members of partners are eliminated, if their numbers and ages are different residing at two different places. This is according to Ibn ʻUrfa from Mālik, the expenses are eliminated for the dependents of both, if they are family members residing at two different prices where the prices are different. According to al-Ṣuqalī, as narrated by Sulaymān from Ibn al-Qāsim, this is when near relations are family members. Al-Tūnsī (Saḥnūn) said, it is necessary that if each partner has family members and the prices are different at two places, then the partners are not provided expenses (Ibn ʻUrfa, Mālik, al-Ṣuqalī, Ibn al-Qāsim, al-Tunsī Saḥnūn).

Ibn ʻAbd al-Salām says that if one of the partners is content with crushed grain food and rough clothing and other partner is opposite of it in the ways of his living, then it is charged from the provision of each partner. It is like charging expenses for the relatives only from his own provision. Ibn ʻUrfa says if one partner has relatives and child and not the other partner, then each one pays for his own provisions (ʻAbd al-Salām, Ibn ʻUrfa).

If one of the partners purchases a female slave for himself to render services for him, or he has intercourse with her or not, and he has paid the price for her from the property of the partnership, then the female servant is abandoned from the partnership and he pays price of her in every case, but if he has bought her in partnership with the permission of other partner, then the profit and loss is for both partners, because his partner has given half of loan in the partnership. Likewise, as Ibn Yūnus and Abū al-Ḥasan have transmitted it, if he has bought her with the permission of his partner to render services for him (Ibn Yūnus, Abū Ḥasan).

If one of the partners has bought female slave for the partnership and unites with her in the intercourse with the permission of his partner and has speedy intercourse with her and whether she becomes pregnant or not, the exposure of the private parts of her body is disapproved. (Thus, he is responsible for her price.)

If he has intercourse with her without the permission of his partner and she does not become pregnant, rectification for the intercourse with her is to be established. This is *mashhūr* legal ruling as described in the chapter "Children of the Slave Women" in the *Mudawwana*. This is consistent with what is in the chapter "Partnership" by Mālik. It is also *mashhūr* legal ruling in the Mālikī school of law (*madhhab*) (Ibn Rushd, Mālik).

PARTNERSHIP IN TRAFFIC

In the partnership known as the partnership in traffic (*al-shirka al-'aynān*), if both partners stipulate usufruct of property of each other in the presence or absence of each other, it is valid. 'Abd al-Salām says that it means that it is valid for both partners to make usufruct in the property of each in the presence or absence of each other. If it is stipulated that one of the partners does not have usufruct in the absence of other partner, except in his presence and with his agreement, it is not considered acting independently in the usufruct of property in partnership (Ibn 'Abd al-Salām, Ibn 'Urfa 'Ayāḍ).

It is valid that one partner has male birds and the other partner female birds with an agreement to hatch the eggs by bringing them together for the poultry in partnership. It is narrated from Ibn al-Qāsim regarding the pigeons bringing together to help hatching. Ibn Salmūn asked for the advice of some jurists regarding a person, who gave rooster and other person gave hens while both partners were in bankruptcy, he said it is not valid, because of the debt. He said that it is valid, if one person brought the female pigeon and the other person the male pigeon to unite them to hatch eggs, because the male pigeon and the female pigeon help each other in hatching (Ibn al-Qāsim, Ibn Salmūn).

If a person says to the other person to buy a thing for him for such and such as his representative on the condition that it is exclusively for the purchase and not for the sale, then his representative is not permitted to transgress, because it is specified only for the purchase. And if he says, "Buy it for me and for you," it is valid to "pay price of his portion" in what he has bought as his representative.

It is not valid to prevent the person who has been commissioned from usufruct in his portion of property, except if the one who has commissioned it says, "Sell it for me and for you and go on paying cash to me until price is paid to you of my portion of it." In this case, it becomes *rahan* with the one who has been commissioned. This is according to the contract of *rahan* pertaining to the property.

If a person commissions to purchase with the price of his portion and says, "Take these *dīnārs* and buy with them for me and for you and cash payment is for me and for you and give me in exchange what is paid to you as it proceeds further," it is valid according to Ibn al-Qāsim for the one who commissions to give it as a loan to the one who has been commissioned, because it is *ma'rūf* (well established) in any circumstance;' it is not valid, however, if it is a loan generating profit (Ibn al-Qāsim).

The purchase of article of food stipulated to trade with it in one place is not to be purchased in another place. It is not permitted to purchase with it for the successors, *mahr*, and ransoming prisoner.

PARTNERSHIP IN WORKMANSHIP

The partnership in workmanship is valid with the agreement between two parties, if they both join in tailoring or in different workmanships, but it is necessary that such a workmanship of one partner is compatible with the workmanship of the other partner such as knitting, spinning, and weaving. If workmanship of one partner is not compatible with the workmanship of the other partner, then it is void because in that case one takes the revenues (earnings) of workmanship of his partner. If both partners work jointly together, then each partner takes earnings in proportion to his work. If the work of one partner is one-third and work of other partners is two-thirds, then one takes proportionally one-third of proceeds and the other takes two-thirds of proceeds.

Or if both partners do not work jointly together as the custom such that one of them works more than half or one-third, then accordin to earnings that flow from it for more than half or one-third. If revenues are needed in the workmanship, they are taken from the partnership in proportion to the performance of work one has performed. If there are no revenues, it is not valid to accuse or blame (*'atabīya)* as in the claim regarding the catch of fish between two partners. One partner says to the other partner that we cooperate (only) for some of things in the partnership, but not in this, thus the share of hunt is only for him and he takes the catch, denying it to give any share of it to other partner and says that was (only) for him and there is nothing of it in the partnership, because of the invalidity of partnership in it. Ibn Rushd says that the partnership in the manual work is not permitted as it requires cooperation when they entered into the partnership in workmanship. Each partner working for himself is deceptive (fallacious). It is corrected by fulfilling stipulations as it was required from the beginning of partnership, if it was at one place. The stipulation in *Mudawwana* is that if the partnership in workmanship between them was combined at two places, then it is considered blameworthy. It is entered by Ibn *Ḥājib* in his register. Ibn Nājī considers it *mashhūr* legal ruling (Ibn Rushd, *Mudawwana*, Ibn Ḥabīb, Ibn Nājī).

Regarding tools such as tools of carpenter and tools of jeweler in the partnership in workmanship remain as the property in partnership after deducting its expenses and profit of each partner. This is the opinion of Saḥnūn, but some jurists interpret the *Mudawwana* differently (Saḥnūn).

It is permitted to lease-hire tool owned by one of the partners in proportion to his portion in partnership. According to 'Ayāḍ and others this is *ẓāhir* in the *Mudawwana* and according to Ibn 'Abd al-Salām, it is *mashhūr*. In the valid partnership in workmanship, it is permitted that the tools are taken care of by owning them by both partners or renting them from someone else. This is the opinion of Ibn al-Qāsim and others. It is also related in the *Mudawwana.* Both interpretations are omitted by Khalīl ('Ayāḍ, 'Abd al-Salām, Ibn al-Qāsim).

It is valid in the partnership in workmanship when two medical doctors combine their medical practice, one of them making medicine and the other selling it. However, al-Lakhmī and others said that if they differ in pursuing medical practice, it is invalid. If two hunters join in partnership in owning or renting two falcons or dogs on the condition that they are not separated in hunting and each of them brings catch and each of them leases-hires half of it to the other with the agreement or each one of them brings prey and leases-hires half of it to the other as preceded before with or without the agreement, and one of them demands and takes it alone, they are not separated (from the partnership) as one finds in some narrations of the *Mudawwana* (*Mudawwana*).

Is it valid or invalid if two persons join hunting in partnership by owning or leasing-hiring from the other, if both hunters are separated being at different places or are in different professions of hunting as narrated in the *Mudawwana*? Al-Bannānī expresses this by interpreting that (i) it is not valid, if they join in partnership on the condition that each hunt with the falcon or dog, except by owning them and guarding each other or (ii) it is valid, if one of them demands that the two dogs or falcons not to be separated from each other, then it is valid. Al-Tunsī, likewise, maintains that if one partner brings falcon and the other partner dog and they help each other in hunting, it is valid (Al-Bannānī, al-Tunsī).

Likewise, it is valid if two persons in partnership join in digging hidden treasures when it is not known whether it is gold or silver, or well, spring, or graveyard, or something else, if they are marked off at one place. Al-Mutīṭī considers that it is not valid to do digging, if the treasures are in a cave and this is only for the cave. If Imam permits a person to perform it and take what is extracted from it for himself and if he dies before completion of digging, then no inheritor is entitled to treasures in it. It is returned to Imam and he gives it to the inheritor of deceased person or others.

If no inheritor is entitled in the remaining treasures and the legator or near relative shows up to obtain treasures, and it appears or nearly it appears that no treasures or some treasures have come out of it, then the entitlement of inheritor in the remaining treasure is void. If the legator dies after treasures have been taken out from it completely, then no inheritor is entitled to the treasures. According to al-Qābasī, it is restricted by the *ḥaṭṭ* or *aṣl* (Al-Qābasī).

The expression in the *Mudawwana* is shortened by Ibn Yūnus. If one of the partners dies after the realization of the attainment of treasures, the inheritor does not inherit any portion from the treasures. The Sulṭān distributes it among Muslims whomever he wishes. Ibn al-Qāsim says if the treasures obtained have been taken out of the cave and are distributed between the partners, then there is nothing in the treasures for the inheritors of deceased except what the Imam distributes to them or others (Ibn Yūnus, Ibn al-Qāsim).

If one partner in partnership works in the absence of the other partner, then according to the contract of lease-hire, it is incumbent on his partner to pay wages for it in proportion to the work his partner has performed in his absence. He said in the *Mudawwana* that what one of the partners receives for his work is incumbent on the other partner to reimburse him when they separate from the partnership as it was in his responsibility (*Mudawwana*).

According to al-Lakhmī, if two partners agree to make contract of lease-hire for the workmanship and then one of them falls sick or dies, then it is incumbent on the other partner to finish remaining work to completion, regardless whether the contract of lease-hire has guaranteed it or not (Al-Lakhmī).

If one of the partners falls sick such as for two days or he is absent during the time of his sickness, it is not considered sickness, and wages are divided between them, but if the duration of sickness or his absence prolongs, then not. He said in the *Mudawwana* that if one partner is absent for one or two days and his partner works, this matter is valid between the partners except that there is no monstrosity committed in prolonging it. It is valid, if the partner who performed work likes to give his partner half of the wages, (even) if it was not stipulated originally in the contract (*Mudawwana*).

If one of the partners becomes sick or absent for a longer time than two days, then the wages for the work performed by the other partner during that period are determined in excess for him for those days. This is according to Ibn Yūnus. According to Khalīl, there is no definite ruling transmitted from the earlier jurists in the following generations (*taruddūd*) (Ibn Yūnus, Khalīl).

PARTNERSHIP IN LIABILITY

The partnership in liability (*shirka al-ḍamam*), which is also called the partnership on credit (*shirka al-wujūh*), is invalid when two persons agree to make purchase without having capital (*māl*). Saḥnūn said that no one makes any purchase on credit in partnership. It is specified in the *Mudawwana* that no one is permitted, except with having capital, or manual workmanship of both partners in the same kind of workmanship. The responsibility without having capital for which each partner purchases on credit is not permitted, regardless if both partners are in the same place or at two different places and rendering services in all business transactions or some of the transactions in partnership. Likewise, it is invalid that both partners join in partnership with little amount of capital by borrowing from each other, one partner says to other partner "you carry (responsibility) for me in half of what I buy" and the other partner says to him "you carry (responsibility) for me in half of what I buy," except if it is a purchase of specified wares in each other's presence or absence, then it is valid, because it was before the contract was drawn between the two of them that one partner is responsible for the other partner. Abū al-Ḥasan considers that it is repugnant. Ibn Rushd says this is as what Abū Ḥasan says, because profit follows labilities, when there is a borrowing from each other. It is like when workmanship brings capital from only one partner and not from the other partner (Saḥnūn, Abū al-Ḥasan, Ibn Rushd).

In the *Mudawwana,* it is said that if the worker sits in a shop for transporting goods and earnings made from it are to be divided between the owner of shop and the worker, then it is not valid. 'Isā heard from a person who said, "Sit in my shop and I would take your goods to sell and the profit is made in half or one third for you," and he decreed it invalid ('Isā).

Secondly, the author explains the difference in partnership on credit when a person, who is known among people, desires to buy wares from a merchant, it is valid and if he is not known, it is invalid. Ibn Ḥājib says that the partnership on credit is not valid and explains that it is considered a sale of unknown property on credit for some profit. It is a liability in the purchase and sale, and the profit between them is without the property between the two partners, it is void and invalidated. Ibn Shās is of the same of opinion and it is related from some of the former men of knowledge and secondly from ʻAbd al-Wahāb (Ibn Ḥājib, Ibn Shās, ʻAbd al-Wahāb).

If it is stipulated in the contract by the owner of hand mill, or owner of house, or owner of animals that his representative works and the revenues generated from it are only for him and he pays wages for the workmanship to his representative, then according to Ibn al-Qāsim, the revenues are not allowed to single out for the owner of animals (Ibn al-Qāsim).

If a partner who has usufruct in a structure or immovable property such as the bathroom and attached fixtures *(barḥa)* needing repair, and his partner wants to inhabit or sell the portion of structure and the Qāḍī orders to repair it and if he refuses, then the Qāḍī rules against him to sell it.

According to Ibn al-Qāsim, regarding an apartment shared by two partners, one partner residing upstairs, and the other partner residing downstairs, and the roof of apartment breaks down, then the owner of part of upstairs repairs it and, likewise, if the wall is destroyed of the lower part of apartment, it is incumbent on him to build it. According to Ibn Rushd, this issue is correctly described as it is described in the *Mudawwana* and there is no difference of opinion in it (Ibn al-Qāsim, Ibn Rushd).

LEASE-HIRE

Hermeneutical General Features as Reflected in Lease-Hire and its Contents[28]

The contract of lease-hire is valid according to the *sharīʻa*. According to Ibn Shās, there are three constitutive elements (*arkān*, pl. of *rukn*): (i) contract between the two parties, (ii) specified amount of wages or recompense, and (iii) usufruct of thing for which it is hired-leased.

The stipulation of wages is incumbent in a valid contract of lease-hire such as the wages of a person for the services rendered for a year and expediting of it is obligatory. Its postponement is a deception. Or if the expediting of it is not specified, then its fulfillment is obligatory according to the stipulation or custom. If its expedition is not specified, then the expedition of it is attended at the time of lease-hire as stipulated. Or if the duration of lease-hire is neither specified nor stipulated, then the wages are the responsibility of lessee such as the wages for sewing cloth for a *dirham* and the worker does not begin work, then obligation for its expediting becomes freed from the very beginning as debt is canceled against debt. If he begins it afterward, then it is not obligatory to expedite it. ʻAbd al-Wahāb said debt against debt is canceled (fulfilled) with the possession of usufruct by the lessor and the possession of wages by the lessee (Ibn Shās, 'Abd al-Wahāb).

Except lessor leases-hires a camel for riding on it or carry load on it for going to pilgrimage during the specified time of season, neither earlier before its timing nor later than that, then the wages for its expediting is incumbent on him. This expediting includes staying at all places. If before the time of travel, it is feared that the camel would run away or its haughtiness at the time of journey would prevent from going to pilgrimage, then the wages for hiring of camel becomes forfeited.

Ibn Muwāz narrates from Mālik that the wages of lessee comprise the payment at a future time as in pilgrimage. During other times it is not valid that the payment is delayed. He continued to say that it is not appropriate, except with one-third of wages is paid in advance of what is incumbent at the time of journey and the rest of it at return, and he said if the leasie-hire is without any intervals or interruptions, it is not appropriate to delay the cash payment in *dīnārs* and their like. However, Abū Muḥammad says if it is intended without a deferred payment and the riding of animal has begun, it is valid without the cash payment. Ibn Yūnus says it is valid, if the lease-hire of an animal comprises riding only on a specified time for cash payment, but if it is for a deferred payment, it is invalid (Mālik, Ibn Muwāz, Abū Muḥammad).

Al-Mutīṭī narrates from Abū Zayd who narrated it from Ibn al-Qāsim that the lease-hire comprising specified time is not described in case of pilgrimage based on the origin (*aṣl*) (Al-Mutīṭī, Abū Zayd, Ibn al-Qāsim).

If the wages are not specified, and if the deferred payment, or the usufruct is not stipulated, the lease-hire does not begin until the lessee receives usufruct of the specified day and pays wages to the lessor on that day.

The lease-hire of a thing at a deferred payment of wages is not acted upon according to the custom. This is according to Ibn al-Qāsim. Ibn Yūnus says it is because the custom is considered like stipulation even if it was not regulated between parties to the contract and they have leased-hired with cash payment or deferred payment. According to Ibn al-Qāsim, the *aṣl* is that the prepayment of wages is not requisite in the contract of lease-hire, except according to the custom or stipulation, contrary to the case of purchase of the specified thing in which cash payment is required (Ibn al-Qāsim, Ibn Yūnus).

Similarly, the lease-hire and the wages in one contract is invalid according to the *mashhūr* legal opinion. Ibn 'Urfa says that this is different from combining the sale and the wages in one contract. According to Ibn Rushd, the wages and the lease-hire are not combined in one contract, because the contract of the lease-hire is not concluded, except with the known wages. It is narrated from Saḥnūn that the contract of lease-hire of an orchard which the lessee undertakes to cultivate in exchange for it he becomes owner of one-half of the yield (*al-mughārasa*) is considered combining the wages and the sale, it is invalid. It is not valid by the *aṣl* to combine the lease-hire and the *salaf* sale in one contract (Ibn 'Urfa, Ibn Rushd, Saḥnūn).

The lease-hire in combination with the sale in one contract is invalid according to the consensus. Likewise, the lease-hire for skinning an animal in exchange for meat is invalid. The lease-hire for grinding flour involves deception, because the quantity or the description of it is not known. The skinning a sheep in exchange for its meat is not valid. According to Ibn Shās, the lease-hire of skinning animal by a butcher in exchange for the meat is not valid. Ibn 'Urfa says, the skinning is regulated as what has preceded before according to the ruling of contract of sale (Shās, Ibn 'Urfa).

The lease-hire is valid for grinding wheat in weight of an *ardabb* in exchange for a *dirham* and a heap of wheat in exchange for thinning it. According to Mālik, what is valid in the contract of sale is valid in the contract of lease-hire (Mālik).

According to 'Abd al-Salām, it is *ẓāhir* in the discourse (*kalām*) of Ibn Ḥājib that there is no difference between alive sheep or slaughtered sheep, it is the same ('Abd al-Salām).

Likewise, it is invalid to lease-hire for weaving cloth not knowing the description of its finished product after it has been woven and the lease-hire for tanning leather or weaving cloth on the condition that after the workmanship is finished half of it is wages. According to Ibn al-Qāsim, this is because one would never know how it would come out and for Mālik this is ruled as what is invalid in the contract of sale is also invalid in the contract of lease-hire. Ibn Muwāz states except if he says, "half of spanned cloth is for you on the condition that after you have woven it for me," it is valid. Ibn Muwāz says,

> I understand that according to the legal opinion (*qawl*) of Mālik, if he leases-hires the part of cloth in exchange for part of cloth after it has been spanned or hides after it has been tanned, it is valid as in the contract of sale for a delayed payment at a future specified time, otherwise it is void (Ibn Qāsim, Ibn Muwāz, Mālik).

Or lease-hire of a female slave for breastfeeding an offspring is not valid except after her own young child has become one year old.

It is invalid if one leases-hires to pick up the fallen olives or pressing them in exchange for the portion from it such as one-third from it or the portion from the extracted olive oil as the wages, because of not knowing the quantity of fallen olives in the first case and in the second case not knowing the description of the extracted olives. If he says, "Shake off my tree and half of the fallen or shaken fruits for you," it is not valid because its quantity is not known. It is invalid, if he says press my olives or sesame and half of the oil from it for you, because one does not know its quantity or description.

Similarly, in leasing-hiring to harvest or thrash crops, he says, "half of it is for you," it is invalid because its quantity and description are unknown.

The lease-hire of the land to cultivate in exchange for food is invalid. It is forbidden, except for the cultivation of wheat, or to grow in it other than the food such as the cotton, linen, flex, except such as the wood. For Mālik, if it is grown for food in it, it becomes like *muḥāqala* (the sale of grain still in growth) not cut off, the cane not cut off to prune, straw, fodder, and milk drawn from the udder of animal which cannot be turned into cheese or such other things. If it is feared that some of the crop would not grow, then it is considered lease-hire of food in exchange for food with a deferred payment (Mālik).

According to Mālik, it is not objectionable to lease-rent wood. He meant by it Indian wood, sandal wood, fire wood, timber, and tree stems. According to Saḥnūn, these things last long time and they are easy to grow. According to Ibn 'Urfa, it is not objectionable to lease-hire to take out water in exchange for the food. Thereafter there are some remarks from the commentators not related to our investigation (Mālik, Saḥnūn, Ibn 'Urfa).

It is invalid to lease-hire to carry food from a specified place for half of the food, because it would be taken into possession at a future specified time in all circumstances, except if it is stipulated to take it into possession after it has been brought to the specified place, then it is valid. If you say, "Carry my food at such and such place and half of it is yours," it is not valid, except if it is given as wages at your place. If the food is given at the place where it is brought, it is not valid, because the sale of food taken into possession becomes at a differed payment. According to Ibn Yūnus, when an ambiguity is found in the matter, it is invalid according to Ibn al-Qāsim, Ashhab and Ibn Ḥabīb (Ibn Yūnus, Ibn al-Qāsim, Ashhab, Ibn Ḥabīb).

Like the last case of invalidity, he said that the lease-hire for sewing cloth, one says, "Sew cloth today for a *dirham* and if you do not sew it today, then the wages for it would be less such as half of it," it is invalid. According to Ibn al-Qāsim, if the wages for sewing the piece of cloth today, then the wages for it a *dirham*, if he does it tomorrow, then the wages for it in half is not valid according to Mālik. Following Saḥnūn, Ibn 'Abd al-Ḥakam says it is preferable by us that if you lease-hire a person for sewing the piece of cloth today for a *dirham* and if he does it tomorrow for half of it, but if you say sew Roman garment for a *dirham* and if you sew Persian garment for half of it, it is not valid, because these are two contracts combined in one contract and the wages for them is more than designated or is less than designated (Ibn al-Qāsim, Mālik).

Similarly, if one says mow grass or gather firewood or draw water from the well and sell or carry it and the wages in half of price received from it, it is void, because of the deception or uncertainty involved in it.

If he says, "Take my animal and rent it and half of the payment for you," then the revenues are considered for the owner and the wages are incumbent on him for the one who has done the work. If he gives to a person camel, sheep, animal, or pigeon to rent and half of payments of it for him, it is invalid, because if the rent would go down, then the wages would go down in the same manner. (Consequently, the amount of wages is not certain.) If he says, "Sell my things and whatever you sell, it is for me and for you or he says if it is more than one hundred *dīnārs*, it is between us", it is not valid, because the price for you and the wages for him should be in the same proportion.

According to Ibn Yūnus, it is the same in case of animals, house, or ship, if he says, "rent it and half of rent is for you," then the revenues from rent is for its owner and the wages in the same amount for the person who rents it, it is right (Ibn Yūnus).

If he gives a ship, or camel, or animal for working on it and whatever gains are made, they are between them, it is not valid. If he works riding on it and the earnings are for the owner and the rent is incumbent on the one who works riding on it. In this case, the gains made between them are invalid and the contract becomes dissolved.

Similar case to the last one of the invalidities is if the owner of an entire property gives it to a purchaser to sell and the wages for sale for him, it is invalid. It is *mashhūr* legal opinion. According to Abū Isḥāq, because he has purchased it without taking it into his possession, except if it is at a future specified time reaching the other place to sell itm and if the place of sale for both is not the same, then it is valid.

According to Mālik, it is valid if one sells to a person half of animals or other such things on the condition to sell the other half later, it is valid if it is set to sell it at the appointed time, except in case of the article of food. According to Saḥnūn, it is not valid because the possession of the wages is not known with specification, then half portion which he has sold for a differed payment becomes hire and loan and, likewise, all of it if it is not known with specification. It is narrated from Mālik that if he sells half of cloth on the condition that the other half of it later, it is not good. It is *ẓāhir* according to Ibn Ḥājib, if he sells article on the condition that he sells half of it and then one-third of it for a differed payment, it is valid. There is no difference if he sells it at the same place or at a different place. Then there are several comments by different jurists in details (Mālik, Saḥnūn, Ibn Ḥājib).

It is valid to hire animal or boat to carry the load of firewood from a certain point to a known place, if the kind of firewood is known by stipulation or custom. It is also valid to carry half of it today and the remaining other half of it later or half of it in five days and the remaining in other five days. Mālik said as narrated by Ibn Muwāz, it is not good that a person pays for carrying load of firewood in exchange for half of it. Muḥammad (al-Shaybānī) meant that the half of price of firewood as the wages for carrying half of load is valid and, likewise, for two loads if it is known (Mālik, Ibn Muwāz, al-Shaybānī).

It is valid to hire a person to grind wheat or squeeze olive (to extract juice) for a *ṣā'* of flour or for a *ṣā'* of juice with the description of produce from them such as it is of good or bad quality. If they are different in description or in their production, it is not valid because of the deception or uncertainty in it. It is not objectionable to grind wheat in the measure of one *irdabb* and for a heap of flour, it is like what is valid in the contract of sale is valid in the contract of rent. If you rent to grind wheat or extract juice from olives for a *dirham* and pay for it in installment, it is valid. It is valid, if you sell a heap of wheat for grinding flour, if the flour is not different in its description. If it becomes destroyed, the seller is responsible for it. If the olive oil and flour of wheat are not different, it is valid. If the juice and the flour are different when they are produced, it is not valid. If a person buys wheat on the condition that the seller grind it and if the flour is slightly different in its description, it is valid (Mālik).

If a person hires a thing to work with it or hires animal to ride on it or carry load or food or cultivate the land and the lessor undertakes on himself to do it, it is valid.

It is valid to hire an instructor for teaching a slave workmanship for a year from the beginning to the end. If your servant paid to the tailor or bleacher to teach him workmanship, it is valid. He said that if the wages are known, it is permitted, and others said it is valid even if the wages are not known. If the servant dies after finishing it, there is nothing and no further discussion (*kalām*). However, if the servant dies before beginning it, then the lease-hire becomes void and the instructor should return wages to the owner in the same amount he had paid to him. If the servant dies during the time of teaching workmanship, it is settled according to such as if the time of teaching was one-third, then it is incumbent on the instructor to return two-thirds of the wages to his owner. If the instructor taught him one-third of workmanship, then it is incumbent on the owner to pay one-third of the wages. If both wages and workmanship are equal, then neither one pays anything to other (Al-Ṣaqlī, 'Abd al-Ḥaq, al-Tūnsī).

According to the *Mudawwana*, it is valid to apply rent to cultivate specified crops on the condition that half of it is for you. Abū Muḥammad restrict it to in case if it is known how much crop is expected to grow, otherwise it is not good. Mālik says, if one says to a person to harvest this crop of mine and half of it is for you or cut my palm date tree and half of it is for you, it is valid. According to Ibn Ḥabīb, likewise for picking olives from the ground. If it is stipulated in the workmanship to prune seed to be divided between the two, it is not valid. If it was made requisite to cultivate it, it is valid. If he says, "Whatever you harvest or pick from the ground, half of it is for you" it is valid, because it is considered as wages (*Mudawwana*, Abū Muḥammad, Mālik, Ibn Ḥabīb).

It is valid to hire animal from Egypt or Medina to stay longer for holding prayer for specified amount of *dīnārs* or *dirhams* on the condition that the lessee would not ride animal to find runaway slave or indebted fugitive.

Mālik said that it is valid if one rents animal for a *dīnār* to go to a certain place on the condition that the rent is calculated at the place of arrival as designated or known. If the place of arrival is not designated and he says, "My slave ran away on the way, then the rent is calculated a *dīnār*." Mālik said if one rents animal to search a fugitive, it is not valid unless the place is designated. If he says, "I found what I needed without it," then the rent is returned in that measure, if it was not the cash payment. According to the word (*qawl*) *of* Ibn Rushd, it is not objectionable if it was not the cash payment. He heard from Ibn al-Qāsim that in renting house for a year on the condition that if the lessee vacates before it, then the rent is calculated according to the duration of his residency in it. There is a ruling like this in the *Mudawwana* that it is considered valid, if a person rents it to sell cloth to him (lessor) on the condition that he can abandon residency as he wishes if it was not the cash payment, because of the additional stipulation of right of option. According to Saḥnūn, it is prohibited, because the stipulation of right of option is in remote time. To this Ibn Rushd said that it is not as if the stipulation of right of option for all times to come after one month has passed (Mālik, Ibn al-Qāsim, Saḥnūn, Ibn Rushd).

It is valid for the lessor to rent his slave, or immovable property, or animal to the lessee, who subsequently subleases to someone else time after time. It is valid to hire representative to sell thing for its usufruct from the sale for a specified time until thing lasts without any change, except the hire-lease of it was to purchase it later at a specified time. According to Ibn Ḥājib, to lease a slave is valid. According to Ibn 'Abd al-Salām, the slave denotes to comprise in this case animals and other things (Ibn Ḥājib, 'Abd al-Salām).

It is valid that the lessor permits the lessee differed payment of rent or exempt it in exchange for any usufruct or exempt it before the next term of lease is transferred, assuming it would in fact remain the same, until the usufruct of property is ended, otherwise it is deception. For this reason, the stipulation to make rent payment of immovable property for two years after its possession is valid, but it is not valid in case of animal, except after a short time such as ten days. According to Ibn Shās, it is valid to rent house restricting it that most likely there would be no change in it and in the payment of rent. However, if it is believed that there would be a change eventually or structure would become weak, then it is not valid to rent it (Shās).

According to Mālik, it is not objectionable to lease a slave for ten and fifteen years nor does Khalīl find any objection in it. It is clearly more valid. And the stipulation of prepayment of rent is valid. According to Ibn Yūnus, it is valid to lease for thirty years in exchange for the cash or differed payment, because it is reliable in such things. According to al-Bannānī, if there is no change in the second term of lease as indicated in the discourse (*kalām*) between them and, then, he said here the context or form (*ṣawra*) is that most probably in the beginning of coming of third year it is safe with the expiration of the second term, there is no change and most probably in both cases it is same (Mālik, Ibn Yūnus, al-Bannānī).

It is valid to rent a thing for two years for the known wages without specifying the rent for each month of the year. According to Ibn 'Urfa, it is valid to rent it for two years without specifying rent for each month of the year. It is valid, if one rents the land for thirty years in exchange for thirty *dīnārs* per every ten years, but he said that it is calculated in the measure of salability of thing. According to Ibn Shās, it is valid if he rents and the portion of rent of each year is not calculated as in the rent for each month in the year (Ibn 'Urfa, Ibn Shās).

It is valid to rent land for using it as a mosque for a certain period of time and if after its expiration the structure is destroyed, it is valid for the owner of land to take stone, wood, rubbles, and debris from its destruction, and make use of it as he wishes. Ibn al-Qāsim said that the owner of land is not forced to keep mosque in existence, if neither the owner of land nor the builder of structure wants to keep it in existence, it is not forced to keep it in existence. According to Ibn al-Qāsim, it is not objectionable to rent land to occupy it as the mosque for ten years. However according to Saḥnūn, when the duration of ten years expires, the land is returned to its owner and the rubble is for the one who wanted to build the structure, if he wants to make use of it for something else. Abū Muḥammad, after following the legal opinion (*qawl*) of Ibn al-Qāsim, said that one is not entitled to build a mosque on the land, if he intends to destroy it to make something different, because it would no longer exist for the worship of God. It is returned after the expiration of lease-hire. According to Ibn Yūnus, it is like returning horse to its owner after the holy war is over (Ibn al-Qāsim, Abū Muḥammad, Saḥnūn, Ibn Yūnus).

It is valid for anyone to carry dead body, taking out blood, or human ordure from a place. According to Ibn al-Qāsim, it is not objectionable to hire for removing the dead body, blood, or human waste (Ibn Qāsim).

It is valid to hire a person for intentional killing, enmity or killing or harming, but if a person kills anyone wrongfully for the wages, there are no wages for him. A person on whom the blood money is obligatory of those people whom he has killed which the Imam has prohibited before, it is not in good manners and there are no wages for him, as it would be the wages for enmity of the murderer. If it is not possible for a person to retaliate himself for the injury and knows someone who can retaliate for the wages, then the wages for it is valid for him. However, a person who kills the inheritor of a person killed is forbidden, because it is simply a game. It is not objectionable to hire a person to retaliate after it has been established with evidence by the verdict of *Qāḍī* for justice. According to Al-Lakhmī, it is valid to hire for killing or injury, when retaliation is in just cause of God, but it is not valid except if one has seen that it is carried out for just cause and not for the game or going beyond the *ḥadd* (Al-Lakhmī).

It is valid to hire anyone for teaching good manners to his slave, child or mate or anyone else. It is not objectionable to beat your slave or child to teach him good manners. However, it is not appropriate to beat one's father or stranger. According to Abū al-Ḥasan, if the owner establishes that his slave does not behave in good manners which are obligatory on him, then is it possible that beating conducted is with or without any reason? There are differences of opinion in it. If the husband or wife testifies that the slave does not behave properly which is obligatory on him, then one should wait to see until the end if that is the case, God knows better (Abū al-Ḥasan).

It is valid to hire the male or female slave for rendering services and such other things for ten days and fifteen days. Khalīl does not find any objection to it. Likewise, in case of house it is obviously valid. The payment in advance is valid with the stipulation. According to Ibn Yūnus, it is valid to rent a house for thirty years with the cash or differed payment in exchange for animal, relying upon its appearance by seeing it if it is small, large, or old and, whether it is strong or weak. According to Al-Lakhmī, the duration of lease-hire differs with the difference in the reliability and fear (caution).

The differed payment comprises in order of lands, then houses, then slaves, then animals, and then cloths. It is valid to lease-hire land for thirty and forty years without the cash payment, except if it is reliable that the water is available in it, then it is valid with cash payment. Likewise, in case of the reliability of a house, if it is newly built. If it is an old house, then in the amount one thinks probable of its reliability of being safe. In case of slaves, it is different. In the book of Muḥammad (al-Shaybānī), it is for twenty years with cash payment, in the *Mudawwana*, it is for fifteen years with cash payment, and Ibn al-Qāsim forbids for twenty years with cash payment. In case of the slave, one sees his age by his looks and, likewise, in case of animal. Regarding the difference in the recompense in case of structure, it is different according to the custom. In case of mules how long their life span would be, in case of donkeys without it and, likewise, in case of clothing (Ibn Yūnus, al-Lakhmī, al-Shaybānī, *Mudawwana*).

It is valid to hire sewer to sew a piece of cloth on the condition that he returns it on a day beginning of the week, month, or year. If the sewing is combined with other workmanship restricting its duration and workmanship in one contract, it is invalid. According to Ibn Rushd and ʻAbd al-Salām, it is invalid according to the consensus. According to one of the *mashhūr* legal opinions, it does not invalidate. Contrary to which answer by Ibn Shās is that the person who is engaged in the workmanship knows approximately the duration of performing such work as in sewing cloth in a day or duration of sewing of certain kind of cloth ('Abd al-Salām, Ibn Rushd, Ibn Shās).

According to Ibn al-Qāsim, it is valid to sell house with the exemption for its usufruct after a year, that is, the buyer takes possession of house after a year without any change in it, but not exceeding one year. It is permitted to sell house with the exemption to reside in it during one year of time most likely without any change. This is one of the seven rulings of the *madhhab* of the *Mudawwana.* Ibn al-Qāsim permits to reside in the house for one year and in between its duration, but not more than that, fearing that change might occur. Ibn Ḥabīb allows one and a half year, if there is no change. He adds by saying that it is contrary to what is now held, but it is not contrary to the *fiqh* (Ibn al-Qāsim, *Mudawwana.* Ibn Ḥabīb).

Or according to Ibn al-Qāsim, it is valid to rent the land exempting to take it into possession for its usufruct after ten years most likely without any change in it. According to Ibn Rushd, it is valid to rent the land with the exemption of less than (ten) years and Ibn Qāsim allows ten years (Ibn Qāsim, Ibn Rushd).

It is valid to hire the female to breastfeed an infant when needed for the known wages for intended purpose. It is permitted according the Qur'ānic textual evidence (*naṣṣ*), regardless if the wages are paid in cash, or in lieu of animal, or wares, or food. If it is for suckling animal which is forbidden to eat such as donkey to suckle it by female donkey, it is not valid. According to Mālik, it is not objectionable to hire the wet nurse to breastfeed an infant for a year or two for such and such wages except, if it is stipulated for food and clothing, it is valid. According to Ibn Ḥabīb, it is *mashhūr* legal opinion that it is determined depending upon how much and how far the father of an infant is rich or poor to afford her service (Mālik, Ibn Ḥabīb).

According to Ibn Yūnus, no food (namely, wheat, grains etc.) is taken in exchange for the article of food (namely, milk taken from the breast of female), because of the forbiddance of it which has become customary among the people. However, the breastfeeding which has become practice is permitted. There is no incongruity in it, because the milk which is breastfed to the child is not measured in terms of price. If her stay with an infant becomes longer and she goes through trouble of breastfeeding and milk becomes less in her breast, there is no price for it (Ibn Yūnus).

If the washing of rage is not stipulated, then the wet nurse does it as currently practiced among the people, namely to breastfeed an infant, fastening him in bed, anoint him, washing the body of infant with warm water, and coloring eyelids with kohl making the child look beautiful. This is all customary among the people (Ibn Ḥājib). The anointing and washing rage and such things is practiced according to the custom and some say it is incumbent on the wet nurse. However, according to the author of the *Tawḍḥī*, all such things are practiced according to the custom. If it is made requisite that father does it, then it is incumbent on him to do it. This is *madhhab* of the *Mudawwana*. If there is no clear ruling, then according to the custom. But according to Ḥabīb, if there is no custom found, then by the textual evidence (*naṣṣ*), it is incumbent on the father and others say that it is incumbent on the wet nurse as the custom (Ibn Ḥājib, *al*-Tawḍḥī, Mudawwana).

If the husband does not permit to breastfeed the child, because of any detriment from it, it is void. If he intends to travel, he is not allowed during the journey to take the infant with him, except with the wet nurse and pays her the wages for it.

Similarly, it is invalid if some relatives of an infant claim that the breastfeeding the child by the wet nurse is harmful for the child. The ruling in the *Mudawwana* is that in case the wet nurse is pregnant and there is a fear for child's death or fever, it is invalid. Furthermore, in the *Mudawwana* he said "yes," if it is not safe for a child as narrated from Mālik. It is said that the breastfeeding by pregnant woman is thought to be harmful for a child (*Mudawwana*, Mālik).

Similarly, regarding invalid claim, if lessee hires two wet nurses together at the same time or the second wet nurse after the first wet nurse, and the first one dies and only the second wet nurse breastfeeds child, then according to Saḥnūn, it is void. The author means that if he hires two wet nurses together at the same time or the second wet nurse after the first wet nurse, and one of them dies, then it is not valid that the other wet nurse breastfeeds the child. If a person hires the first wet nurse and then the second wet nurse and she dies, then it is incumbent on the first wet nurse to breastfeed the infant as she did before the second wet nurse was hired. If the first wet nurse dies, then it is incumbent on the second wet nurse to breastfeed the child. According to Abū al-Ḥasan 'Abd al-Ḥaq, this is if the second wet nurse knew at the time when she was hired with the first wet nurse. If she did not know, then there is no further discussion (*kalām*), because she came to breastfeed the infant as the only one. So also narrates Ḥamdays (Saḥnūn, Abū al-Ḥasan, Ḥamdays).

Similar claim of invalidity to last one is that if the father hires the wet nurse (and has given the wages) for two years and in the meanwhile he dies, then the wet nurse does not take the wages for the completion of breastfeeding for the duration of two years. If the father has left behind him no property (capital) and there is no longer any money left from him, then the lease-hire is void in every circumstance, except if the wet nurse does it voluntarily with no wages. If the father is killed, then the portion of the wages for the remaining duration of breastfeeding which he has given beforehand from his property is returned to him, because the maintenance expenses which he has given beforehand is no longer incumbent on him, except so long as he was alive. The breastfeeding of the infant is incumbent on the father and not the mother. According to Ibn Yūnus, if the separation between father and mother takes place, then the breastfeeding is not incumbent on the father. However, if he has given the wages beforehand thinking that he would be alive, and at that time breastfeeding was incumbent on him, then the wages are returned to him (Ibn Yūnus).

If the father dies without paying wages for his child's breastfeeding and the wet nurse has not taken any wages from him, the lease-hire becomes void. If anyone pays her wages voluntarily, then it is not void. The wages for the wet nurse are not obligatory from the property of the father. His responsibility for the wages of the wet nurse has already expired, meaning if the wages have been taken and then the father dies, then nothing is returned to his inheritors and the contract of lease-hire becomes void. The portion of wages is taken from the property and placed in the authority of the representative of infant.

According to Ibn Yūnus, the intermediary position between the two rulings (*qawlayn*) is preferable (*istiḥsān*), contrary to the preceding case when the father has paid the wages for schooling of his son while he was alive or after he dies. The difference between these two is that the schooling of the child is not incumbent on him, he has obligated upon himself to it while he was alive or after he dies as in the preceding case of breastfeeding which was obligatory on him (Ibn Yūnus).

Similarly, the invalidity of claim as in last case, he said that if a person hires anyone to perform services or tend to or guard animals for the wages paid in food only or with food equitable to the amount of *dirhams* and if the servant asks for more food in quantity, then lease-hire of him is void, except if he agrees food to be in the measure which is equitable to what is usual, then it is not void.

According to Ibn Yūnus, if the lessee finds worker eating too much food not usual among the people, then the lease-hire is void, because it is like he found defect in him, except if he agrees that the wages in food to be average (equitable). However, if he marries a woman whom he finds eating too much food which is unusual, then it does not invalidate his marriage with her, either he can satiate her, or divorce her, because it is not a defect (Ibn Yūnus).

It is prohibited for the husband of wet nurse to cohabit with her, if the breastfeeding by her for the child would be harmful, but if it is not harmful, then according to the ruling (*qawl*) by 'Abd al-Ḥakam, it is valid, regardless whether it was stipulated in the present contract or not. Būlū indicates the opinion of Aṣbagh that it is not prohibited, except if it is stipulated with the occurrence of harmfulness. The Prophet prohibited to breastfeed the infant while the mother or the wet nurse is pregnant or compressed. If the husband of wet nurse prevents her to travel to the place of infant, it is invalid. According to Ibn 'Abd al-Ḥakam, if the husband wants to travel with her and she lets herself hired with his permission, then he has no right to prevent her from letting herself hired for the breastfeeding. If she does it without his permission, then he has right to cancel the lease-hire. Similarly, it is invalid that the wet nurse breastfeeds other infants, even if the milk in her breast is enough for all, regardless if it was stipulated or not. If it was stipulated to breastfeed other children, then there is no prohibition. According to Ibn al-Qāsim, if one hires wet nurse for breastfeeding an infant, then it is not valid that she breastfeeds other children with him. She should breastfeed the infant with safety and serve him with care. Similarly, if she is not asked to pursue breastfeeding with safety and care, then it is not incumbent on the wet nurse. However according to Ibn Shās, the lease-hire of wet nurse for breastfeeding the child does not obligate it and vice versa (ʻAbd al-Ḥakam, Būlū, Ibn al-Qāsim, Ibn Shās).

It is valid for the rightful owner that the seller sells his wares such as for one hundred *dīnārs* on the condition that if he sells it for one hundred *dīnārs* a year and profit is for him only, since the purpose is to sell the wares for one hundred *dīnārs* and to pay wages for trading for a year and the seller buys and sells for one hundred *dīnārs* for all or some of commodities, it is valid according to the consensus, if it is stipulated in the present contract that the price of all or some wares become reduced by continuing to trade for a year. If it is not stipulated, it is not valid because of the higher degree of uncertainty.

According to Mālik, it is valid that the owner of wares sells it to a person on the condition that he trades with them for the specified price in one year by stipulating in the contract that if the price declines, he continues to work until the end of year, if it is not stipulated it is not valid. Likewise, it is valid if he hires you to work with these one hundred *dīnārs* for a year with the stipulation that if it is destroyed, then the wages are incumbent on him. If it is not stipulated, the contract of lease-hire becomes invalid (Mālik).

Mālik said, if one hires anyone to tend to his animals for one year, then the stipulated wages are incumbent on him, if in the meanwhile animals are destroyed, sold, or lost, the contract continues for the remaining time of it. If it not stipulated, it is not valid. If it is stipulated and animals become destroyed before the lease-hire is completed, then the owner has an option either to restore the contract or not. According to Ibn al-Qāsim, if the owner hires anyone to tend to his animals for one hundred *dīnārs* without any stipulation and the animals become destroyed, then he must restore the contract of lease-hire. If it is stipulated, then it is inevitable to restore it according to the stipulation. Saḥnūn said that it is valid in case of animals or *dīnārs* not stipulated to restore the contract of lease-hire, then by ruling it is made incumbent on him to restore it. Based on the ruling (*qawl*) of Ibn Ḥabīb, Ibn al-Māgshūn and Aṣbagh, Khalīl concurs with. According to Ibn Yūnus, it is valid (right). If the lessee hires an animal to carry the load of food or goods, it is not necessary to stipulate to restore it in contract of lease-hire, if the animal is destroyed. The ruling is made to restore it. Likewise, one finds such a case in the *Mudawwana* and in the book of Muḥammad al-Shaybānī (Mālik, Saḥnūn, Ibn Ḥabīb, Ibn al-Mājshūn, Asbagh, *Mudawwana*, Khalīl al-Shaybānī).

According to al-Bājī, Ashhab said that if one hires a person to harvest specified crop and it becomes destroyed, the contract of lease-hire becomes void whereas according to Ibn al-Qāsim, it is not void. According to Ibn 'Urfa, this is contrary to the opinion if there is an excuse for not plowing land, because of pouring rain, then the lease-hire is void. According to Ibn al-Qāsim, if there is an excuse that plow broke by plowing land or animal dies while plowing, then the lease-hire does not become void. For Saḥnūn, if the worker is prevented because of rain from building or harvesting or working, then the wages for him according to the work he has performed for the day, according to the opinions of others all wages are paid to him (Al-Bājī, Ibn al-Qāsim, Saḥnūn, Ibn 'Urfa).

Similarly, the validity in the contract of lease-hire for tending animals, it is valid if it is not stipulated to restore the contract, if animals die or become destroyed, except if it is specified not to restore it. If the guard dies, then the wages become incumbent for the work he has performed.

Similarly, in case of riding an animal if one hires without stipulation to ride it to a place and it dies before reaching it or in the stretch of journey, then it is incumbent upon the owner of animal to restore the contract of lease-hire, according to all commentators. To make it possible to ride, it is incumbent to restore it as the lease-hire is not invalidated. Mālik said, if people lease-hire an animal on the night of wedding ceremony and they are not able to ride on it on that night, the rent is incumbent on them. If one hires an animal with the co-rider to escort with him to a certain place or instead he rides on it to a known place, the rent is incumbent on him (Mālik).

If one hires a camel riding on it to go to pilgrimage, or Jerusalem, or Prophet's mosque and the sickness hinders him, or he falls, or dies, or the debt befall him, and he is obstructed on the way, the rent is incumbent on him. The rent is obligatory for his inheritor as it was for him. The owner of camel is a fortiori creditor among all other creditors.

It is valid to lease-hire for constructing wall to annex border on the side of river so that the water flows beneath it. If the river of someone flows to your land, the rent is incumbent on you for border, which is built between the lands of both.

It is valid to rent path to lessee to pass though it to his house, otherwise it is like one encroaches upon the property of people wrongfully. Abū al-Ḥasan narrates (copies) it from Ashhab. According to Ibn al-Qāsim, it is not objectionable to rent the border of your river to the one who builds the house or set up hand mill on it, and to rent path leading to his house. It is valid to lease drainage passing to the water basin from the house. However, it makes one wonder if the draining water from rain to the river would be in abundance or less. According to Ibn Yūnus, one of our shaykhs, makes a distinction between the answer to the question regarding the drainage to the water basin and the drainage to the riverbed. However, they agree that there is no difference between the two. It is as if one hires water basin to drain it into the river as if he buys the water from it (Abū al-Ḥasan, Ibn al-Qāsim, Ibn Yūnus).

It is valid to rent rivulet to discard excess of water flowing to the open country. It is valid to sell water from the rain flowing to the drainage by bringing the tool to expedite it along the edge of surface to run the water collected from rain.

It is valid to rent mill to set the water for rotating seedling for the food or something else. According to Mālik, it is not objectionable to rent the water mill for food and other things. According to Ibn al-Qāsim, if the water is cut off from it, it is the reason to invalidate lease. If the water is restored, then the lease for the remaining duration is obligatory as the opinion of Mālik regarding a slave who becomes sick and then regains his health, he is called upon to rotate the water mill (Mālik, Ibn al-Qāsim).

It is valid to lease-hire for the teaching of *Qur'ān* for the known amount of wages for each month, or year, or week, or day without describing duration, otherwise it is pursued as in all times or on the condition of memorization of whole *Qur'ān,* or some known portion of it such as the *Sura Yāsin,* or one-third of *Qur'ān,* or teaching art of reciting *Qur'ān* (*qira't*). According to Ibn al-Qāsim, it is not objectionable to hire anyone for teaching *Qur'ān* for the duration of whole year, or month for such and such wages, or the memorization of *Qur'ān,* or reading whole of it, or one-sixth part of it with proficiency for such and such wages. Ibn Wahb narrated that it is not objectionable to stipulate the wages for the known thing (meaning teaching of *Qur'ān*) for the whole month of *Ramaḍān* or *Zu'lhijja* (Ibn al-Qāsim, Ibn Wahāb).

The wages of instructor for the teaching of *Qur'ān* are stipulated depending upon the of proficiency of the instructor. However, if it is not stipulated, then according to Ibn Ḥājib, it is not objectionable that the instructor takes the wages for the teaching of *Qur'ān*. Saḥnūn was asked of a person teaching child without stipulation of his wages for one or two *dirhams* for each month and when the instructor demanded the wages for it the father declined it, then in that case the wages are determined according to the ability and the financial condition of father. If the child attends puberty and has learned three fourth of *Qur'ān*, then it is obligatory to plan for completing it. If the mother and the father of the child are deprived of money because of the sickness of father, nothing is taken from them. If the father abandons miserly child's memorization of *Qur'ān*, it is repugnant. If there is any property left, the guardian or *Qāḍī* of the place or community to leave it for the teaching of *Qur'ān* to the child. If there is no property, it is directed to appoint guardian or relative to overtake the teaching of *Qur'ān* to the child. It is a collective duty (*farḍ al-kifāya*) (Ibn Ḥabīb, al-Mutīṭī, al-Qābasī, Saḥnūn, and others).

According to al-Qābasī, if the teacher weeps a child with the lash in his foot for not memorization of *Qur'ān* enough and wound occurs in his foot causing no suspicion that death befalls him, and if one pushes a child mildly and the coarseness does not become filled tenfold, it is not objectionable. He said it is right considering the condition of children. The weeping a child by our instructors twentyfold or more is correct, if our instructors weep in bones twenty times or more causing injury to the child on the surface below his foot, it is prohibited to suppress the lump (clotting) for diminishing it. It is valid (correct) that some of them do it if the *Qāḍī* permits, in case the child has capacity to restrain it. There are several commentaries on minor secondary details by some jurists (Al-Qābasī).

It is valid to rent the pot (kettle), sieve, and hoe with the specification or not. Ibn 'Aṭṭār said that it is prohibited to rent without knowing the specification of the earthen ware and if the pots are not fumigated, except if they are engraved. According to Ibn 'Urfa, this is inadequate (Ibn 'Aṭṭār, Ibn 'Urfa).

It is valid to lease-hire anyone to dig a well specified with the description of how deep or shallow. If it becomes destroyed in the meanwhile, then the wages are determined in proportion to the work performed and if after the work is finished, all wages are paid and if it was not specified, nothing of wages for the workmanship, except if all digging is completed in the freehold land or uncultivated land. According to Ibn Yūnus, it is because the lease-hire in case of freehold land and any other waterless desert land is valid, except if the wages in amount of *dirhams* are known on the condition that the digging is done by riding on the camel of lessor for such and such amount of *dirhams* and if half of the digging is done and then it becomes destroyed, then no wages are paid for the workmanship. It is paid (only) after the digging is finished. Mālik said there are no wages paid to him for digging well, unless after digging is finished. According to Ibn al-Qāsim, it is not valid to lease uncultivated land. According to Ibn Yūnus, if one abandons work after beginning it, then the wages for the remaining work are for the one who completes it (Mālik, Ibn al-Qāsim, Ibn Yūnus).

It is repugnant to lease-hire for embellishing an ornament, because it is considered not exactly ethical nor is it quite unlawful, but it falls somewhere in between the two. According to Ibn al-Qāsim, it is not objectionable to lease-hire for embellishing golden ornament in exchange for gold or silver. Mālik finds it of his disliking and considers it not ethical among the people (Ibn al-Qāsim, Mālik).

Similarly, if a person rents an animal for riding to a specified place or rents a piece of cloth to wear it for the specified time and if traveling by riding animal or wearing piece of cloth makes it lighter or heavier, it is repugnant. According to Ibn al-Qāsim, if one rents a piece of cloth to wear it for a night, and if he gives it to someone else to wear it, it is invalid because of the differences in wearing cloth by different persons. If it becomes damaged in your possession, you are responsible for it, but if you give it to someone else to wear it, he is responsible for it. If the owner of an animal leases it to the lessee for riding on it and he leases it to someone else and animal becomes little lighter by traveling or something similar, then the lease is not invalidated. If it is destroyed, he does not become responsible for its present condition of little lightness, if it shows any deflect caused from journeying. Likewise, in case of wearing piece of cloth of living beings or dead persons (Ibn al-Qāsim).

However, it is repugnant to lease-hire anyone for teaching science of *fiqh* (*'īlm al-fiqh*) and teaching divine precept (*farā'iḍ)* and to sell the books of *fiqh* and *farā'iḍ*. According to Ibn al-Qāsim, it is repugnant to hire anyone for teaching *fiqh* and *farā'iḍ* (Mālik), and more repugnant to sell books of *fiqh* with the stipulation of teaching them. However, according to Ibn Yūnus, it is valid to sell other books than *fiqh* and teaching them is right (valid) (Ibn al-Qāsim, Ibn Yūnus).

It is repugnant to lease-hire anyone for teaching the recitation of *Qur'ān* (*qirā'a)* with the appropriate nasal sonorous voice to tune according to what is known in the music. According to Ibn al-Qāsim, it is repugnant to hire anyone for teaching tambourine, drumming instrument, and string instrument. According to 'Ayāḍ, it is repugnant to lease-hire anyone for singing on the wedding feast. According to Ibn al-Qāsim, it is not appropriate to hire anyone for playing tambourine, string instrument on the wedding feast. For Mālik, it is repugnant because it is not a deed of pious persons. 'Ayād adds further that playing of string instrument on wedding feast is neither permitted nor its hiring (Ibn al-Qāsim, 'Ayāḍ, Mālik).

It is repugnant that Muslim leases-hires slave to an unbeliever in the valid workmanship such as construction and tailoring and in the invalid workmanship such as wine and guarding pigs.

It is repugnant to lease-hire land to build mosque. According to al-Bājī, it is not permitted because of forbiddance. It is not valid to build mosque to rent it for the people to hold prayers in it or rent house to the people for holding prayers in it. According to Ibn Yūnus, it is not valid for anyone to build mosque for renting it to the people for holding prayers in it. Ibn al-Qāsim said that anyone who rents his house to the people to hold prayers in it during the month of *Ramaḍān* does not induce admiration in me. It is the same as renting mosque. However, others have said that it is not objectionable to rent house for holding prayers. According to Ibn 'Urfa, it is not valid to build mosque to rent it for holding prayers by the people and to rent house for that purpose. However, it is permitted to rent any other place than the house. 'Ayāḍ said that it is not very noble. However according to al-Lakhmī, anyone who builds mosque to rent it, it is invalid. Khalīl says that this is not based on any legal opinion (*qawl*). Thus summarily, it is not permitted and is not appropriate (Al-Bājī, Ibn Yūnus, Ibn al-Qāsim, Ibn 'Urfa, 'Ayāḍ, al-Lakhmī).

It is to be avoided (guarded) to hire mute or blind person to cultivate dry land or overflowing of it, but the *madhhab Mudawwana* permits it in the end, if it is not cash payment. According to Ibn Shās, if it is stipulated to be accepted in the form of usufruct is valid as decreed by the *sharī'a*. It is forbidden to hire a mute person for teaching and a blind person for guarding and for killing innocent person or for cutting the parts of his body or cleaning mosque (Ibn Shās).

According to Ibn 'Urfa, it is valid to stipulate usufruct of an article on the condition that it is not destroyed. According to Ibn Shās, it is not valid to rent trees for their fruits and sheep for littering and milking, because it is the sale of a thing before its existence. Ibn 'Urfa says that I do not know this subsidiary ruling (*far'*) by the adherents of the *madhhab* (Ibn 'Urfa, Ibn Shās).

If usufruct of a thing such as cutting someone's body or beating someone out of enmity is prohibited, then it is not valid to rent anyone for it, because it is forbidden by the *sharī'a*. According to Ibn 'Urfa following al-Ghazālī, the ruling lacks strength with the good reason in its invalidation. If one hires to extract tooth or to cut hand, it is valid. However, if the hand is with which one eats, or the pain is caused in the tooth, it is not valid. According to Ibn Wahb and Ashhab, if one cuts palm of hand keeping the hand, it is not objectionable that he cults it from the joint, if there is no fear of death. According to Ibn Rushd, if death is feared in keeping the remaining hand, it is valid to cut it. According to 'Ayāḍ after al-Ṭabarī, to cut the excess of finger of hand is not valid. Such cutting is considered changing the creation of God, except excess is hurting or causing pain in the finger or in case of wisdom teeth, then it is not objectionable to cut the finger or pull out the wisdom teeth (Ibn 'Urfa, Ibn Wahb, Ibn Rushd, 'Ayāḍ, al-Ṭabarī).

If the usufruct is not specified and if it is not seeking or desired as loan for an animal for the occasion of sacrificial feast, fasting on the tenth of month of *Muḥram*, voluntarily performing minor or major pilgrimage, preparing and furnishings for the dead and if it is feared that there is a cheating in it, then the lease-hire is not valid and there are no wages for the hireling. According to Ibn Rushd, the wages for hireling are not valid, if he keeps on cheating. However, it is valid if he does not go on cheating any longer. If one asks wages in such and such an amount for suggesting to marrying a woman, there are no wages for him, meaning for his suggestion and advice in the matter, there are no wages. If he asks no wages for it, then it is valid. According to Ibn Shās, the wages are valid for performing pilgrimage for someone as substitute, carrying the dead body to the grave yard, digging the grave, and bathing dead man's body (Ibn Rushd, Ibn Shās).

It is valid to lease-hire Imām (prayer leader) to lead prayers including prayer calls, but not for one's compulsory or supererogatory individual prayers and anyone as representative for substituting acts of religious worship such as prayers and fasting. But, it is valid if anyone leases-hires anyone to recite *Qur'ān*. According to Ibn al-Qāsim, Mālik and many of his disciples it is permitted, but Ibn 'Abbas says so long as you do not make business of doing it. Būlū indicates that Ibn Ḥabīb forbids hire of it (Ibn al-Qāsim, Mālik, Ibn Ḥabīb, Ibn 'Abbas).

It is not valid to lease-hire land in which water overflows and disappears (vanished) from it. According to Ibn Ḥājib, it is not valid to lease land for cultivation which is overflowing with the water and it disappears from the land. According to Ibn 'Urfa, it is valid according to the *Mudawwana*. It is *ẓāhir*. Based on the textual evidence (*naṣṣ*), if one leases land submerged under water for such and such and, if the water disappears, it is not valid. This is contrary to lease-hire land from which the water does not disappear from it, if it is not with the cash payment. However, with cash payment it is not valid if it is believed that the water disappears from the land. Others have said, if it is feared that water from the land disappears, it is not valid even if it is not with cash payment (Ibn Ḥabīb, Ibn 'Urfa).

According to 'Abd al-Salām, it is valid to lease tree which is cut off to grow back based on one of the legal rulings (*aqawāl*, pl. of *qawl*) described by Ibn Ḥājib. Ibn 'Urfa following Ibn Ḥājib and Ibn Shās describes two legal rulings (a*qwāls*). Khalīl says that he does not know any legal ruling that prohibits it. According to the *madhhab*, it is permitted as in the lease-hire for draining water into the basin and to pick up the wood from orchard. According to Ibn Shās, it is not valid to lease tree for fruits still growing on it, or sheep producing milk in future or giving birth to her offspring in future, or growing its wool in future, because it is the sale of an object before its existence. According to 'Abd al-Salām, if one leases-hires an animal for milk, it is absolutely not forbidden. If he decides to sell milk, it is valid with the stipulation of number of sheep to be milked. If the milk is measured, it does not need to be stipulated. It is not appropriate to apply forbiddance to it. In the *Tawḍīḥ*, the fulfillment of the validity of stipulations is well known (*ma'rūf*). Then Ibn Ḥājib carries discourse (*kalām*) further that it is not forbidden in case of sale of fruits and wool ('Abd al-Salām, Ibn Ḥājib, Ibn 'Urfa).

It is valid to rent house with the fruits of Dahlia plant or palm trees for which the wages in the amount of not more than one-third is retained from the rent for watering Dahlia plant or palm trees and other related services. According to Ibn al-Qāsim, one who rents house or land or portion of it in which there are lotus trees or Dahlia plants, or trees with no fruits now at the present or fruits not yet set to be picked up and they are one-third or less, they belong to the lessor, except if it is stipulated for the lessee. It is established by well-known ruling (*ma'rūf*). According to Aṣbagh, if it is known that the fruits of tree are good before the end of the lease term, then it is valid to lease it. If it is not known, it is not valid. According to Ibn Yūnus, it is valid in case of need that lessee enters the house for mending or restoring fruits and cutting them (Ibn al-Qāsim, Aṣbagh, Ibn Yūnus).

It is not valid to hire anyone to teach music and, likewise, to teach music instruments such as the *'Ūd* and the *Mūzmār* (*Lūṭ*) for the entertainment.

NOTES

1. 'Abd al-Ḥayy al-Laknawi, "Introduction" in the *Muwaṭṭa' of Mālik in the Narration of Muḥammad al-Shaybānī* (UK: Turath Publishing, 2004), pp. 11–12.
2. Al-Laknawī, "Introduction," p. 4.
3. Norman Calder, *Studies in Early Muslim Jurisprudence* (Oxford: Clarendon Press, 1993), p. 27.
4. Norman Calder, *Studies*, p. 20.
5. Al-Laknawī, the *Muwaṭṭa' of Mālik*, pp. 19–22.
6. Muḥammad bin Muḥammad 'Ulaysh, *Manḥ al-Jalīl Sharḥ Mukhtaṣar Khalīl* (Beirut: Dār al-Fikr, 1989), vol. iv, p. 8.
7. 'Ulaysh, *Manḥa*, p. 8.
8. 'Ulaysh, *Manḥa*, p. 8.
9. 'Ulaysh, *Manḥa*, p. 9.
10. Abū 'Abdallah Muḥammad bin Muḥammad bin 'Abd al-Raḥmān al-Ḥaṭṭāb, *Mawāhib al-Jalīl lī Sharḥ al-Mukhtaṣar*, vol. I (Beirut, Dār al-Fikr, 1992), p. 35.
11. See Bāqillānī, chapter 2, p. 25n11.
12. Al-Ḥaṭṭāb, *Mawāhib,* p. 35.
13. Al-Ḥaṭṭāb, *Muwāhib*, pp. 35–36.
14. Al-Ḥaṭṭāb, *Muwāhib*, p. 37.
15. Joseph Calder, *Studies*, p. 1.
16. Adolf Grohman, *First Encyclopaedia of Islam*, vol. vii (Leiden: E. J. Brill), pp. pp. 64–65.
17. Calder, *Studies*, p. 17.
18. We have followed throughout the entire text of all chapters of Khalīl's *Mukhtaṣar* in *Manḥa* al-Jalīl, edited by Muḥammad Aḥmad 'Ulaysh with the explanations and notes (*tā'līqāt*) in the main text in which Khalīl's *Mukhtaṣar* is reproduced at the top on the upper margin, pp. 275–339; *Mukhtaṣar Khalīl* edited by Ṭāhir Aḥmad al-Zāwī (Cairo: Dār al-Aḥyā Kutub al-'Arabīya, 1980), pp. 187–200; Occasionally we have also used Muḥammad bin Muḥammad bin 'Abd al-Raḥmān al-Ḥaṭṭāb's explanations from the *Mawāhib al-Jalīl lī Sharḥ al-Mukhtaṣar* (Beirut: Dār al-Fikr, 1992).
19. *Taraddud*, hesitation or suspension of judgment. Here the reference is to a situation where either the contemporaries of Abū Ẓayd al-Qayrawānī were unable to

transmit a consistent legal view of the predecessors to later scholars or early jurists raised no legal opinion, Ajetunmobi, "A Critical study," p. 280.

20. This would include anyone who is not able to exercise his judgement in the matters of selling and buying such as minors, a person possessed by madness.

21. *Tarjīḥ*, the preferable. This is a reference to what is contained in the Commentary on *Mudawwana* by Abū Bakr Muḥammad bin Yūnus. His commentary contains comparative views to justify the legal verdict in the *Mudawwana*. Hence the use of *Tarjīḥ*, Ajetunmobi, *A Critical Study*, p. 288.

22. *taraddud* meaning hesitation or indecision as no definite verdict has reached to us from the jurists in earlier generations, *Musa Ali Ajetunmobi, Islamic Studies* vol. 25, 1886, p. 280.

23. Reference is to the preferred view which was presented by al-Lakhmī among the views expressed by different commentators on the *Mudawwana*, be that view arrived at through their personal *ijtihād* or that of another jurist which they approved.

24. *Gharẓa*, a palm tree that becomes dry and having no head on the orchard wall.

25. 'Ulaysh, *Manḥa al-Jalīl*, vol. v, pp. 71–104; al-Zāwī, *Mukhtaṣar Khalīl*, pp. 200–209.

26. 'Ulaysh, *Manḥa al-Jalīl*, vol. v, pp. 211–232; *Mukhtaṣar al-Khalīl,* pp. 214–220.

27. 'Ulaysh, *Manaḥ,* vol.vi, pp. 162–195; Al-Ẓāwī, *Mukhtaṣar Khalīl*, pp. 239–243.

28. Muḥammad bin Aḥmad bin Muḥammad 'Ulaysh, *Minaḥ al-Jalīl*, vol. viii, pp. 282–326; Ṭāhir Aḥmad al-Zāwī, *Mukhtaṣar Khalīl,* pp. 273–282.'Ulash and Zāwī have a separate section on the Renting of House, Animals, Bathrooms and Land, which is mostly covered in the section of Lease-Hire.

Chapter 7

Differences of Opinion (*Ikhtilāf al-Fuqhā*ʿ) among the Jurists from Hermeneutical Perspective in the Formation of Islamic Legal System

In the classical literature, the differences of opinion among the jurists of four Sunni schools of law are generally discussed under the heading "Differences of Opinion among Jurists" (*ikhtīlāf al-fuqhā'*). This was understood as if they are differences of the tenets among four Sunni schools of law without raising the question if the legal rulings in each Sunni school of law are determined by the same sources of revelation provided in the *Qur'ān* and the prophetic *Ḥadīth* reports why such differences of opinion could be because of the different tenets of school of law. These differences of opinion are in reality the result of hermeneutical process of interpretations in determining the legal ruling according to the canons provided in the *Qur'ān* and the prophetic *Ḥadīth* reports.

I would first describe in general the juristic differences of opinion in the rulings of Ḥanafī, Shāfi'ī, Mālikī, and Ḥanbalī schools of law as they have been narrated by the translator and commentator Jamīl Aḥmad Sakrawdhwī in al-Marghīnānī's *Hidāya*[1] and explain briefly their reasons. Secondly, I would describe the juristic differences of opinion between Mālikī and Ḥanafī jurists as narrated by Muḥammad al-Shaybānī in the *Muwaṭṭā'* in chapter *al-Buyū'*. The main idea is to clarify and establish that these juristic differences of opinion in different schools of law are actually because of the application of the hermeneutical process of interpretations and not because of the different tenets of schools of law. Our forgoing accounts of the civil and commercial law in the compositions of *Mukhtaṣar* manifest that from the very inception of the formation of Islamic law, one finds such differences of opinion among the jurists of the same school as well as from the opinions of the jurists of other schools of law. In short, they are the result of the continuity of hermeneutical interpretations in the formation of Islamic law.

Al-Marghīnānī's *Hidāya* and al-Shaybānī's *Muwaṭṭā'* of Mālik these differences of opinion are mostly from the earlier times and confined mostly to the legal opinion of jurists of that time. They do not contain the differences of opinions that have been developed from over the course of time such as we find progressively developing further in the compositions of *Mukhtaṣar* from one author to the next as in al-Muzanī's *Mukhtaṣar* and al-Shīrāzī's *Tanbīh* in the Shāfi'ī school of law, al-Ṭaḥāwī' *Mukhtaṣar*, al-Qudūrī's *Mukhtaṣar* and al-Marghīnānī's *Hidāya* in the Ḥanafī school of law, al-Khiraqī's *Mukhtaṣar* in the Ḥanbalī school of law, and finally culminating this process of hermeneutical interpretations in the composition of Khalīl's *Mukhtaṣar*. Thus, this process of hermeneutical formation of Islamic legal system continues in the genre of *Mukhtaṣar*.

DIFFERENCES OF OPINION ACCORDING TO THE HERMENEUTICAL INTERPRETATIONS BY JURISTIC REASONING

In general, first I would state the opinion of Marghīnānī from the *Hidāya* according to the Ḥanafī school of law, which are different from the opinions of al-Shāfi'ī, Mālik, Ibn Ḥanbal. From all differences of opinion in juristic rulings, I found approximately thirty in number, out of which twenty-two are because of hermeneutical interpretations and, only seven are due to the employment of the doctrine of *istiḥsān* (juristic preference).

CONTRACT OF SALE

If it is said to the seller to pluck fruits from the tree and deliver them to the purchaser and, in the same manner, if there is any cultivation in the field, then it is incumbent on the seller that he does it accordingly. Al-Shāfi'ī maintains that the fruits should be left unplucked until they are ripe to be plucked and the field is cleaned up by the purchaser.[2]

According to Abū Ḥanifa, the sale of fruits is valid after they have become ripe or before becoming ripe. In both cases, the fruits are useful currently or later. According to al-Shāfi'ī, Mālik, and Ibn Ḥanbal, it is not valid.[3]

The sale of fruits exempting a certain amount of *riṭls* is not valid, because of not knowing the quantity of the remaining fruits. Mālik says it is valid. Al-Ṭaḥāwī, a Ḥanafī jurist and the author of composition of *Mukhtaṣar*, is also of the same opinion,[4] because according to Mālik one has knowledge of it after having experience in such a kind of business.

The sale of wheat and rice growing in the ears is valid. Al-Shāfi'ī considers it invalid and according to al-Shāfi'ī, same applies in the contract of sale of almond, walnut, and pistachio with thick skin.[5]

RIGHT OF OPTION

According to Abū Ḥanīfa, it is valid to reject (annul) or accept contract within a specified time and one can annul a contract without informing or the presence of the other party to the contract. But according to al-Shāfi'ī, it is invalid. Al-Shāfi'ī's contention is that in such a case it may result in an eventual loss for the other party to the contract. Thus, the annulment of the right of option by one party rests upon the other party.[6]

A person having the right of option dies, then the sale is considered complete and right of option is void. It is not transferred to his inheritors. According to al-Shāfi'ī, the right of option descends to the inheritors as in case of defect. For Abū Ḥanīfa, the right of option is only a desire or disposition that is not transferable to others, unlike in case of defect.[7]

RIGHT OF OPTION OF INSPECTION

According to Abū Ḥanīfa, if a person purchases a thing without seeing it, he has right of option after seeing it. For al-Shāfi'ī, such a contract is by its origin (*aṣl*) invalid, because of the invalid stipulation as article of sale is not known.[8]

The sale or purchase of an article by a blind person is valid. According to al-Shāfi'ī, if only that person was not blind by birth and then he became blind. If he was not blind by birth, the sale or purchase of it is valid. If one was blind by birth, then it is invalid.[9]

The *salam* sale of an article is invalid, unless it exists from the time when it was contracted and the time when it is to be delivered. Al-Marghīnānī cites prophetic *Ḥadīth* report in support of it: "You shall not sell fruit by way of the *salam* sale, until their ripeness is apparent." Al-Shāfi'ī maintains that the existence of article at the time of its delivery is sufficient.[10]

The sale of *umm al-walad*, *muddabir*, and *mukātab* is not valid. The *umm al-walad* has a claim to emancipation based on the prophetic *Ḥadīth* report: "Her child sets her free." The cause of emancipation with respect to the *muddabir* slave has not been established upon the death of his owner, and the *mukātab* has right of emancipation which is binding upon his owner. According to al-Shāfi'ī, in respect to it there are two narrations (*riwāya*): apparent (*ẓāhir*) in which case the sale is valid, and not in case of restricted (*muqayyad*) emancipation to the nonrecovery of owner from illness when emancipation would be granted (*tadbīr*).[11]

The sale of honeybees is not valid if they are not protected. Al-Shāfi'ī maintains that it is valid, because of the usefulness (benefit) of honey though bees are not eaten.[12]

The sale of milk of a woman filled in a cup is not valid. According to al-Marghīnānī, because the breast of the woman is considered a revered part of the body of a woman. According to al-Shāfi'ī, it is valid because milk is pure.[13]

If a person purchases a female slave in exchange for one thousand *dirhams* with cash or delayed payment to a future specified time and takes her into his possession, and then sells her for five hundred *dirhams*, this (second) transaction of the sale is considered invalid. Contrary to it al-Shāfi'ī maintains that after the sold article has been taken into possession, the contract of sale is complete, and the purchaser can sell it to anyone he pleases.[14]

RIBĀ

According to Marghīnānī, *ribā* is unlawful in respect to the unequal rate of measurement or weight of one article of exchange for another article when they belong to the same species. The juristic reasoning (*'illa*) in this case is that the measurement or weight is united with the species. According al-Shāfi'ī, *ribā* takes place only in respect to esculent articles.[15]

The sale of milk of cow in exchange for the milk of goat at an unequal rate is valid, because they are of different species. According to al-Shāfi'ī, it is not valid because they are not of different species.[16] In this case, Al-Shāfi'ī classifies cow and goat of the same species, whereas the Ḥanafī jurists classify them belonging to the different species.

PARTNERSHIP IN TRAFFIC

According to al-Marghīnānī, it is valid in respect to the partnership in traffic, the capital of each partner is equal, and yet the profit unequally shared. The profit is shared between two partners as specified in the contract. According al-Shāfi'ī, it is invalid, because if an inequality of the profit is admitted, then it would induce the profit upon capital concerning which there is no responsibility. Al-Marghīnānī maintains that it is based upon the prophetic *Ḥadīth* report: "The profit between them is according to their agreement and their loss in proportion to the property of each, and no distinction is made between equality and inequality of their capital."[17]

According to al-Marghīnānī, it is valid for two persons to engage in the partnership in traffic, where the capital of one person is *dirhams* and *dīnārs* of another partner (so long as they are equal in values). According to al-Shāfi'ī, it is not valid because the difference of sentiments in respect of the admixture of capital. For al-Shāfi'ī, the capital is essential to the partnership and that does not take place when capital is not of homogeneous nature.[18]

LEASE-HIRE

The recompense in contract of lease-hire is not due immediately. It becomes claimable on one of the three grounds: it is claimable in advance, in virtue of previous agreement, or independent of such an agreement. Al-Shāfi'ī maintains that it becomes due immediately upon concluding the contract.[19]

It is invalid to receive recompense for the performance of summoning people for prayers or for the performance of pilgrimage. Likewise, it is invalid to receive recompense for leading prayers in the capacity of an Imām and for the teaching of *Qur'ān*. Al-Marghīnānī cites prophetic *Ḥadīth* report and narration from early Muslims: The Prophet said: "Recite *Qur'ān*, but do not receive for it any recompense." When 'Uthmān, the third Caliph, was appointed as the call prayer *(mu'ḍḍin)*, he was asked not to receive any recompense. According to al-Shāfi'ī, one can receive wages for the performance of any religious duties, which is not required.[20] Al-Shāfi'ī's view was gradually accepted in the Ḥanafī and other schools of law.

It is invalid that a person hires anyone to cultivate land in return that he has right to cultivate other land for the wages. Al-Shāfi'ī maintains that it is valid, because the advantage is the same in substance.[21]

In articles of food between two persons in the partnership, one partner hires other person or his donkey to carry his share of load to a certain place, he is not entitled to either the specified recompense or proportionate recompense. According to al-Shāfi'ī, he is entitled to the specified recompense. It is like when a person hires building in the partnership between himself and another person for keeping grain or slave in the partnership between him and the other person for making apparel.[22]

The reserve in right of option by the lessee is valid in the contract of lease-hire. According to al-Shāfi'ī, it is invalid because it would be impossible for the lessor to complete the contract because the lessee can prolong it indefinitely to make the contact complete. Abū Yūsuf and Muḥammad al-Shaybānī maintain that contract of lease-hire is like the contract of sale in which it is not required that the article has been taken into possession at the meeting of contract and in which the condition of option may legally be inserted in it.[23]

Differences of Opinion due to the Ḥanafī Doctrine of Juristic Preference (Istiḥsān) considered Invalid in other Sunni Schools of Law.

RIGHT OF OPTION

The right of option exceeding three days is invalid according to the opinion of both Abū Ḥanīfa and al-Shāfi'ī. However, according to Abū Yūsuf and Muḥammad al-Shaybānī, it can be extended exceeding three days to facilitate transactions. This is according to the doctrine of the juristic preference (*istiḥsān*). According to al-Muzanī and al-Shīrāzī it can be extended exceeding three days.[24]

A person having purchased an article stipulates the right of option to a third person, then the purchaser or third person who has right of option can accept the contract of sale or annul it. It is valid according to the doctrine of the doctrine of juristic preference, though according to the *qiyās*, it is not. According to Abū Yūsuf and Muḥammad al-Shaybānī, such a right of option can be establishment by a way of appointing agent by the purchaser to act as his substitute.[25]

It is valid if a person purchases two pieces of cloth on the condition that within three days of right of option, he may determine which piece of cloth he may approve. Such a stipulation is called the option of determination. It is valid according to the doctrine of the juristic preference. According to al-Shāfi'ī, it is invalid, because the subject of sale is unknown at the time of concluding contract.[26]

A person purchases a slave and afterward emancipates him, or the slave dies in his possession and if he comes to know that the slave was defective, he is in either case entitled to the compensation for it from the seller. Similarly, in case if slave is dying not from any act of the purchaser, but because of unavoidable calamity. This is according to the doctrine of the juristic preference, though according to the *qiyās*, the purchaser is not entitled to the compensation.[27]

It is not valid to sell one piece of cloth out of two pieces, in such a case it is not known which piece of cloth is sold. However, if the seller says, "take either one of them," it is valid according to the doctrine of juristic preference.[28]

PARTNERSHIP

The partnership in reciprocity is valid according to the doctrine of *istiḥsān*, but not according to the doctrine of *qiyās*. Al-Shāfi'ī and Mālik maintained that it is not valid. As already mentioned in chapter 3, al-Shāfi'ī said, "I know not what partnership in reciprocity (*shirka mufāwaḏa*) is."[29]

LEASE-HIRE

According to the doctrine of the juristic preference, it is valid to lease-hire a wet nurse to suckle an infant in return for the food and clothing. This is according to Abū Ḥanīfa. However, Abū Yūsuf and Muḥammad al-Shaybānī as al-Shāfi'ī maintains that it is not valid, because the recompense is not known with the specification. If the recompense can be ascertained, it is valid.[30]

REASONS FOR THE DIFFERENCES OF OPINION AMONG JURISTS

As we have already mentioned, the jurists do not always describe explicitly reasons for their juristic opinions, which as a student of the *fiqh* one needs to figure out making it explicit. At the cost of some repetitions, we would here attempt to describe explicitly the reasons for differences of opinion among the jurists in the Ḥanafī, Shāfi'ī, Mālikī, and Ḥanbalī schools of law. As already mentioned, the main purpose is to establish that these differences of opinion among the jurists are the result of the continuity of hermeneutical different interpretations by the jurists and not because of the different school tenets.

According to al-Marghīnānī, the sale of fruits before or after they are ripe is valid, because they are useful. According to the jurists in Shāfi'ī and other schools of law, it is invalid. According to Marghīnānī, only difference is if they are ripe, they are useful at present and if they are not ripe now their usufruct would be later.

According to al-Marghīnānī, the sale of wheat and rice still growing in the ears is valid. Contrary to it, al-Shāfi'ī maintains that it is invalid. The reason for this difference of opinion is that according to al-Shāfi'ī uncertainty or risk is involved, but not for al-Marghīnānī. This is because the people who are engaged in the business of farming know such matters by experience.

According to al-Marghīnānī, the purchaser and the seller both have right of option to accept or reject the contract without informing the other party. According to al-Shāfi'ī, it is invalid, because it might result in an eventual loss for the other party to the contract.

According to al-Marghīnānī, if a person having right of option dies, then the right of option is void. It is not transferred to his inheritors. Contrary to it, for al-Shāfi'ī it is transferred as in case of defect. The reason is, according to Abū Ḥanīfa, right of option is only a desire or disposition. Thus, it is not transferable unlike in case of defect.

According to Abū Ḥanīfa as narrated by al-Marghīnānī, the right of option is valid in a purchase of thing without seeing it. According to al-Shāfi'ī, it is invalid, because of the invalid stipulation in its origin *(aṣl).*

According to al-Marghīnānī, the sale or purchase by a blind person is valid, contrary to which al-Shāfi'ī restricts it that if he was not blind by birth and then he became blind, because when he was not blind previously he would have knowledge of the matters of sale and purchase.

According to al-Marghīnānī, the *salam* sale of thing is invalid unless it is existing from the time when the contract was concluded and at the time of its delivery. For al-Shāfi'ī, it is sufficient if the thing exists at the time of delivery. The reason is that a manufacturer knows how much thing would cost and how long it would take to make it.

According to al-Marghīnānī, the sale of honeybees is invalid, if it was not under the protection. Al-Shāfi'ī maintains that it is valid, because of the usefulness of honey, though one does not eat bees. The honey is the main object of the contract of sale and not the bees. For al-Marghīnānī, the protection is desired, because of the safety of purchaser.

The sale of milk of woman filled in a cup is invalid, because the breast of a woman is revered part of her body, but al-Shāfi'ī considers that it is valid because the milk is pure, which is the main object of contract of sale. In this case, both al-Marghīnānī and al-Shāfi'ī's reasoning is based on the valid ground. This shows that the differences of opinion can arise when one jurist considers one element and the other jurist considers another element in the interpretation of his ruling. Hence, one can clearly state that the differences of opinion are the result of hermeneutical interpretations rather than the different tenets of schools of law as such.

According to al-Marghīnānī, if anyone purchases a thing in exchange for one thousand *dirhams* with cash (*naqd*) or with delayed payment at a future specified time and after taking it into possession sells it for five thousand *dirhams,* then this second transaction is considered invalid. For, al-Shāfi'ī, it is valid, because after the article of sale has been taken into possession, the contract of sale is complete, and purchaser can do with it whatever he pleases.

According to al-Marghīnānī, the *ribā* is unlawful in respect to an unequal rate of exchange of the article to that of other article belonging to the same species. Al-Shāfi'ī restricts it to the esculent articles.

According to al-Marghīnānī, it is valid to sell the milk of cow in exchange for the milk of goat at an unequal rate, because they belong to two different species. According to al-Shāfi'ī, it is invalid because he considers that they belong to the same species. Here it becomes a fortiori manifest that it is the matter of hermeneutical different interpretations of the same object regarding al-Marghīnānī and al-Shāfi'ī conceive of which articles belong to the same species or different species.

According to al-Marghīnānī, in the partnership in traffic capital of each partner in equal proportion and the profit shared in an unequal amount is valid based upon the prophetic *Hadīth* report. However, al-Shāfi'ī disagrees with it, because if the profit at an unequal rate is admitted, it would induce the profit on capital concerning which there is no responsibility.

According to al-Marghīnānī, it is valid if one partner in partnership in traffic brings *dīnārs* and other partner brings *dirhams*. For al-Shāfi'ī, the admixture should be of homogeneous nature. For al-Marghīnānī, it is valid so long as the *dīnārs* and *dirhams* contributed to the partnership are of equal value.

According to al-Shāfi'ī, the recompense in contract of lease-hire is paid immediately upon concluding the contract. According to al-Marghīnānī, the recompense can be paid immediately upon concluding the contract, in advance, or by agreement. For al-Shāfi'ī, immediate payment would make contract of lease-hire certain, whereas in other case it may not be that certain.

According to al-Marghīnānī, it is invalid if a person hires anyone to cultivate land in return that he has right to cultivate other land as the recompense for it, because the amount of recompense remains unspecified and uncertain. For al-Shāfi'ī, it is it is valid, because advantage is the same in substance.

According to Abū Ḥanīfa, it is valid that the hirer reserves right of option to take the article into possession in the contract of lease-hire. Abū Yūsuf and al-Shaybānī maintain that such a right of option may legally be inserted in the contract itself. For al-Shāfi'ī, it is invalid. The reason is that this would be something extraneous to the contract.

The differences of opinion in the rulings based upon the doctrine of juristic reasoning (*istiḥsān*) in respect to (i) the right of option exceeding three days, (ii) the right of option in the contract of sale in respect to stipulate a representative to accept or reject the contract, (iii) if a person purchases piece of cloth from two pieces of cloth on the condition that he may determine within three days which one piece of cloth to purchase and other to return, (iv) partnership in reciprocity is valid according to the doctrine of the juristic preference, and (v) validity of hiring a wet nurse for suckling an infant for the food and clothing as a recompense. They are considered by the Ḥanafī jurists valid according to the doctrine of juristic preference, because *istiḥsān* is considered also a kind of *qiyās*. The jurists in the Shāfi'ī, Ḥanbalī, and Mālikī schools of law, reject the validity of it. In substance, the differences of opinion are as such the result of hermeneutically different juristic interpretations rather than school tenets. In general, the doctrine of juristic preference is associated with only the Ḥanafī school of law, but in fact sometimes it is also used by the jurists of other schools of law.

DIFFERENCES OF OPINION BETWEEN MĀLIK AND MUḤAMMAD AL-SHAYBĀNĪ

Muḥammad al-Shaybānī in his treatise discusses the agreements and differences of opinion between Ḥanafī and Mālikī schools of law. Out of twenty-four items, we find there is an agreement in nineteen items and there are five items where they differ in their juristic opinions.

SELLING OF ANYTHING BEFORE IT HAS BEEN TAKEN INTO POSSESSION

According to Shaybānī, Abū Ḥanīfa allows sale of immovable property such as the houses and lands which have not been substantially altered before they have been taken into possession, contrary to the opinion of Mālik.[31]

SELLING FOOD ON DEFERRED PAYMENT FOR GOLD, AND BUYING DATES WITH ITS PRICE BEFORE TAKING IT INTO POSSESSION

According to Mālik, it is repugnant to sell food at a deferred payment for gold and later buying dates with that gold before it has been taken into possession. Al-Shaybānī does not see anything objectionable in buying dates with it before taking gold into possession if they are actual and not debt. This is the verdict of Abū Ḥanīfa.

THE LIABILITY AGREEMENTS OF THREE DAYS AND OF A YEAR

Mālik informed us that Abān ibn ʻUthmān and Hishām ibn Ismāʻīl used to teach people about the liability of agreements of three days and of a year.

Al-Shaybānī said: "We do not recognize liability agreements of three days, nor liability agreement of a year unless the person stipulates this option of returning goods in three days or in a year." As for the verdict of Abū Ḥanīfa, only the option of returning goods in three days is valid.

PERMISSIBILITY OF BARTERING ANIMALS TO BE DELIVERED AT A FUTURE SPECIFIED TIME PERIOD

Yāḥya related from Mālik that ʻAlī ibn Abī Ṭālib sold one of his excellent camel (ʻuṣ*fūr*) for twenty camels to be delivered later.

Yāḥya related from Mālik that 'Abdallah ibn 'Umar bought female riding-camel for four camels and guaranteed to deliver them in full to the buyer at Rabaḍha.

Al-Shaybānī said that something different reached us from 'Alī ibn Abū Ṭālib, who forbade the sell one camel for two camels in exchange for a differed payment. It has reached us that the Prophet forbade to sell animals on a differed term and we adhere to it.[32]

THE REASONS FOR THE DIFFERENCES OF OPINION BETWEEN AL-SHAYBĀNĪ AND MĀLIK

According to al-Shaybānī, regarding the permissibility to sell immovable property which have not been altered substantially before it has been taken into possession is that in such properties generally no changes occur. In this case, for Mālik the possession of property of sale provides certainty of transaction.

According to Mālik, to sell article on a differed payment and to buy another article with its price is considered not good, because it is buying without paying price. If there is a differed payment in transaction, there is a lack of certainty. For al-Shaybānī, there is no harm.

The reasoning from the side of Mālik and al-Shaybānī concerning the liability agreement for a year are based on the reliability of transmitted prophetic *Ḥadīth* report transmitted to Mālik of which al-Shaybānī claims having no knowledge.

The validity or invalidity of bartering of animal in exchange for a differed payment for more animals is again claimed from both sides as based on the prophetic *Ḥadīth* reports depending upon the reliability of their confirmation.

NOTES

1. Jamīl Aḥmad Sakrawdhwī, *Sharḥ Hidāya* in *Urdu*, vol. viii (Lahore: Maktaba Rahmanya).
2. Burhān 'Alī bin Abū Bakr al-Marghīnānī, *al-Hidāya Sharḥ Bidāya al-Mubtadī*, vol. iv (Cairo: Dār al-Salām, 2000), p. 945.
3. Al-Marghīnānī, *al-Hidāya*, p. 946.
4. Al-Marghīnānī, *al-Hidāya,* p. 947.
5. Al-Marghīnānī, *al-Hidāya*, p. 947.
6. Al-Marghīnānī, *al-Hidāya*, p. 949.
7. Al-Marghīnānī, *al-Hidāya*, p. 953.
8. Al-Marghīnānī, *al-Hidāya,* p. 957.

9. Al-Marghīnānī, *al-Hidāya*, p. 960.
10. Al-Marghīnānī, *al-Hidāya*, p. 1020.
11. Al-Marghīnānī, *al-Hidāya*, p. 972.
12. Al-Marghīnānī, *al-Hidāya*, p. 976.
13. Al-Marghīnānī, *al-Hidāya*, p. 977.
14. Al-Marghīnānī, *al-Hidāya*, p. 979.
15. Al-Marghīnānī, *al-Hidāya*, p. 1003.
16. Al-Marghīnānī, *al-Hidāya*, p. 1010.
17. Hamilton, *The Hidāya, Commentary,* vol. ii, p. 550.
18. Hamilton, *The Hidāya,* vol. ii, p. 551.
19. Al-Marghīnānī, *al-Hidāya*, p. 1269.
20. Al-Marghīnānī, *al-Hidāya*, p. 1280; Hamilton, The *Hidāya*, vol. ii, p. 218.
21. Al-Marghīnānī, *al-Hidāya*, p. 1285; Hamilton, The *Hidāya*, vol. ii, p. 224.
22. Al-Marghīnānī, *al-Hidāya*, p. 1285; Hamilton, The *Hidāya*, vol. ii, p. 224.
23. Al-Marghīnānī, *al-Hidāya*, p. 1295; Hamilton, The *Hidāya*, vol. ii, p. 240.
24. Al-Marghīnānī, *al-Hidāya*, p. 949.
25. Al-Marghīnānī, *al-Hidāya*, p. 953.
26. Al-Marghīnānī, *al-Hidāya*, pp. 953–954.
27. Al-Marghīnānī, *al-Hidāya,* p. 964.
28. Al-Marghīnānī, *al-Hidāya*, p. 971.
29. Hamilton, *The Hidāya, Commentary*, p. 541.
30. Al-Marghīnānī, *al-Hidāya,* p. 1282.
31. Al-Shaybānī, *The Muwaṭṭa'*, Item 766, pp. 336–337.
32. Muḥammad al-Shaybānī, *The Muwaṭṭa'*, Item, 799 and 800, p. 350; Mālik, *al-Muwaṭṭa'*, Items, 31.25.59 and 31.25.60.

Conclusion

The main contention of our investigation is that the compositions of *Mukhtaṣar* are authored texts by individual jurists claiming independently to personal hermeneutical interpretations in their writings. Our forgoing account of these compositions of *Mukhtaṣar* shows that they are not as it has been traditionally understood just the abridgement, which the literal translation of the word '*mukhtaṣar*' suggests. They are not authored just to reproduce the legal opinions of the eponyms of schools of law in an abridged form. The nature of compositions of these *Mukhtaṣar* is highly complex unfolding itself in several aspects, incorporating all the entailed expanded additional elements that had been developed over the course of time. Foremost, the main purpose for which they were composed was to provide the hermeneutical account of the formation of Islamic legal system. The authors of these compositions of *Mukhtaṣar* in their production and reproduction continue the hermeneutical interpretation in the formation of Islamic legal system. This shows the part played by the hermeneutics of the compositions of *Mukhtaṣar* in the formation of Islamic law.

In the classical *fiqh* literature the differences of opinion among the jurists of four Sunni schools of law were discussed under the title "Differences of Opinion among the Jurists (*ikhtilāf al-fuqhā*)." They were understood as if they are the differences of opinion due to the different tenets of four Sunni schools of law without raising the question as to how if the legal rulings in each of these four schools of law are determined according to the canons provided in the *Qur'ān* and prophetic *Ḥadīth* reports. They are, *in reality*, the result of hermeneutically different interpretations by the jurists, regardless from which individual jurists and which school of law they belonged.

The exploration of different compositions of *Mukhtaṣar* in the forgoing chapters manifests the significance of al-Shāfi'ī's concept of continuity of hermeneutics in the formation of Islamic legal system in the composition of one *Mukhtaṣar* to the next composition of *Mukhtaṣar,* culminating finally in the composition of Khalīl's *Mukhtaṣar.* Thus, to conclude one can describe in a general statement that the compositions of *Mukhtaṣar* are the continuous hermeneutical formation of Islamic legal system and not just the abridgements of legal opinions of eponyms of the school of law.

Appendix

As mentioned In Chapter Seven, Khalīl's *Mukhtaṣar* defies comparison with the ordering of material with Mālik's *Muwaṭṭā'*. Khalīl arranges material, in most part, after Saḥnūn's *Mudawwana al-Kubrā'* incorporating all the additional expanded elements as indicated in parenthesis in our Text.[1] But, on the whole, Khalīl's arrangement of material is independent of Saḥnūn's *Mudawanna al-Kubrā.* Khalīl packs all expanded elements in an abridged form such as in the *ṣarf* sale, *salam* sale, lease-hire, partnership, etc., which have been developed over the course of time by the earlier jurists in succeeding generations.

I have selected here randomly some passages as an illustration from Khalil's *Mukhtaṣar* and Saḥnūn's *Mudawwan al-Kubrā'* chapter Lease-Hire (*Ijāra*).

LEASE-HIRE OF WET NURSE

According to Khalīl, it is valid to lease-hire the wet nurse to breastfeed an infant for the known wages with the additional expanded elements. Likewise, it is valid to stipulate food and clothing according to Mālik and for husband not to cohabit with her.[2]

According to Saḥnūn, it is valid to lease-hire a youngling for such and such wages. It is valid to stipulate food and clothing for the wet nurse. If she lets herself hired with the permission of her husband, he should not cohabit with her.[3]

According to Khalīl, if the husband does not permit to breastfeed child, it is void.[4]

According to Saḥnūn, if the wet nurse lets herself hired to breastfeed child without the permission of her husband, it is void.[5]

According to Khalīl, the hire of wet nurse is not valid, if she is pregnant because of the fear of child's death or fever.[6]

According to Saḥnūn, if breastfeeding child by the wet nurse is harmful, it is not valid.[7]

According to Khalīl, if father dies without paying wages to the wet nurse, the hire becomes void for remaining period of hire. If anyone pays her wages voluntarily, it is not void. The wages for the wet nurse are not obligatory after the father dies. Khalīl brings additional expanded elements from Ibn Yūnus that the wages were obligatory on the father while he was alive, but the wages for schooling the child are not obligatory whether in his life time or after he dies. He has taken it on himself of the schooling of child while he was alive.[8]

According to Saḥnūn, if the child dies, the hire of breastfeeding becomes void and the wages are incumbent on the father in proportion to the period wet nurse has breastfed child. If the father dies without paying wages and someone else pays wages for the completion of breastfeeding period of lease-hire, it is valid.[9]

According to Khalīl[10] and Saḥnun,[11] if one hires two wet nurses together at the same time or the second wet nurse after the first wet nurse, and the first wet nurse dies and only the second wet nurse breast-feeds the child, the hire is void. Khalīl brings additional expanded element from Abū Ḥusan 'Abd al-Ḥaq and so is narrated by Hamdays that if one hires the first wet nurse and then the second wet nurse and if she dies, then it is incumbent on the first wet nurse to breast child. This is when the second wet nurse knew it at the time she was hired.

TEACHING OF QUR'ĀN

According to Khalīl, it is valid to hire anyone to teach *Qur'ān* with proficiency for the whole month or year, or week, or day with the known wages.[12]

According to Saḥnūn, it is not objectionable, if a person hires someone to teach his child *Qur'ān* with proficiency for the whole month for a *dirham* or for the whole *Qur'ān* for the known wages. It is not objectional to hire someone to teach *Qur'ān* to his servant.[13]

Strangely enough we find in Khalīl's text mention that it is not objectionable, if a teacher whips the child with lashes mildly for not memorizing *Qur'ān* and other such details that had developed over the course of time.[14]

LEASE OF MOSQUE

According to Khalīl, it is valid to rent the land to build mosque for a certain period and then destroy it. The stone, wood, bricks from it are the property of the owner for whatever he wishes to do with them after the expiration of lease.

According to Saḥnūn, it is not valid to build mosque to rent it for the people to hold prayers in it.

HIRE OF IMAM

According to Khalīl, it is valid to hire an Imam (prayer leader) to lead prayers, including prayer calls, but not for one's compulsory or supererogatory prayers, and anyone as the representative for substituting the acts of religious worship, and fasting. Ibn al-Qāsim, Mālik, and his many disciples permit it, but Ibn 'Abbas says so long as you do not make business out of it. Būlū indicates that Ibn Ḥabīb forbids hire of it.[15] There is no corresponding narration of the hiring Imam in Saḥnūn's *Mudawanna*.

We have narrated above these few examples to show that Khalīl indicates the additional expanded elements incorporated in the composition of his *Mukhtaṣar*.

NOTES

1. Saḥnūn, bin Sa'īd al-Tanūkhī, *Mudawwana*, vol iv, part, ix (Dār al-Ṣādīr: Beirut, 2005.
2. Khalīl, *Minḥa,* vol. viii, p. 305.
3. Saḥnūn, *Mudawwana*, p. 441
4. Khalīl, *Minḥa*, p. 305.
5. Saḥnūn. *Mudawwana*, p. 441.
6. Khalīl, *Minḥa*, p. 305.
7. Saḥnūn, *Mudawwana*, p. 442.
8. Khalīl, *Minḥa*, p. 306.
9. Saḥnūn, *Mudawwana*, p. 442.
10. Khalīl, *Minḥa*, p. 306.
11. Saḥnūn, *Mudawwana*, p. 444.
12. Khalīl, *Minḥa*, p. 311
13. Saḥnūn, *Mudawwana*, p. 419.
14. Khalīl, *Minḥa*, p. 316.
15. Khalīl, *Minḥa*, p. 323.

Bibliography

Abū Ya'la, Ibn al-Farrā, *Mu'atamad fī Uṣūl al-Dīn*, Beirut, 1974.

Ajetunmobi, Musa Ali, "A Critical Study of *Mukhtaṣar* Khalīl" in *Islamic Studies*, vol. no. 3, 1986, pp. 275–288.

Al-Ḥaṭṭāb, Muḥammad bin Muḥammad, *Kitāb Mawāhib, al Jalīīl lī Sharḥ Mukhtaṣar*, vol. 1, Beirut, 1992.

Al-Muzanī, Ismā'īl, Ibn Yaḥyā, *Mukhtaṣar al-Muzanī*, Beirut, 1993.

Al-Qudūrī, Abū Ḥasan Aḥmad bin Muḥammad, *Mukhtaṣar*, Beirut, 1997.

Al-Shāfi'ī, *The Risāla* translated with an Introduction by Majid Khadduri, Baltimore: The John Hopkins Press, 1961.

Al-Shāfi'ī, Muḥammad Idrīs, *K al-Umm*, vol. iii, Beirut: Dār al-Kutab-al-'ilmīya, 1993; Al-Shāfi'ī, *K al-Umm*, vol. iii, Cairo: Bulāq al-Shu'ab, 1998.

Al-Shaybānī, *The Muwaṭṭa'*, UK: Turath Publications, 2004.

Al-Shaybānī, Muḥammad, *Jāmi' al-Ṣaghīr*, Beirut: Turath, 1979.

Al-Shīrāzī, Abū Isḥāq Ibrāhim, *al-Tanbīh*, Cairo, 1951.

Al-Ṭaḥāwī, Abū Ja'far Aḥmad bin Muḥammad, *Mukhtaṣar*, Cairo, 1951.

Bāqillānī, Abū Baker, *Taqrīb wa Irshād al-Ṣaghīr*, Beirut, 1998.

Bernard Marie, Marie, "Ḥanafī *Uṣūl al-Fiqh*" through a Manuscript of al-Jaṣṣāṣ", in *American Oriental Society*, vol. 105, no. 4, 1985, pp. 623–635.

Brockopp, Jonathan E, "Early Islamic Jurisprudence in Egypt: Two Scholars and their *Mukhtaṣar* in Journal of Middle East Studies, Cambridge University Press, 1988.

Calder, Norman, *Study in Early Muslim Jurisprudence*, Oxford: Clarendon Press, 1993.

Cheneb, M. Ben, "Al-Khalīl ibn Isḥāq", in *Encyclopaedia of Islam*, vol. 4. Leiden: E. J. Brill.

Dutton, Yasin, *The Origins of Islamic Law: The Qur'ān, Muwaṭṭa' and Madinan,* New York: Routledge, 1999.

Epistle of Legal Theory with Arabic Text edited and translated by Joseph E. Lowry, Leiden: E. J. Brill, 2007.

Fadl, Khalid Abu El, *Speaking in God's Name*, Oxford: One World, 2005.

Fadl, Muhammad, "The Social Logic of *Taqlīd and the Rise of Mukhtaṣar*" in Islamic Law and Society, vol. 3, no. 2, 1996.

Gleave, Robert, *Islam and Literalism*, Edinburgh: Edinburgh University Press, 2002.

Hallaq, Weal B., *Authority, Continuity, and Change in Islamic Law*, Cambridge, 1997.

Hallaq, Weal B., "Was al-Shāfiʿī the Master Architect of Islamic Jurisprudence" in *International Journal of Middle East Study*, 4, 1993.

Hallaq, Weal, B., *A History of Islamic Theories*: *An Introduction to Sunni Uṣūl al-Fiqh*, Cambridge, 1997.

Hamilton, Charles, The *Hidāya*, Commentary on Islamic Law, vol. II, Karachi, Dār al-Ishāʿat. 1993.

Ḥanbal, Aḥmad, *Masāʾil riwāya inhu ibn Aḥmad* Beirut: Kutab al-ʿIlmīya, 1971.

Heffening, W, "Al-Muzanī" in *First Encyclopeadia of Islam,* vol. vii, Leiden: E. J. Brill, 1993.

Kassim, Husain, *Sarakhsī: The Doctrine of Juristic Preference in Islamic Jurisprudence*, San Francisco, London, and Austin: Winfield, 1995.

Khalīl ibn Isḥāq, *Mukhtaṣar al-Khalīl*, Cairo, 1951.

Khiraqī, ʿUmar bin Ḥusayn, *al-Mukhtaṣar*, Cairo, 1980.

Lowry, "The Legal Hermeneutics of al-Shāfiʿī and Ibn Qutayba: A Reconsideration" *Islamic Law and Society*, 11, 2004, 1–41.

Lowry, Joseph E, *Early Islamic Legal Theories*, Leiden: E. J. Brill, 1997.

Mālik Ibn Anas, *al-Muwaṭṭa'*, vol. ii, edited by Fuwād ʿAbd al-Bāqī, Beirut: Dār al-Kutab al-ʿArabīya, 1951.

Mālik, *al-Muwaṭṭa',* translated by Aisha Abdurrahaman Bewly, Scotland: Madinah Press Inverness, 2004.

Marghīnānī, Burhān al-Dīn ʿAlī Abū Bakr, *al-Hidāya*, Cairo, 2000.

Melchert, "Traditionists-Jurisprudence and Framing of Islamic Law" in *Islamic Law and Society*, Brill, 2001.

Melchert, *Aḥmad ibn Ḥanbal*, Oxford: One World, 2006.

Melchert, Christopher, *The Formation of the Sunni Schools of Law*, Leiden: Brill, 1997.

Meron, Yakov: The Development of Islamic Thought" in *Studia Islamic*, 1969.

Nyazee, Ahsan Khan, "Introduction" in *al-Hidāya*, translation and commentary, Bristol Press, 2006.

Saḥnūn, Saʿīd Tanūkhī, *Mudawwana al-Kubrā'*, vol. iv, part ix, Dār al-Ṣādir, 2005.

Sarakhsī, Muḥammad ibn Aḥmad, *Mabsūṭ*, vol. I, Cairo: Dār al-Maʿārif, 1906–12.

Schacht, "*Aṣḥāb al-Raʾy*" in Encyclopeadia of Islam, vol. v, New Edition, Leiden: Brill, 1997.

Schacht, Joseph, *Origins of Muhammadan Jurisprudence*, Oxford: Clarendon Press, 1996.

Shamsi, "Al-Shāfiʿī's Written Corpus: A Source of Critical Study" in *The Journal of the American Oriental Society,* 2002.

Shamsi, Ahmad E., *The Canonization of Islamic Law: A Social and Intellectual History*, New York: Cambridge University Press, 2013.

Spectorsky, Susan A., "Ibn Ḥanbal's Fiqh" in *Journal of American Oriental Society*, vol. 102, no. 3, 1962.

ʿUlaysh, Muḥammad bin Aḥmad, *Sharḥ ʿalā Mukhtaṣar*, vols. iv, v, vi, viii, and viii, Beirut: Dār al-Kutab al-ʿIlmīya, 2003.

Vishanoff, David R., *The Formation of Islamic Hermeneutics*, New Haven, CT, 2001.

Index

About the Author

Husain Kassim is emeritus associate professor, University of Central Florida. He has taught as a Fulbright Scholar at the University of Bremen, served as Distinguished Chair in Intercultural Theology and Religion at the University of Salzburg, and as visiting professor at the University of Karachi. Dr. Kassim is the author of *Sarakhsī: The Doctrine of Juristic Preference in Islamic Jurisprudence*, *Aristotle and Aristotelianism in Medieval Muslim, Jewish, and Christian Philosophy*, *Legitimizing Modernity in Islam*, and *Islamicate Societies*, as well as several articles in Islamic Studies.

www.ingramcontent.com/pod-product-compliance
Ingram Content Group UK Ltd.
Pitfield, Milton Keynes, MK11 3LW, UK
UKHW041632031026
15587UKWH00001B/234

9 781498 512152